Martial Rose Library
Tel: 01962 827306

The Theatre of the Bauhaus

Routledge Advances in Theatre and Performance Studies

The Theatre of the Bauhaus

The Modern and Postmodern
Stage of Oskar Schlemmer

Melissa Trimingham

Routledge
Taylor & Francis Group
New York   London

First published 2011
by Routledge
270 Madison Avenue, New York, NY 10016

Simultaneously published in the UK
by Routledge
2 Park Square, Milton Park, Abingdon, Oxon OX14 4RN

Routledge is an imprint of the Taylor & Francis Group, an informa business

Typeset in Sabon by IBT Global.
Printed and bound in the United States of America on acid-free paper by IBT Global.

Library of Congress Cataloging-in-Publication Data

Trimingham, Melissa, 1955–
    The theatre of the Bauhaus : the modern and postmodern stage of Oskar Schlemmer /
by Melissa Trimingham.
        p. cm. — (Routlege advances in theatre and performance studies ; v. 16)
    Includes bibliographical references and index.
    1. Schlemmer, Oskar, 1888-1943—Criticism and interpretation.   2. Theaters—
Stage-setting and scenery—Germany.   3. Bauhaus.   I. Title.
    PN2096.S26T 75 2010
    709.2—dc22
    2010009271

ISBN13: 978-0-415-40398-6 (hbk)

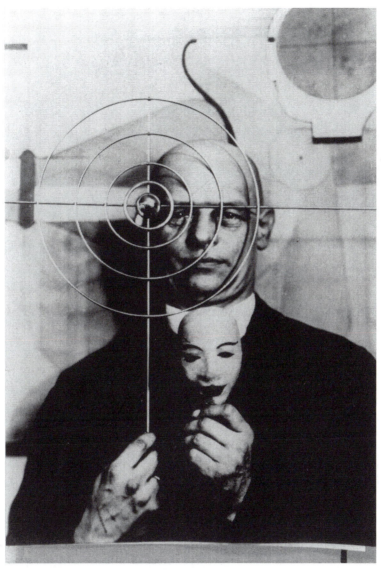

Portrait of Oskar Schlemmer with mask [Oskar Schlemmer mit Maske, Koordinatenelement (Sonne), vor 'Mythischer Figur'], 1930. Photo Archive, C. Raman Schlemmer, IT-288824 Oggebbio (VB) Italy.

*For my father, Oswald, and
my children, Lucian and Eloise*

Contents

Figures

Preface

This book is the culmination of many years' study beginning with my doctorate in 2001, 'The Practical Application of Principles Underlying the Work of Oskar Schlemmer at the Dessau Bauhaus, 1926–1929', a body of work which now seems very long ago. On the one hand, little of my original thesis has found its way into this book verbatim; on the other hand, my practical doctorate research and its conclusions, and indeed my current teaching, remain fundamental to every word I write. I am convinced that the ideas realised on the stage of the Bauhaus, under the directorship of Oskar Schlemmer, are seminal to a huge body of experimental stage and performance work in the twentieth and twenty-first centuries. Yet few artists of the twentieth century actively knew of and used Schlemmer's work, though many undoubtedly did. I came to understand that Schlemmer's influence is both less specific and more pervasive than this. Far from the Bauhaus stage being a Modernist curiosity, there is an unbroken line, as Nick Kaye has argued, between Modernist performance and postmodernism (Kaye 1994). Schlemmer is one hitherto largely unrecognised thread in this line, and a vital one.

An approach to early twentieth century German Modernist thought that accommodates change, time and organicism in terms of 'Gestalt' ideas enables a more holistic and visionary interpretation of the Bauhaus as a whole, both at Weimar and Dessau, and especially of its stage throughout its existence under Schlemmer. This interpretation of the stage work links directly with a visionary postmodernism that celebrates Bergsonian flux at the heart of our existence.

Chapter 1, 'The Theatre of the Bauhaus', begins with a history of the Bauhaus that concentrates on its theatre, since there are plenty of art and design histories in English that give extensive information about the art school, its cultural context, origins, progress and achievements, its impact on industrial design and the troubled course of its history, but few that offer insights into its stage.

Chapter 2, 'Modernism', breaks new ground laying open for the first time the thinking that shaped the Bauhaus stage in terms of German 'Gestalt' ideas; it establishes the historical intellectual context for subsequent chapters and argues for a less Constructivist and machine orientated interpretation of Bauhaus Modernism and its theatre work.

Chapters 3–7 do not analyse the stage work chronologically but rather under topics, so that insight into Schlemmer's approach to space, objects and sound can more easily inform and illuminate our understanding of subsequent performance work by others. The work is analysed under these subjects: Chapter 3, 'Space: Light and Scenery'; Chapter 4, 'Body and Motion'; Chapter 5, 'Body and Objects'; and Chapter 6, 'Sound'. Chapter 7, 'Time', deals almost entirely with contemporary performance work that explores in part or wholly the same resonant themes and ideas as the theatre of the Bauhaus. Chapter 8, 'Afterword', summarises the journey undertaken from the stage of the Bauhaus, via happenings and Alan Kaprow, to the postmodern stage.

For me, as a doctorate student, Schlemmer opened up the possibilities of non-naturalistic performance space, imbued it with the metaphysics of space and time, and confronted fundamental questions about the nature of our being-in-the-world, our agency and our power to effect change. These questions fascinated me then and do so now, and I see them continually played out in theatre today. I hope that this book will contribute to Schlemmer taking up his rightful place as a genius, an original thinker, and someone who changed the function of the performance space forever.

Acknowledgements

My research has been supported by the University of Kent, from which I was generously allowed two terms study leave to complete the bulk of the manuscript. Thanks are due to several members of staff and students there who have generously given of their time to check my translations, format my script, and offer support when I most needed it, including Dr Peter Boenisch, Professor Paul Allain, Denise Twomey, Angela Kennett, and above all, Professor Patrice Pavis for reading the manuscript and offering invaluable commentary on it. I am especially grateful to the School of Arts Research Committee who supported me in my pursuit of photographs and other material from the Schlemmer Archive.

I would also like to thank Professor Christopher Baugh, University of Hull, who has taken an interest in the manuscript over several years, offering invaluable advice and support, and who kindly read through the draft manuscript.

I would like to thank Raman Schlemmer: Oskar Schlemmer photographs are courtesy of Photo Archive C. Raman Schlemmer, IT-288824 Oggebbio (VB) Italy. Photographs of Cie 111 Aurélian Bory and Phil Soltanoff, Plus ou moins infini, and Cie 111 and Scènes de la Terre, Les sept planches de la ruse de Aurélian Bory, are courtesy Aglaé Bory. Photographs of Sòcietas Raffaello Sanzio, Inferno and Purgatorio, are courtesy Luca del Pia. Photographs of Robert Lepage The Anderson Project are courtesy Erick Labbé. Photographs of Robert Wilson Strindberg's The Dream Play are courtesy Lesley Leslie-Spinks.

The author would like to thank Erick Labbé, Lesley Leslie-Spinks and Luca del Pia for their generosity in offering photographs and material freely and without charge, and thanks to John Collins for generously allowing me to quote him.

Oskar Schlemmer quotations courtesy the late Jaïna Schlemmer, Bühnen Archiv Oskar Schlemmer (The Oskar Schlemmer Theatre Estate). The Secretariat Schlemmer does not take any responsibility for the accuracy of the translations of any texts by or relating to Oskar Schlemmer included in this publication.

Three paragraphs in Chapter 4, 'Body and Motion', are reprinted courtesy of Cambridge University Press. They first appeared as part of an article, 'Oskar Schlemmer's Research Practice at the Dessau Bauhaus' (Trimingham 2004a: 128–142).

I also owe thanks to those who helped me with my original doctorate thesis including Dr. Philip Butterworth and the students I worked with; and thanks to Dr. Stephanie Bunn of St Andrews University for unending inspiration and ideas, and to Jude Mazonovicz for support and to Jeremy Martin, Daniel Martin, Dr. Rosemary Klich and Dr. Rachel Hann for proof reading. With grateful thanks to Dr. Alison Harcourt for her extensive help in translation work. Thanks to Sebastian Grau, currently a postgraduate student at the University of Kent, for his help in translating extracts from Oskar Schlemmer's 'Mensch und Kunstfigur', 'Bühne' and *Briefe und Tagebücher.* Thanks also to Ulrike Kraemar for help with translation. Other translations are acknowledged in the text, or where there is no acknowledgement, they are my own.

1   The Theatre of the Bauhaus

It is time for a complete reappraisal of the stage in the Bauhaus. Moreover, to adapt Oskar Schlemmer's own words, the theatre of the Bauhaus may lead us to the keyhole to the riddle which the Bauhaus poses.[1] The Bauhaus-trained architect Hubert Hoffmann described the Bauhaus as the 'workshop of the future'. He made the claim that just as the ideas of the Renaissance lasted longer than 300 years, so the ideas of the Bauhaus would shape our future for another 300 years and more (Bogner 1997: 15). As notions of 'Modernism' in architecture hijacked the complex ideals of the Bauhaus, a cultural, ethical and social vision of the future was reduced to a simplified functionalism known eventually as the International Style.[2] As our age challenges our ability to ground ourselves in the fast changing and perishing world around us, confused by rapid advances in technology that have opened up a new dimension of virtual space and digital realities in less than thirty years, it is time, in the words of Pelle Ehn, once again to 'unite the two sides of Enlightenment: the hard (technology and natural sciences) and the soft (values, democracy, art and ethics)' (Ehn 1998). The stage, a laboratory for the imagination, occupied a central a place within the Bauhaus, and its presence has been too long unaccounted for and forgotten, not only by theatre historians but by architects and designers. The stage and its work undermine many myths about the Bauhaus's 'International Style' and its functionalist levelling. It is a necessary and vital antidote, since 'Bauhaus' ideas on architecture and the built environment have been so firmly rejected over the past thirty years or more. This book provides the first full-length history of the Bauhaus stage under its 'Master Magician'[3] Oskar Schlemmer, and in doing so grounds its ethos and that of the Bauhaus as a whole in values that give the lie to clichés about Bauhaus rigidity, purism, lack of imagination and pervasive 'Fordism' (one size and colour fits all) in its architectural ideals.

The process of reappraising the stage work is well underway in France and especially Germany, but English-language criticism has scarcely begun to change its impression of the Bauhaus stage under the directorship of Oskar Schlemmer at the Dessau Bauhaus. In the history of theatre and in journalism[4] there is still a pervasive insistence on defining early twentieth-century Modernist theatre through texts and their more or less radical new staging (e.g., the controversial content of Ibsen or Strindberg, the naturalism of Chekhov, the staging of Craig's Hamlet in Moscow, Brechtian alienation, Meyerhold's Constructivist productions *et alia*) which has consigned the non-narrative ('abstract') theatre of the Bauhaus to the outer fringes of Modernist eccentricity. Lack of information and a dearth of commentary in English have compounded the problem. Alternatively, when the Bauhaus stage is placed in the history of performance art and the avant-garde as Roselee Goldberg first did in 1977 (Goldberg 1977) it stands out as strangely anomalous in the line of development she later traces in her seminal book *Performance Art from Futurism to the Present* (Goldberg [1979] 1988). Schlemmer's tight-knit form sits uneasily amongst the stimulating ill manners and anarchy of the Futurists, the Expressionist and political excesses of the Dadaists and the bullying avant-garde tactics of the Surrealists. This study is aware of the pitfalls of placing Oskar Schlemmer's work within the history of any genre, but it acknowledges to some extent the sense of interpreting Schlemmer alongside Adolphe Appia and Gordon Craig in their attempts to revitalise the theatre stage (see Kirchmann 1997; Louppe 1999; Schober 1994, 1997). However, arguably Schlemmer demands equally to be considered within the history of dance (Rousier 2001), happenings and the American avant-garde (Pawelke 2005), performance art (Louppe 1999, Niimi 1999, Rasche 1994), postmodern dance (Moyniham and Odom 1984, Blistène 1999, Niimi 1999, Fabbri 2001), contemporary dance and digital performance (Norman 2001, Duhm 2008) and even kinetic and pop art (Krystof 1994: 55–7). Schlemmer's stage work is, it seems, an enigma. Persistently mentioned usually as little more than a name in the avant-garde historical canon, Schlemmer is rarely well or even fully explained. It seems he has affinities with a range of avant-garde performance that came after him, yet these affinities have so far remained elusive and difficult to define.

Commentators on the theatre of the Bauhaus up to the late 1980s contributed to three unhelpful clichés: that Schlemmer's stage work is robotic and mechanical, that he suffers from the fatal split between the 'Apollonian' discipline of his paintings and the 'Dionysian' freedom of performance; and finally that the presence of a stage at the Bauhaus is an example of the Wagnerian urge towards the 'Gesamtkunstwerk'. These myths allow little scope for identifying any synergy between our contemporary stages and the 'abstract' space of the Bauhaus stage. Dirk Scheper, writing in 1988, does make a short attempt at the end of his long study to link Schlemmer with, amongst others, figures such as Alwin Nikolais and Rebecca Horn, but although affinities are demonstrable between his work and theirs, the issue is scarcely explored by him in any depth (Scheper 1988: 279–89). Eric Michaud in the 1970s, though he has softened his judgement since (Michaud 1996: 184–187), makes no bones about it: he interprets Schlemmer as fatally limited in his stage work, straitjacketed by the Bauhaus philosophy, particularly that of Kandinsky, and takes a restricted view of Bauhaus ideas as linked to a rigid and unrealistic Utopia that could never be attained; as a result, the stage figures are ultimately robotic and mechanical (Michaud 1978a). Art historians tended before around 1990 to lament the fact that Schlemmer spent so much of his time on the ephemeral art form of performance, and because Hildebrandt in 1946 (see Krystof 1994) unfortunately identified the Apollonian/Dionysian split in Schlemmer between painting and the stage (roughly equivalent to control and freedom) this has become somewhat of a cliché, and a misguiding one. Despite the words originating from Schlemmer himself, it is simply inaccurate to divide Schlemmer's consciousness and work in this way: it is more accurate to say that his stage work actually constituted the successful fusion of these two impulses. Another falsehood is that the Bauhaus stage is a 'Gesamtkunstwerk' or unified work of art; recent commentators in German such as Thomas Schober (Schober 1997: 124) and Kay Kirchmann (Kirchmann 1997: 88) have correctly pointed out that Schlemmer's method, at least, was the exact opposite to this: an abstraction, honing down and synthesising of elements peculiar to the stage, rather than a wider inclusive approach. It is exactly this minimalism that has been recognised as distinctive of his work by dance commentators such as Debra McCall (Moyniham and Odom 1984) and later critical commentators Laurence Louppe (1999) and Ryu Niimi (1999).

The workshops of the Bauhaus were dynamic powerhouses fuelled by ideas from some of the greatest artists of the twentieth century such as Wassily Kandinsky, Paul Klee, Johannes Itten, Walter Gropius, Lyonel Feininger and Oskar Schlemmer himself. All these artists were extraordinarily well read and deeply involved in contemporary debates on culture, history, aesthetics and philosophy. They believed themselves, correctly as I shall argue, to be helping to shape the century to come and beyond. Schlemmer's stage workshop was an essential part of this, the 'beating heart of the Bauhaus' as Goldberg describes it (Goldberg 2003). European Modernists in all their various guises, Futurists, Constructivists, Dadaists, Surrealists, from Moscow to Paris, Berlin to Rome, dispersed into the New World as émigrés becoming artists and teachers who consequently impacted upon the arts, design and architecture. Today, Bauhaus influence on industrial design is fully acknowledged. Similarly, Bauhaus architectural style, as manifested in the Dessau building, and supposedly developed in the New Bauhaus in Chicago, seems to define Modernism. Bauhaus pedagogical influence within art schools was and is pervasive. However, artists from the 1950s onwards who privilege(d) the visual, plastic and aural qualities of the stage and performing body above character, narrative and themes also owe much to the peculiar mix that was Bauhaus Modernism and in many ways their work brings to fruition the unrealised potential of the Bauhaus stage and its highly original and radical recasting of stage semiotics. Moreover, the 'International Style', with its stress on functionalism, actually denies many of the values held dear within the Bauhaus until about 1928 when Hannes Meyer took over from Walter Gropius, values epitomised in the stage work. This book will trace the history of such values.

Artists at the Bauhaus were coming to terms with flux, change and motion in a world that longed for certainties. Walter Gropius declared (retrospectively) that the purpose of the Bauhaus was finding an 'objective common denominator of form', 'general superpersonal laws' and 'universally acknowledged basic concepts' within a 'science of design' (Gropius in Neumann [1970] 1993: 21). A recent publication on the stage of the Dessau Bauhaus similarly interprets the original stage work of the Bauhaus as looking for 'universal, generalising models' (Akbar 2008: 17). These fixed points of reference, however, were persistently seen within the Bauhaus, certainly up to 1928 when Gropius left, and probably persistently in individuals beyond then, very much in terms of Gestalt thinking.[5] It is hard to underestimate the impact of Gestalt concepts not only within the Bauhaus but more generally within late nineteenth- and early twentieth-century German aesthetics and philosophy; yet they have been little addressed by commentators. Wensinger quotes T. Lux Feininger as saying:

> The term "Gestaltung" is old, meaningful and so nearly untranslatable that it has found its way into English usage. Beyond the significance of shaping, forming, thinking through, it has the flavor of underlining the totality of such fashioning, whether of an artifact or of an idea. It forbids the nebulous and the diffuse. In its fullest philosophical meaning it expresses the Platonic eidolon, the Urbild, the pre-existing form (Wensinger in Gropius and Wensinger [1961] 1996: 50).

The more recent definition by Arne Naess of Gestalt structures is also useful: 'wholes that are perceived to have an organic identifiable unity in themselves, as a network of relations that can move as one' (Naess 1989: 6), and 'identity is inherent only in the *relationships* which make up the entity'. Change, energy, dynamism within Gestalt thinking in the early twentieth century was accounted for and understood within the fusion and 're'-fusion of these 'fundamental' elements into continually changing new 'wholes'. Kandinsky in *On the Spiritual in Art* (Über das Geistige in der Kunst) ([1912] 1982) clearly describes the combination of colours in his paintings as 'Gestalten' without ever using the word. His 'red', for example, has a particular character that itself changes, depending on the combination of colours within which it is placed, as well as its position on the canvas, mass and tone, and so on (Kandinsky [1912] 1982: 162). This is returned to in Chapter 2. Gestalt ideas, from Goethe onwards, enjoyed a revival in this period, and provide a key to understanding the aesthetics of early German Modernism and especially the Bauhaus. Gestalt ideas provide a counterweight to the prevailing functionalist tone of Constructivist thinking, the latter spreading rapidly from Russia around the late 1910s and impacting on the Bauhaus quite early on through De Stijl in Europe and Theo van Doesburg's and László Maholy-Nagy's arrival in Weimar in 1922 and 1923 respectively. Gestalt thinking, however, pervaded the Bauhaus workshops even after 1925 in the reformed Bauhaus in Dessau, and especially on the stage of the Bauhaus, which utilised not only a practical approach to realising 'Gestaltungen' but one that also placed the body itself at the centre of its research. As a result of using a live art form, the experiments of the Bauhaus stage anticipated many later developments in aesthetics and philosophy, and introduced uncertainty and slippage alongside the dynamism and idealism of Gestalt thinking.

Outside the Bauhaus, Gestalt thinking, with its notion of an 'Urbild' or pre-existing form, played a role in early phenomenology that claimed an 'essence' or 'eidios' in perception, its ideas slowly developing from the mid-nineteenth century onwards within philosophy departments of German Universities; phenomenology was nurtured particularly by those scientific cuckoos in the philosophical nest, the (Gestalt) psychologists. At times Gestalt thought is indistinguishable from vitalism, a movement as equally reviled as it was adored, that attempted, like Gestalt thinking (and like the Bauhaus itself), to be both scientific and holistic in the early years of the twentieth century. An approach to Modernism that accommodates change, time and organicism, identified within the heart of the Bauhaus, enables a more holistic and visionary interpretation of the Bauhaus, and especially of its theatre throughout its existence under Schlemmer. The visionary affinity between the Modernist avant-garde, strongly manifested at the Bauhaus, and aspects of later (postmodern) theatre and performance is identified and celebrated most notably by Bonnie Marranca in her book *Ecologies of Theater* (Marranca 1996). It is also recognised and restated by recent scholarship on Schlemmer himself in German and French (e.g., Bossmann 1994, Rasche 1994, Schober 1997, Blistène 1999 and Niimi 1999). None of these commentators, however, clearly identify how the aesthetic idealism of the 1920s, at least as it is commonly presented, can be squared with its continual and insistent manifestation via the body on the Bauhaus stage. Beginning with Heidegger in the 1920s and later Maurice Merleau-Ponty in the 1940s, stress upon the embeddedness of the body in the world moves phenomenology and embodied thinking towards increasingly existential interpretations. This book argues that Schlemmer unwittingly unravelled the very idealism he 'bodied forth' on stage; but in doing so he opened up a far richer seam of exploration, whereby our very uncertainties about our being in the world and the ever present hope of transcendence are held in a delicate and perpetually enriching balance. His journey into the materiality of objects, their handling, their use, and his insistent deployment of all the material aspects of the stage moves his idealism far from the Platonic Utopianism that Michaud describes and closer to a Cagean minimalist aesthetic of the holiness of the ordinary. The visionary is not lost, but recast into modes we can more easily accept, and establishes a rapport between

Schlemmer's practice and our own that in part explains the fascination that his extraordinary work is able continually to provoke.

Doris Krystof demonstrates in her survey of Schlemmer's reception in Germany since his death in 1943 how specifically in his case the past has been interpreted according to the present in which it is received (Krystof 1994: 50). We are as we interpret, and we interpret as we are. The phenomenological method is at the heart of this book, and is closely linked to hermeneutics; and (despite Marxist- and Feminist-led criticisms of its supposed essentialism) the phenomenological approach is acutely aware of the accretions of culture, prejudice and familiarity that cloud the phenomena we study. It is our business as researchers to recognise these contexts and our 'lenses'. Paradoxically, we search out as much as possible about the phenomena we study precisely in order to ask better and more open questions. Accordingly, in this study, historical research sits alongside what is in effect a phenomenological 'reduction' of Schlemmer's work, stripping back his work to the common threads that bind us to him today. This chapter gives a history of the stage at the Bauhaus and is followed by the history of ideas in Chapter 2, but thereafter the material is not structured chronologically. Rather, Schlemmer's work is analysed by grouping together the stage elements with which he 'painted' space: light, scenery, body, motion, object, sound, time. The method is always to start with the historically specific progressing into the phenomenologically direct, that is, by describing the physical effect his applications have on our experience of the stage and our formulation of meaning from that experience. What emerges is that Schlemmer opened up his own and the Bauhaus's essentialist notions to a permeable and shifting art form using space, time and the body; my suggestion is that we have far more in common with Schlemmer than has hitherto been recognized. As a consequence in this study Schlemmer's manipulation of the stage elements will continually be set alongside numerous twentieth century and contemporary performances, some from major directors and others not so well known, who also utilise all elements of the 'Schaubühne' (Schlemmer 1925: 10) or visual stage.[6]

These words by Oskar Schlemmer's widow and literary executor Tut Schlemmer in a lecture given in 1949 in Berlin at the America House on Schlemmer's stage work, which she repeated several times all over Europe, give some flavour of the enormous variety of theatre which permeated the Bauhaus from its earliest days.

> Since there was the urge to perform, a stage was available from the first day of the existence of the Bauhaus. This urge to perform—described by Schiller in his wonderful letters about the aesthetic education of man—is the power from which flows the truly creative values of man, undemanding, naïve joy of creating and designing, without distinguishing between the worthy and the unworthy, sense or nonsense, good or bad (T. Schlemmer in Neumann [1970] 1993: 162).

Many are surprised, even today, to learn that the Bauhaus undertook theatre and performance work which eventually became part of its official
curriculum. We need here to distinguish carefully the more anarchic and
freewheeling stage work at Weimar from the later more orderly experiments on a purpose-built stage at Dessau when the stage elements were
carefully and systematically deployed on a single stage. The result of the
Dessau work was the touring programme of the *Bauhaus Dances* (*Bauhaustänze* 1929) and an accompanying demonstration or lecture, and these
constitute the main stimulus for this study. The early years at Weimar,
however, and *The Triadic Ballet* (*Das Triadische Ballet*) also illuminate
Schlemmer's aims and intentions, which cannot be understood solely in
terms of the later so-called Constructivist ethos of the Bauhaus, an era
which is characterized (on the whole) by bald simplicity, lack of decoration
and, above all, an apparently strictly analytical approach shown in Schlemmer's Dessau dances.

The Bauhaus art school was established in Weimar in 1919 through the
energy and vision of one man, Walter Gropius, already well known as an
architect before World War I. Following the devastating destruction he
experienced as an officer in World War I, he had a vision of a better future
in Germany that might begin with training artists more suited to the twentieth century and discovering an art relevant to the age and openly ethical in
its intent. The existing Academy of Arts and the School of Arts and Crafts
at Weimar were amalgamated and renamed the 'Staatliches Bauhaus' with
Gropius as its Director. The name 'Bauhaus' is a rich German compound
generated to communicate a resonant idea, and it indicates the central aim
of finding a building style or architecture for the age. Its literal translation
is 'building house' but it echoes the old German name for the craft guilds of
stonemasons, the 'Bauhütten'. 'Bauhütten' were the guilds of skilled crafts-
men in the Middle Ages that helped build cathedrals,[7] and this deliberate
reference in the name 'Bauhaus' was further reinforced by Feininger's woodcut of a cathedral that fronted the Program of the Staatliches Bauhaus in
April 1919. The woodcut is visionary in its overtones, looking down on the
building from above with geometric patterning behind that represents shafts
of sunlight but also perhaps suggests other buildings and stars gleaming out
where the diagonal shafts cross in the sky. By the time the Bauhaus was shut
by the Nazis in 1933 it had contributed richly to the new style of design and
architecture known as Modernism, the avant-garde of the twentieth century, with its clean lines and lack of decoration, where form followed function, and new materials were incorporated in airy glass and steel structures,
functioning machines for living.[8] But in these early days, the chosen image
was a cathedral and moreover a 'Cathedral of Socialism'. The Bauhaus was
the first art school in Germany to fuse the two great pedagogical traditions
in Germany: 'Bildung', the traditional approach to education in schools and
universities, that is, theoretical study; and 'Ausbildung', the experiential,
hands-on method of training undergone by apprentices.[9]

In 1918, following the defeat of Germany in the war, there was more hope than material resources. It is a massive achievement that Gropius got the school off the ground at all. He succeeded in securing the funding for a new art school in Weimar from the Thuringen government. Some staff he had to take on from the existing institutions, but he planned completely new structures for teaching. He proposed workshops in various crafts (such as stone work or bookbinding) to be headed jointly by a master journeyman (craftsman) and an artist. He invited some of the leading so-called Expressionist painters of the day to Weimar over the next two or three years, including Johannes Itten, Lionel Feininger, Paul Klee, Oskar Schlemmer and Wassily Kandinsky. Expressionism of course has nothing to do with expressing emotion; put simply, the Expressionist impulse strives to touch the invisible transcendent 'beyond', a state outside the here and now, the level of existence which Immanuel Kant dubbed the 'noumenon' or 'Ding an sich'. This metaphysical state of being is separate from the object or phenomenon we commonly know by our senses. These painters were expected to find a working relationship with the journeymen, giving some kind of ethical and spiritual basis to the search for a new direction. Useful as this arrangement may have been for communicating necessary practical skills, such as book binding, ceramics, metal work and so on, the partnerships were difficult, and the idea was dropped when the Bauhaus left Weimar in 1925 and moved to Dessau. As Bruno Adler remarked looking back on his association with the Weimar Bauhaus, above all it was the 'painters who lent lustre to the Bauhaus' (Adler in Neumann [1970] 1993: 27).

Schlemmer himself arrived at the Bauhaus in 1921 having signed his contract in December 1920. He continued to be distracted by stage design work outside the Bauhaus[10] and most especially the time-consuming preparations in Stuttgart for his premiere of *The Triadic Ballet* which finally took place there in September 1922. Schlemmer was, at the time Gropius invited him to the Bauhaus, quite well known in Germany at least as a painter, and active in reforming circles around the academy in Stuttgart. He was embedded in Stuttgart artistic life with a larger profile than he perhaps cared for. In the turbulent times after World War I, it was hard to separate art and politics and he became embroiled in a major dispute over the successor to his teacher Hölzel at the Stuttgart Academy, a position which he ultimately found distasteful to be in. He was even arrested at one point (on political grounds as a suspected left-wing activist) but released. This experience left him with a determination to avoid active involvement in politics. He met and married (in October 1920) his beloved wife, Helena Tutein. She was affectionately known as 'Tut' to her family and friends. A Schwabian by birth, Schlemmer retained his loyalty to the south of Germany all his life. His love of punning and word play, which makes some of his work at times virtually untranslatable for the tortuous wit and puns contained in it, made much use of Schwabian dialect variations. As T. Lux Feininger commented, 'He possessed the most individual vocabulary I have ever heard' (T. Lux Feininger in Neumann

[1970] 1993: 194). Schlemmer had a deeply religious streak which probably has its origin in the strict Protestant background in which he was brought up.[11] It is important to remember that during the 1910s, when he was not away in the war, Schlemmer's circle in Stuttgart where he was an art student included a close friendship with Joahnnes Itten who was a key figure in the early Bauhaus at Weimar. In 1916, a trio of three friends, Schlemmer, Helge Lindberg and Johannes Itten shaved their heads as a joint gesture of spiritual asceticism: Schlemmer's hair, further punished beneath heavy military helmets, never grew back, giving him the characteristic appearance he has in most published photographs of him. In 1922, on his arrival at the Bauhaus, he was initially put in charge of the Wood and Stone Workshop, later the Sculpture Workshop. Music and performance formed a large part of Bauhaus social life. Unusually, at that time, theatre had some sort of official status in the art school, since Lothar Schreyer, a well-known Expressionist theatre director, was designated in charge of the Bauhaus theatre although no actual stage existed. Schlemmer did not get involved in Schreyer's work but happily associated himself with other student work, often humorous and irreverent puppet shows shown on the Saturday night entertainments at the Bauhaus parties and at the Festivals—which in turn, Schlemmer helped to organise. Schlemmer wrote in March 1922: 'By the way, the door is gradually being opened to the theatre in the Bauhaus. Schreyer was the push—as both poet and painter, but in the realm of the "sacred". What is left for me are the dance and the comic, which I gladly and graciously confess to be my own' (March 1922) (Schlemmer [1958] 1977: 56). This situation continued until 1923 when Schreyer left.

Lack of facilities and compromise, especially concerning the roles of and the relationships between the journeymen and the artists, were to dog the functioning of the workshops at Weimar. But the Bauhaus, taken together including the ateliers of the painters, the stimulating and rigorous Preliminary Course run by Itten, and the flourishing theatrical and social life, was a powerhouse of energy and ideas. It was also often unruly and eccentric. The internal divisions, however, did not prevent a show of total unity against the deeply conservative and bourgeois town people they were foisted upon in Weimar.

In Germany as a whole, it was a time of upheaval and near anarchy. In the latter years of the nineteenth century and the early years of the twentieth century, Germany experienced rapid industrialisation in a very short period of time. Before war broke out in 1914, the old regime under the Kaiser was buckling under pressure to accommodate change and a rapidly increasing population. Before the First World War, the conservative values of the Wilhelminian regime had been satirised by the cabarets of Frank Wedekind and others (who had often ended up in prison for their efforts) and in some quarters blame for the disastrous war was attached to the old (repressive) regime. Germany was about to enter, in 1918, a very unstable period of rioting and near revolution, and hyperinflation, only brought under control in 1924. The 'cathedral of Socialism', as the Bauhaus boldly called its harmonious vision in 1919, proved a liability in the early years of the 1920s and the word 'Socialist' had to be eventually censored from the publicity for the widely advertised and well-attended Bauhaus Exhibition in 1923 at Weimar, the public display of Bauhaus works and achievements. The far right National Socialists, aggressive in their repressive intolerance of all things liberal, new and potentially destabilizing, gained ground rapidly in local government and eventually forced the Bauhaus, far too Bohemian and left wing for their taste, to move north to Dessau, then to Berlin, and they eventually closed the institution in 1933. In these dark days it was hard to imagine just how much the Bauhaus had become or would prove to be a living and influential force in the twentieth century. As ex-Bauhaus student Hubert Hoffmann stated in a round table discussion in 1997 on the occasion of the huge exhibition on Schlemmer's stage work in Vienna[12], the Bauhaus was for life and living and should never be a museum piece, but something living and useful (Bogner 1997: 16). Tut Schlemmer had similarly declared in 1949 that the Bauhaus 'is no legend' (T. Schlemmer in Neumann [1970] 1993: 164). It created a new style of homes, metal, glass, pottery, lighting, carpentry, printing, posters, wallpaper and photos. There is a danger here in attributing everything in twentieth-century Modernist design solely to the Bauhaus,[13] but nonetheless its influence was huge particularly through the émigrés, both students and staff, to the United States, and especially in the arts via Black Mountain College in North Carolina and in industry, technology, design and architecture through the New Bauhaus in Chicago.

Yet there was a respect for history in the Bauhaus: in the words of Tut Schlemmer, 'To have linked the ambiguity of art to the reality of handcrafts and to have *reinstated the old line of descent of the arts* will always be attributed to the Bauhaus' [my italics] (T. Schlemmer in Neumann [1970] 1993: 164).[14] This concern in the Bauhaus with rooting the institution in history, and indeed philosophy, not simply throwing out the old in favour of the new, permeates the early years of the Bauhaus. Gropius, on the other hand, was also driven by a desire to impact genuinely and practically on the new Germany of the machine age and its industrial design base. In this he eventually succeeded, but not for several years, and certainly not in the Weimar years up to 1924. In 1925, he was compelled to move the Bauhaus north to Dessau and to force through practical output from the workshops, and some money was made from sale of design work (though never enough!).

The students at Weimar were less reverent than their masters concerning the past. Tut Schlemmer recalls: 'We celebrated our festivals on the suburban stages, and everything smelling of pathos and ethics was ridiculed. We made parodies of operas and plays and Punch—usually Felix Klee presented Bauhaus satires' (T. Schlemmer in Neumann [1970] 1993: 165). This was the age of Dada, which had hit Berlin after the war. By that time in Germany, Dada, having largely shed the openly mystical and

Expressionist aspirations of Hugo Ball, appeared to be an anarchic, political and humorous avant-garde of instant appeal to the students. Politics was never long off the Bauhaus agenda, whether local politics criticising the Council of Masters, or national politics of the left, and in later years a strong political left-wing atmosphere permeated the Bauhaus. In the end, Schlemmer left in 1929 because of pressure to produce left-wing political theatre, in addition to a strong lurch into pure functionality within the Bauhaus under Hannes Meyer (Findeli 1989/1990). But in the early years at Weimar, the touch was lighter if the hardships were greater. As Schlemmer described in 1927, 'There was . . . a distinct inclination for satire and parody' (Schlemmer 1927c: 1). Much of this was performed at the Bauhaus festivals and parties—of which there were many, all eagerly attended by students and staff alike. Schlemmer played a major role in organising entertainments for these occasions. Every weekend there was a small party and every month a costume party on some theme, held outside Weimar in inns of the neighbouring Oberweimar (Ackermann 1999). These events eventually at the end of the Weimar years spawned the famous Bauhaus band ('Die Bauhauskapelle') to which everyone danced, and whose dancing anticipated fashions fifty or so years later: 'It was a passionate stamping . . . We danced in couples not embracing but separated' (Felix Klee in Neumann [1970] 1993: 42). 'Die Bauhauskapelle' jazz band was an important aspect of Bauhaus life at Dessau, and considering the innumerable testimonies to their skill and passion, it is frustrating that not a single score of their seventy-odd compositions remain, though of course much would have been improvised in performance anyway (Bogner 1997: 16). Just as important were the Festivals at Weimar held four times a year. For these, processions with lanterns and banners would always be planned. For the Kite Festival, for example, elaborate homemade kites were designed and built. These events (Fiedler and Feierabend 2000: 127) would not have been out of place in a community event in England in the 1980s by, for example, Welfare State Theatre, or perhaps a Bread and Puppet Theatre in the United States any time in the past thirty or so years.[15] The aesthetic here was very different to the end on stage and rigid control of space that Schlemmer later employed in Dessau and much looser than the carefully orchestrated parties he directed there. At Weimar he encouraged students to develop the German tradition of processions and outdoor festivals, giving them a decidedly Bauhaus twist, full of humour and Dadaesque irreverence about current art theories in vogue. Felix Klee, one of the youngest students to enter the Bauhaus at Weimar recalls:

One month later [after Gropius's birthday celebrations] we celebrated the pagan Midsummer-night Festival. Once it was held halfway to Belvedere in the little coffee [sic] valley. Hirschfeld and Schwerdtfeger presented their reflecting light play *The Story of Creation*. I contributed to the festivities with a puppet show in which Emmy Galka Scheyer tries to talk my father into buying a Jawlensky. My father, however, doesn't want to and Emmy breaks the Jawlensky on his head. The real Emmy and Klee arrived at the festival just as the performance was over, and the audience welcomed the originals, both unaware of the show, with applause. Later the bonfire was lit, and we jumped bravely and daringly over the flames (Felix Klee in Neumann [1970] 1993: 43).

This was a small community of masters and students, making their own entertainment, living and working in a town that separated itself from their rather Bohemian goings-on. On 18 May, an annual Festival of Lanterns served to celebrate Gropius's birthday (referred to by Felix Klee in the preceding quote). The enthusiasm bears testimony to genuine affection for him. The Dragon Festival in October prompted more feverish making and finally at Christmas, imagination and creativity made up for lack of money. Felix Klee again describes the scene:

A stepladder lent by the wall-painting workshop, with candles on cross-battens, served as a pseudo-Christmas tree. With great hue and cry a student dressed as an angel dragged a wash basket to the door, tore it open, and practically threw presents into our midst. There were large and small packages with names on them. We unwrapped one in high expectation, and there was another, a smaller package, with another name on it. Each package was handed round until finally the very last one produced the gift itself. Gertrud Grunow, the good spirit of the Bauhaus, got a pot with the inscription 'If you think yellow she'll (sic) make tea, if you think brown there'll be coffee.' The Schlemmers had just had two daughters, Karin and Jaina [sic],[16] born in the coach-house of the Belvedere palace. That night Oskar received thirteen more daughters with marvellous imaginary names (Felix Klee in Neumann [1970] 1993: 43–4).

To fully appreciate the joke about Gertrud Grunow's teapot, one perhaps should have been an attendee at her harmonisation classes on the power of thought, or read 'The Creation of Living Form through Color [sic], Form and Sound' (Wingler 1969: 69–71). In these social events, Schlemmer, who was not officially in charge of the theatre at that time, played a major role. On the other hand, Lothar Schreyer, who did carry this responsibility at the Weimar Bauhaus, seems little engaged with these celebrations and took a very different approach to performance.

Schreyer was a well-respected theatre director in the more experimental fields of Expressionist drama in Hamburg (where he founded the Kampf-Bühne, which had strong links with the Expressionist 'Sturm' group in Berlin) when Gropius invited him to the Bauhaus in 1921. Schreyer's work has had bad press, at least within the Bauhaus, since his methods were found to clash horribly with the prevailing mood there. His productions (three short pieces between 1921 and 1922 and the final piece *Moonplay* (*Mondspiel*) in early 1923) are interesting manifestations of the Expressionist stage then being produced in Berlin and other German cities. In some ways his work had much in common with Wassily Kandinsky's Expressionist piece *The Yellow Sound* (*Der Gelbe Klang*), which Kandinsky had published in 1912 in the Expressionist bible, *The Blue Rider Almanac* (*Der Blaue Reiter Almanach*) (Lindsay and Vergo 1982: 229–283). *The Yellow Sound*, like Schreyer's scripts, presents very symbolic action on stage, apparently charged with portentous meaning.[17] All that was presented on stage by Schreyer was solemn, almost religious in its overtones, using costume and masks marked with esoteric symbols and Christian imagery. One of its characteristics was the poetic half-sung, half-spoken language ('Sprechstimme') which overlaid the solemn rites on stage.[18] The detail of these productions is perhaps hard to envisage, but one thing is clear. The symbolism remained distant and did not speak to the Bauhaus students, inclined as they were towards satire and Dadaesque humour. Moreover, they instinctively wanted and created performances that connected to the ethos of the Bauhaus as they perceived and lived it, and it was not this brand of Expressionist mysticism. In spring 1923, Schreyer left the Bauhaus, after *Moonplay* was badly received and his work formed no part of the 1925 Bauhaus theatre book.

Perhaps the hostility to Schreyer's work seems confusing as Itten's Preliminary Course, which all students had to complete before progressing to the workshops, was at first glance as equally saturated in mysticism and spiritual aspirations as Schreyer's productions. Gertrude Grunow, for instance, undertook lengthy 'harmonisation' classes and Itten himself practised breathing exercises before allowing students to touch materials. Itten's strange religion—Mazdaznan—so dominated the Bauhaus at one point that it threatened to destroy the school under a welter of bizarre practices and domination by one man. Indeed, looking at some of the eccentric extremes present in the Bauhaus then, it seems Schreyer's mysticism should have suited the prevailing mood very well. Itten's Preliminary Course, however, which all students undertook, also taught the students in a very practical and engaging way. A gifted teacher who had studied pedagogy and developed nineteenth-century ideas around the need to engage the body with the mind in learning (Lupton and Abbott Miller 1993), Itten insisted in his classes on a physical engagement with a range of materials, exploring their strengths, weaknesses and creative potential, literally pulverising, stretching and cutting materials and building them up again into new structures or 'Gestalten' (forms) as exercises in class. Many of these materials were culled by students picking up rubbish: hair, scrap metal pieces, bits of wood. Whilst students, like Schreyer, may have been interested in discovering a spiritual and intellectual truth for their time, many were equally determined to find this through hands-on experimentation with the basic building blocks of material form and thoroughly practical means. Stage work needed to be similarly anchored to practical work and skills that might interest a visual art student. As a result, the performances created by students and Schlemmer himself in these early years, in contrast to Schreyer's official productions, concentrated on playing with the materials and material technologies (however basic) of theatre; and they demonstrated much needed humour in the face of religious pretensions, hunger, van Doesburg's rival 'Constructivist' classes held in town and straightforward isolation.

The 'mechanical, the grotesque and formal matters' in student theatrical experiments as Schlemmer described them (June 1923) (Schlemmer [1958] 1977: 66) explored mechanical stage devices and puppetry. It is only slowly being recognised how much puppetry enjoyed a revival by the avant-garde at the beginning of the twentieth century (Bell 2008, Segel 1995). At a basic level, puppetry and the manipulation of objects on stage enabled visual artists, who were keen on making and sometimes not so keen on appearing on stage as actors, to engage with performance. Schlemmer at this time went along with this more technically based performance. Kurt Schmidt's *Mechanical Ballet (Das Mechanische Ballett)* used large cutout coloured card figures of abstract shapes and moved them across stage, propelled by hidden human beings behind each cutout. His *The Adventures of the Little Hunchback (Die Abenteuer des kleinen Buckligen)* in 1923 was a marionette puppet show that used more or less geometric shapes to make the puppets, and grossly exaggerated their characters through the forms they took (Scheper 1988: 92). Marcel Breuer's *ABC Hippodrome (ABC-Hippodrom)* was inspired by parodying a dressed shop window and consisted of abstract cutouts placed in the frame of the stage (Michaud 1978a: 86–7).[19] Light and sound were also explored by students; for example, *Reflected Light Play (Reflektorische Lichtspiele)* by Hirschfield Mack, whose live performance anticipated later films such as those of Viking Eggeling and Hans Richter (Scheper 1988: 110). 'Marionette Theatre Design' ('Entwurf einer als Rundbühne gedachten Marionettenbühne') in 1922 by Ilse Fehling was an elaborately engineered design for a puppet stage that apparently played like a large kaleidoscope with effects of abstract shapes (Michaud 1978a: 95).[20] Many productions were laced with humour and drew on popular theatre forms (fairground booths, shooting galleries and the like) such as Xanti Schawinsky's *Circus (Circus)* in 1924 which managed to present an entire circus using cutouts and human performers, right down to the lion droppings being hastily swept up. Schlemmer's own *Figural Cabinet (Das Figurale Kabinett)* was first presented in 1922 and reworked into a more elaborate version in 1923. The piece was based on the idea of a side show or shooting gallery in a fair, and used cutouts, many whizzing around on wires, or being moved up and down in slots, together with revolving and sliding moving parts, all presided over by a 'master of ceremonies' that was a human being/puppeteer (Gropius and Wensinger [1961] 1996: 40–2). The script reveals much about ambiguous attitudes to mechanisation at the Bauhaus at this time, as needless to say, it all goes (deliberately) wrong in the course of the performance and descends into (orchestrated) chaos. Schlemmer enjoyed making jokes at his own expense about his interest in metaphysics, or, to put it bluntly, the world that lies 'beyond' ('meta') the physical one around us: as the script for the *Figural Cabinet* says: 'Meta [a character] is physically complete: head and body disappear alternately'. In his piece *Meta: or the Pantomime of Places* (*Meta oder die Pantomime der Örter*) the joke continues by reducing a dramatic plot to its basic structure, or 'Ur- form', with performers holding signs at fixed spots (Enter, Exit, Intermission, suspense, 1st, 2nd, 3rd crisis and so on). The result was highly 'physical', but hardly 'meta'physical. The joke further turns on the subtlety of Gestalt structures (explored in the next chapter) contrasted with clumsy dissections of this sort of ham-fisted, logical analysis. In a similar vein, Schlemmer a few years later in 1927 organised a 'catch-phrase' or 'slogan' party celebrating the first anniversary of the opening of the new building at Dessau, a satirical but very humorous hit at Bauhaus attitudes in teaching that he considered were in danger of becoming entrenched, unquestioned and so, to his mind, undermining of free thought and creativity. In December 1927, Schlemmer wrote a letter to his wife in which he describes the eager preparations by the students (their making large posters which they put up in the cafeteria) and a play which they put together satirising Maholy-Nagy. Maholy-Nagy is depicted as part of the Weimar era of Expressionistic excesses, since the playlet is called 'The Weimar Affair' ('Die Sache von Weimar'), as if it were a continuing puzzling case for a detective in a novel. Like 'Meta' it draws on the idea of a 'climax', 'conflict' and so on, except here the target was unthinking acceptance of Bauhaus 'Holy Cows'. One joke Schlemmer describes is almost impossible to translate, turning as it did on a pun between 'Leiter' as leader or director (i.e. Maholy-Nagy as teacher) and 'Leiter' as 'ladder'.

> For example, the director [Leiter] becomes the ladder of feelings, and the leader of feelings [Gefühlsleiter] (Maholy), each step on the ladder being a material—sausage, wire, broom, wool. Maholy uses such 'ladders of feeling' in the Introductory course: on a piece of wood different materials are attached over which you run your fingers, eyes closed, and 'feel'. Incidentally, of course, the word 'co-operative, Meyer's slogan, will come in for it hard. The entire architecture department in fact!
>
> It's going to be great fun. We're going to make all sorts of topical jokes (December 1927) (Schlemmer 1990: 184–5).

Satire and humour laced the Bauhaus performances especially when in party mood.

From a mix of student-led mechanical theatre productions and his own work, Schlemmer, by now in charge officially of the theatre workshop, replacing Schreyer, put on a good show for the Bauhaus Week in August 1923. The week of lectures and performances was the centrepiece of the much longer show-piece Bauhaus Exhibition which ran from 15 August 1923 to the end of September. On the Tuesday evening of the opening week, *The Triadic Ballet* was presented at the German National Theatre in Weimar, and on the Friday, a 'Mechanical Cabaret' (*Das Mechanische Kabarett*) (which consisted of a medley of 'mechanical theatre' as described previously, and included Kurt Schmidt's *Mechanical Ballet* and Schlemmer's *Figural Cabinet*) was presented at the theatre in nearby Jena. This performance, where the scenery almost literally fell down, was held together by the extraordinary and humorous improvising efforts of the Master of Ceremonies, Andreas Weininger. Tut Schlemmer, who was in the audience, describes it: 'The intermission between numbers became longer and longer, one could hear excited debates from behind the curtain, hammering and cursing' (T. Schlemmer in Neumann [1970] 1993: 166–7). Weininger, forced to make frequent impromptu appearances in front of the curtain, made some very apposite jokes about the 'new unity between art and technology', Gropius's carefully thought up slogan for the Exhibition. The evening, which of course had all the worthy burgers of Weimar watching, passed off more or less humorously. Bauhaus students, who had had little time to 'tech' their pieces on the Jena stage, learnt the hard way that puppetry and mechanical effects are fraught with hazard for the under-rehearsed and the unprepared, and indeed the lack of professional stage expertise within the Bauhaus always frustrated Schlemmer. Of these two performance events in the Bauhaus Week, the 'Mechanical Cabaret' is most closely connected to the actual output of the Bauhaus stage at Weimar; whereas *The Triadic Ballet* connects closely with its ideals, at least as understood by Schlemmer.

Both *The Triadic Ballet* and Weimar mechanical productions feature in the Bauhaus theatre book *Die Bühne im Bauhaus* (1925), published in the hiatus in 1924/1925 when the new Bauhaus at Dessau was still being planned, and the Weimar Bauhaus was already closing down. This book formed the basis for the later English expanded edition *The Theater of the Bauhaus* (Gropius and Wensinger [1961] 1996).[21]

Scheper makes a useful point about the 1925 book, that it really represents more hopes for the future of the Bauhaus stage than any consistent achievements at Weimar (Scheper 1988: 95). Comic and mechanical productions such as those described above may at first seem to have little to do with the deeply serious intentions and ideas which Schlemmer expressed in 'Man and Art Figure' ('Mensch und Kunstfigur') (Schlemmer 1925), the leading essay in this publication. It would be a mistake, however, to dismiss the comic as not serious: Schlemmer's personal philosophy of the comic as 'holy' disorder and as one (vital) end of the spectrum of the stage that was as worthy of respect as the 'holy' end that Schreyer represented, probably gave the students constant support and encouragement in their humorous stage productions (Blistène 1999: 265). Moreover, Schlemmer always advocated play as a mode of working, open ended, creative and (unconsciously) 'purposeful'.

'Man and Art Figure' was a manifesto for a new German theatre, visionary in intent, quite new in its approach, metaphysical in its profundity; the
comic would be an intrinsic part of this 'Gestalt', as well as a means of
discovering it.[22] The clown, according to Schlemmer, is a sort of 'priest':
man the actor becomes a tragic actor in theatre or a clown in circus. Even
so, whilst he approved of comedy and understood why the students rejected
Schreyer's 'poetic' theatre, he regrets the lack of interest in the 'poem of our
times' ('das Zeitgedicht') (March 1923) (Schlemmer [1958] 1977: 65):

> Literature is avoided almost on principle; therefore, it's all to do with
> form. Moveables, collapsible flats. Anything mechanical, lighting ef-
> fects. At the most, dance. All this is nearer of course to the handcraft
> of the Bauhaus students than acting. I regret that a little. The poem for
> our times slumbers. The poets fail us (June 1923) (Schlemmer [1958]
> 1977: 66).

What is little understood is that Schlemmer saw the poet as part of his
vision for a new theatre, and that poetry was very much part of the future
of his 'total theatre'; it was never just a 'Schaubühne' or visual stage, characterised by Schlemmer in 1924 as the designer's component within the
stage ('the builder of form and colour'), the other components being the
'Spielbühne' ('play stage') of the actor and the 'Sprechbühne' ('voice stage')
of the author (Schlemmer 1925: 10).[23] He considered Shakespeare and later
Schiller to have touched the height of theatre in the past, lost high points
where the aesthetic, cultural, ethical and political were one, which he was
hoping to reach again in Germany via dance and popular theatre. He felt
that theatre itself had become debased into representative imitative stages
and offered no hope of renewal. He admired post-revolutionary Russian
stages before social realism set in, in particular Meyerhold's work, Taïroff's
Blue Bird and Vaktangoff's *Dybuk*, having seen the Russian theatre ensem-
ble in Berlin, and having heard of them by repute before that (Scheper
1988: 245–8). What he says in the letter to Otto Meyer quoted previously
is that the kind of 'mechanical theatre' the students were producing in the
end lacked the profound idea, the metaphysical dimension, that Schlemmer
himself thought central to any revival of German theatre.[24]

The idea of a specifically German aesthetic as opposed to say French
or Russian was particularly dear to his heart. He felt there were certain
German qualities, found in German Gothic architecture and art, that lent
themselves to a spiritual dimension in art and philosophy and would ultimately shape a German theatre. These did not include the unrestrained
'hand wavings' (as Schlemmer called them!) (Schlemmer [1929] 1965: 13)
and emotional outpourings of (German) Expressionist Dance of the time.
And he felt German aesthetics to be more robust than those of the French
who lacked the mysticism permeating German visual art and were (he felt)
excessively interested in form without the soul that such form expressed

(a formalism exemplified by Cubism). The idea of developing a noble and even spiritual (and thereby ethical and purposeful) theatre for the times runs through 'Man and Art Figure' and drives his subsequent work at Dessau. One phrase Schlemmer was very fond of when describing his art was 'Gebrauchsgegenstände der Seele' (Kunz 1991: 91) which roughly translates as 'objects of practical use for the soul'; this applies equally to his ideal (German) theatre as much as it does to this paintings and sculptures. The ideas which he held on developing a new German theatre were influenced by Schiller's writings and those of William Worringer (Worringer [1908] [1948] 1953). Worringer was analysing the significance and meaning of the cycles of abstract tendencies in visual art, and what these indicated about the spiritual state of a culture. Schlemmer felt he was in a cycle that cried out for the discipline of the abstract form of expression.

Schlemmer had formulated his ideas about the particular German approach to the stage over the two years or so following the successful debut of *The Triadic Ballet* at Stuttgart in 1922. This is shown by the outline for the stage workshop (never on the official curriculum at Weimar) which Schlemmer drew up sometime in 1923 following Schreyer's departure, and submitted to the Council of Masters for approval.

> *The Stage Workshop of the Bauhaus in Weimar*
> Direction: Oskar Schlemmer
> Technical Direction: The mastercraftsmen of the Staatl. Bauhaus
> *Internal Department*
> Field of activity: investigation of the basic elements of stage production and design: *space, form, color, sound, movement, light.*
> Practical experiments.
> Independent designs (Schlemmer in Wingler 1969: 59).

He later used this as the basis for setting up the Dessau workshop. Space and spatial manipulation and understanding is central to it, and it is noteworthy that Spengler in his then recently published book *The Decline of the West (Der Untergang des Abendlandes)* (Spengler [1918] [1922] [1921–2] 1932) had designated space as the primary embodied manifestation of Western civilisation, and the Gothic as the height of this particular cultural 'Gestalt'. Schlemmer read Spengler (April 1920)[25] (Schlemmer 1972: 77) and admired the German Gothic hugely.

Yet little of this theatre work came to pass in the Weimar Bauhaus, despite the 'trumpet blowing' in the Bauhaus theatre book published in 1925. Part of the problem was that in 1923 Schlemmer was very busy with the mural paintings he prepared for the Bauhaus Week in September that year. Then he had an unsuccessful and financially draining production of *The Triadic Ballet* at Dresden after the Bauhaus Week performance at Weimar. That autumn, as an active up-and-coming stage designer in 'mainstream' theatre, he designed a Carl Hauptmann play at the Berlin Volksbühne, *The*

Disloyal Tsar (*Der abtrünnige Zar*). In 1924, Schlemmer was also designing two stage productions at the Berlin Volksbühne: Leonid Andrejew's *King Hunger* (*König Hunger*) and Friedrich Wolf's *Poor Konrad* (*Der arme Konrad*).[26] By May 1924, he was already helping Maholy-Nagy prepare the Bauhaus theatre book.[27] The Bauhaus at Weimar closed that year.

As a result, Schlemmer and Maholy-Nagy in 1924 had to put together the book on the theatre of the Bauhaus when, as far as Schlemmer was concerned, the job had scarcely begun.

So there was a difference between aspirations and reality. The book has in addition two 'Utopian' essays on the theatre of the future, one by Maholy-Nagy ('Theatre, Circus, Variety' ('Theater, Zirkus, Varieté')) and one by Farkas Molnár on 'U Theatre'; these also have little to do with the practical reality of the Bauhaus stage at Weimar.[28] Maholy-Nagy's very different approach to space compared to that of Schlemmer is apparent in his essay that set out his stage vision, packed with action, technology and complex dynamic movement. Schlemmer's masterly, complex and densely argued essay 'Man and Art Figure', which heads the 1925 book and the 1961 English-language edition, is more easily understood in connection with ideas already realised in *The Triadic Ballet* rather than work not yet undertaken at Dessau, yet, dense and difficult as it is to understand, it also provides a key to all Schlemmer's work on stage. There is a stress on transformation of the human body through costume (as there is in *The Triadic Ballet*) as one way of realising the new theatre to come, but other forms of theatre using other means are also anticipated; but Schlemmer does not specify how these are to be created. Dessau was just the start of his investigations which were cut short in 1929 when he left. These theatre types are:

Abstract Technical Theatre and the Colour Stage
The Static, Dynamic, and Tectonic Stage
The Mechanical, Automatic, and Electric Stage
The Gymnastic, Acrobatic, and Equilibristic Stage
The Comic, Grotesque, and Burlesque Stage
The Serious, Sublime, and Monumental Stage
The Political, Philosophical, and Metaphysical Stage (Schlemmer
    1925: 19).

When watching some contemporary theatre pieces these labels often uncannily describe what one sees. For example, Need Company's *The Porcelain Project* (Barbican Centre, London BITE09) is a 'Comic, Grotesque' (even 'Burlesque') piece created through material form (here ceramics) and visual and bodily play with it; the work of the French director Aurélien Bory in 'Les Sept Planches de la Ruse'(Barbican Centre, London BITE09) can be described as 'The Static, Dynamic and Tectonic Stage', and the work of Elizabeth Streb might be described as this or equally 'The Gymnastic, Acrobatic, and Equilibristic Stage' (for example, *Streb*, Barbican Centre, London BITE99): both Bory and Streb play with large structures on stage. The viscerally sensuous and optically rich work of Socìetas Raffaello Sanzio could well be described as 'the Serious, Sublime and Monumental' (*Inferno, Paradiso* and *Purgatorio*, Barbican Centre, London BITE09), and at times 'The Political, Philosophical, and Metaphysical' (as could much of Robert Wilson's work). Part of the methodology of this study is to develop these first tentative links between Schlemmer's vision and our contemporary stages across the gap of eighty years and more, and many of these artists will be returned to in the course of later chapters.

The Triadic Ballet was a far more subtle and visually stunning piece, and far more professional, than any of the 'mechanical theatre' pieces featured alongside it in the 1925 Bauhaus theatre book. Its choreography was forged out of the material form of the built-up, geometrically inspired costumes, which directed and controlled the movements of the dancers. As such, it was in tune with the ethos of the Bauhaus as outlined earlier, where material texture, strength and tensile qualities were a lived experience and informed the creation of artwork.

Raman Schlemmer emphasises the central importance to his grandfather of *The Triadic Ballet* (Schlemmer 2001: 23). Although the Bauhaus tended to take credit for *The Triadic Ballet*, not least in the several photographs gracing the pages of *The Theater of the Bauhaus* book, on the whole it was always financed with a great deal of hardship by Schlemmer himself, and was largely built in the early 1920s outside the Bauhaus, in a workshop in Canstatt, Stuttgart, with help of Casca, his brother. More expense was caused through the years by storage, and essential remakes and repairs were always a struggle to finance. When Schlemmer fell out with his co-dancers Albert Burger and Else Hötzel in the mid-1920s they took several of the costumes with them, a body blow from which he never quite financially recovered. The piece was only performed in its entirety two or three times in his lifetime, and during the 1930s the costumes, incomplete and in need of expensive repairs, languished in storage in Berlin, a source of huge frustration to him. When he sent several figures to New York for the 1938 Museum of Modern Art Exhibition on the Bauhaus, the coming war meant they stayed there, and were only recovered through the efforts of his widow Tut Schlemmer in the 1950s (Bogner 1997: 29). Despite all this, *The Triadic Ballet* plays a central role in Schlemmer's artistic *oeuvre* and it is the piece he is best known for. In a sense, both the essay 'Man and Art Figure' and *The Triadic Ballet* together articulate Schlemmer's vision of an ethical and efficacious theatre for the twentieth century. They are dealt with more fully in Chapter 4, 'Motion'.

The 1961 English edition of *The Theater of the Bauhaus*, edited by Gropius and Wensinger in America thirty-six years later, adds Schlemmer's 1927 essay/lecture 'Bühne' and many photographs of later Dessau work to the original 1925 edition, in order to give more complete coverage of the Bauhaus stage as a whole. The Dessau stage work, with its minimalist smoothed out bodies and featureless head masks, created from a limited palette of colour and movement, where bodies in motion engage with held geometric objects and materials, looks quite different from the rich colours and built-up geometric costumes of *The Triadic Ballet*, and from the 'mechanical theatre' work of Weimar. The Dessau Bauhaus is often called 'Constructivist' in approach.

Constructivism originated in Russia before and after the Revolution of 1917,[29] and after the revolution advocated an approach to art that was strongly analytical and utilitarian; it opposed 'easel art' and paintings (as practised persistently by many of the Bauhaus artists), and developed the idea of industrial design. In other words, artistic talent and sensibility should be turned to creating prototypes that were fit for their purpose, economical to produce, and used the most suitable material for their function. The prototype could then be mass manufactured. That Constructivist thinking was applied on the Russian stage is clear from the work of Meyerhold and others with their pared down stagings and 'boiler suit' costumes. To say it was applied by Schlemmer on the Bauhaus stage is to risk missing the way his continuing Romantic aesthetic philosophy permeated the analytical and controlled approach he took. It is also true that Constructivism in Dessau was always tempered by Bauhaus sensibilities and even by Maholy-Nagy's own personality, which was not at all the dry unimaginative soul he is sometimes mistaken for.[30] It is telling that Maholy-Nagy left when Hannes Meyer took over from Gropius because he could not endorse the new harder functionalist approach to design and architecture.

The freewheeling days of the 'Wandervögel' (literally 'roving birds') of the Weimar Bauhaus came to an end at Dessau (Michaud 1978a: 50, Bogner 1997: 20). But even before then, the Bauhaus was under pressure to change. One source of constant criticism was the presence of Theo van Doesburg in Weimar from 1921. As leader of the De Stijl movement and advocate of strongly Constructivist ideas, van Doesburg seemed to make it his mission to sharpen up thinking at the Bauhaus, encourage Dadaesque scepticism of Itten's and Gropius's regime, and turn the Bauhaus into a Constructivist stronghold.[31] However, instead of employing van Doesburg, who clearly thought he was the man for the job, and who had been holding alternative lectures for disaffected students in Weimar (and there were plenty of those) Gropius employed instead the Hungarian Maholy-Nagy. Maholy-Nagy replaced Itten, sweeping away the harmonization classes of Gertrude Grunow, Itten's breathing exercises and the self-mortifying practices of Mazdaznan.[32] However, much of what was best in Itten's classes—the pulverisation and analysis of materials and their reconstitution into material structures and forms—remained. And despite van Doesburg's criticisms, the painters themselves at the

Bauhaus had been teaching analysis of form, breaking down the tools of their work, in a way that was not unsympathetic to Constructivist ideals of analysing and understanding the building bricks of artistic creation using a quasi-scientific approach.[33] The crucial difference however, and one which will be explored in the next chapter, is the prevailing and thoroughly German idea of Gestalt thinking, and this ensured a deeply spiritual and philosophical bent to Bauhaus teaching which was never eradicated. The unique and powerful synthesis of Expressionist idealism and Constructivist analysis, which Schlemmer worked hard to preserve, speaks loudly of the humanitarian ideals of the Bauhaus, especially under Gropius, though perhaps less so under Hannes Meyer who took over in 1928 and Mies van der Rohe from 1930.

In autumn 1924, even though Gropius had sacked Itten and had Maholy-Nagy in post, driving the Bauhaus towards some more hardheaded realism, the Weimar Bauhaus finally had its funding withdrawn by the right-wing Weimar government, and Gropius had to close the institution. He negotiated a new host for the Bauhaus, north in the industrial town of Dessau. In this he achieved another miracle considering the economic state of the nation, since not only would the town fund the running of the Bauhaus but it also agreed to construct a new building for it. However, budgets were impossibly tight. In the course of 1925, work began on a structure of steel and glass on a vast empty field outside the town, fashioned following the new Constructivist principle of 'form follows function', where extraneous decorative details were cut out in favour of clean lines, and huge glass windows were hung like curtains on a steel structure, forming sheer walls letting in light.

The impact of the new building which was finally opened in December 1926 is hard to gauge today. Here is Hoffmann describing his first view of it: 'I was accompanied there by an assistant; he showed me the first introduction to the Bauhaus building. I found it sensational: how could anyone put such a raw structure in a field!' (Bogner 1997: 15). Rudolf Arnheim gives an account some years later of his visit in 1927 saying the building was kept apart from the 'dingy crotchety small town houses' by the railway tracks, and is thus isolated: 'two glaringly white giant boxes, the one upright, the other horizontal, on a grassy plane. A few red balconies and windows subdivide the surfaces; otherwise the whole is bald and flat.' He concludes, however, that the 'practically useful' is at the same time 'the beautiful' (Arnheim 1997: 60).

The style of the building did not spring ready formed from Gropius's head but evolved from his own previous work, of course, and from similar buildings and architectural ideas around in Europe and Russia at that time. Although the Bauhaus is chiefly associated with this Modernist style, it did not develop it in isolation but as part of a Europe-wide change of style. Its widespread roots outside the Bauhaus explain the huge impact of the Modernist architectural style in America and beyond.[34]

In addition to the two wings of the main building (with an accommodation block for students), there were six houses for the masters and their families, and ambitiously and eventually, the Törten housing estate in the South of the city. This estate also applied all the principles of modern architecture, ethical and utilitarian, that Gropius advocated, and which he had been developing in conjunction with ideas from the rest of Europe and Russia (Bogner 1997: 18). In other words, mass housing, desperately needed by ordinary people, could be well designed and pleasant to live in, if only the prototype were carefully enough thought out. As students drifted back to the Bauhaus and workshops were opened in temporary buildings in the town, fittings and accessories for the new Bauhaus were designed and sent for manufacture, under the guidance and inspiration of Maholy-Nagy and Gropius himself.

Schlemmer in the meantime pursued his own work and wondered if he would be invited to join the new Bauhaus. Schlemmer never got on particularly well with Gropius though he respected the difficult task he faced. Schlemmer, a deeply moral man, and happily married,[35] disapproved of some of Gropius's sexual liaisons, and Gropius in turn never really understood Schlemmer. Gropius considered him, it seems, rather unworldly financially and took advantage of this, since when Schlemmer returned eventually to the new Bauhaus he was never on a full contract that paid as much as the other masters were earning, even though he had a family to support. In addition, he had had a row with Gropius at Weimar towards the end of 1924, when Gropius had a contract to refurbish the theatre at Jena. Schlemmer had been commissioned by Gropius to paint the auditorium and did so using geometric shapes and contrasting colours. The story goes that van Doesburg came in and saw it, declared how horrible it was and how it clashed with the interior of the theatre. Gropius heard of this and at once ordered the ceiling to be painted over. Naturally this caused great ill feeling between Gropius and Schlemmer (Bogner 1997: 35). As the new Bauhaus building took shape, some students began agitating for Schlemmer's return and the establishment of theatre in the Bauhaus once again (Schawinsky 1971: 34). After some negotiations, a small 'framed' stage was planned in the new building, in the main hall, tempting Schlemmer back to the Bauhaus. He had never had such a dedicated space, however small, at the Weimar Bauhaus. He arrived in the autumn of 1925 when the building was of course not yet finished. Indeed it was December 1926 before the new building was completed and dedicated in an evening's celebrations, which included, of course, a performance from the theatre. Schlemmer always rather dryly and humorously described his theatre as the 'flower in the buttonhole' of the Bauhaus, always on display on special occasions to stun and amaze the local officials and funders. Elsewhere, somewhat bitter about his own half wages and general underfunding, he referred to it sardonically as the fifth wheel on the Bauhaus wagon (December 1926) (Schlemmer [1958] 1977: 90).

At first, in Dessau during 1925, Schlemmer was busy ensuring the stage was built to his (very modest) specifications and planning the research he would undertake on it. He wrote to his wife in November 1925:

> Schmidtchen is very busy in matters around the stage. Yesterday a great debate with Gropius over equipping the theater. Schmidtchen wants the entire theatre mechanised. No chance, as I had anticipated; and besides I don't want it anyway . . . I am going to push through my plan, which is for an absolutely basic stage[36] (November 1925) (Schlemmer [1958] 1977: 83–4).

And 'Gropius is building me a stage which it will be a pleasure to get hold of, despite its small size' (December 1925) (Schlemmer [1958] 1977: 85). 'Schmidtchen' is a more or less affectionate term for Joost Schmidt who ran what was in effect a mechanical theatre workshop ('Die Plastische Werkstatt') throughout the Dessau Bauhaus period, completely separate to Schlemmer's stage workshop (Schmidt 1984: 44–76). Relations were not always totally harmonious (Schlemmer [1958] 1977: 92).

The stage was a small framed stage (see Moyniham and Odom 1984: 52) which opened on to the hall on one side (the configuration most used by Schlemmer) and the dining hall on the other. It had some wing space and a three or four track system for suspending and sliding flats and so on across the stage. This basic space was supplemented by rostra that could be built up into various combinations. He also wanted 'a curtain, leotards, fabric' (November 1925) (Schlemmer [1958] 1977: 84). In 1927 he said: 'Although originally meant for lectures and smaller events, it [the stage] nevertheless provides the most elementary tools to undertake serious experiments into stage matters' (Schlemmer 1927c: 1). This stage needs to be seen in the context of what was available in the way of stage lighting and stage technology in the 1920s, a context that has been fully and ably explored by Baugh (2005). Baugh demonstrates how many scenic artists at that time, within the Bauhaus and outside, such as Craig, Appia, Meyerhold, the Futurists, and especially the Italian designer Mariano Fortuny (107) were developing the 'overall plasticity of a constructed theatrical event' (123), and especially the capacity of light to go beyond 'the function of illumination' and to take on 'a material quality in its own right' (119). Light is returned to in Chapter 3, but it is important to stress here that although Schlemmer shared these aims, his stage including the lighting was very simple and nothing was really available to him beyond flats, drapes, rostra, costume and few basic lights; and there was no cyclorama of course and probably no dimmer (Meier 2006).

Schlemmer worked at Dessau between 1925 and 1929 when, under pressure to produce the political left-wing theatre that came to dominate its stage until the closure of the Bauhaus in Berlin in 1933, he left for a new post at Breslau. In that time, he transformed the possibilities of stage space in fundamental ways. He introduced the body, time and motion into the static painterly space that had hitherto constrained him. It is a transformation that is present in *The Triadic Ballet* but was deliberately and systematically undertaken at Dessau. The stage elements of the body, motion, space and light, objects, and costume were isolated, analysed and deployed on a minimalist stage at Dessau with few or no resources. Schlemmer cut the dynamics of stage space down to the barest of stage elements. The main body of work which Schlemmer achieved at Dessau was *The Bauhaus Dances*, eleven short pieces developed over four years from 1926, and which he took on tour around various German cities in 1929, supplemented with a lecture (Schlemmer 1927c).[37] The major pieces consisted of neutralised figures dressed in white padded body suits and full head masks. Coloured stockings, body vests and so on were added as necessary. The pieces were called 'dances' as Schlemmer said for 'want of a better term' (Schlemmer [1929] 1965: 16). Of necessity he was forced to work with students with little or no movement training, so he developed techniques to overcome this. As a result, Schlemmer investigated the fundamental building blocks of performance and completely escaped working within the narrow bounds of Western genre terms such as 'dance'. *Space Dance (Raumtanz)*, for example, is interested in motion but there is no dancerly skill as such required to execute it, simply sensitivity to space. Motion is an element common to all stage work. *Form Dance (Formentanz)* sets the body in motion working with 3-D objects that are held (see Figure 1.1). Again, no nimble virtuosity is required, merely a sensitivity to space and object. Other 'dances' (*Metal Dance (Metalltanz)*, *Glass Dance (Glastanz)*, *Stick Dance (Stäbetanz)* and *Hoop Dance (Reifentanz)*) use material objects, shapes and forms in a similar way. There are two pieces that play humorously with the dynamics of stage scenery transforming space, *Box Play (Kastenspiel)*, reworked on occasion as *Building Problems (Bauprobleme)*, and *Flats Dance (Kulissentanz)*,[38] with more than a nod to contemporary silent comic films that Schlemmer loved so much. These pieces and others (*Gesture Dance (Gestentanz)* and *Three Women (Frauentanz)*) attempt to mix narrative in with these 'type' figures in different ways, and were highly comic in their impact.

Other work was also undertaken at Dessau. At one point in 1927 Schlemmer tried to incorporate the 'word' into his work in a piece called *House of Pi or The House of Stars (Haus Pi oder das Sternheim)* but abandoned it, feeling it required far more work than he had time to devote to it at that particular point. In *House of Pi* it seemed the 'word' tended to mask the direct physical perception of space which Schlemmer successfully explored in several of *The Bauhaus Dances* and he needed more time to develop his ideas on language as part of the total stage Gestalt: time which he never got. He always longed to find the link between his work on space and 'poetry'. Another piece by Schlemmer in these years was *Treppenwitz* or *Staircase Joke* in 1925 (Michaud 1978a: 152). We cannot really understand the title as we have no word for this in English. It refers to the *bonmot* or witty response you remember too late, presumably on the stairs on your way out, but Schlemmer would have made full use of the idea of the staircase as both a practical

Figure 1.1   Oskar Schlemmer, *Form Dance* [*Formentanz*] (dancers Werner Siedhoff, Albert Mentzel, Fisher), 1928. Photo Archive, C. Raman Schlemmer, IT-288824 Oggebbio (VB) Italy.

and 'mystical' pathway and played with real stairs (a smaller set of theatrical treads and sometimes much larger sets of stairs) on stage. In fact, there are innumerable pieces created for the Bauhaus at Dessau which we know little about because they would be done once and abandoned, or bowdlerised and remade in different versions. For example, Schawinsky (1971: 43) describes his production of *Olga Olga* which clearly turned on ideas first developed in *Flats Dance* by Schlemmer but developed into a more content driven piece. He calls *Olga Olga* an example of 'equilibristics' (usually meaning circus tricks involving balancing): 'You use the things of daily life in reference to the imagination without giving an answer to anything. You go further—you jump out of the frame with your idea' (Schawinsky 1984: 43). Circus tricks, action and humour were a vital impulse for the avant-garde as a whole in this period and the Dessau stage was no exception, since no 'meaning' as such could be extracted from them, no plot, no characters, no imitation or reproduction of life, but they were still pure performance. Play and its fluid forms of creativity were vital here. *Light Play* (*Lichtstück*) (1927) played with scale and shadow perhaps developing some of the ideas of Hirschfeld-Mack's Weimar 'mechanical theatre' piece *Reflected Light Play* using simple lights and screens but with the human figure added (Scheper 1988: 162). The letters also make it clear that pieces such as *The Figural Cabinet* were reworked and performed within the Bauhaus to great acclaim and that figures from *The Triadic Ballet* were being utilised to make one-off pieces.

Figure 1.2   Oskar Schlemmer, *Metal Party* [*Metallisches Fest am Bauhaus*], February 1929. Photo Archive, C. Raman Schlemmer, IT-288824 Oggebbio (VB) Italy.

Most importantly of all, Schlemmer was in effect director and designer of the various major parties that took place at the Dessau Bauhaus. Of course there were also many smaller parties that regularly took place, some organised by students, and many dances and performances by the 'Bauhauskapelle' or band. The major parties that Schlemmer organised can be considered participatory performances, works of art in themselves that aimed at the cultural, social and aesthetic harmony striven for in the Bauhaus, where at times audience and performers merged as one. These themed parties involved the whole Bauhaus in making and designing décor and costumes. Schlemmer made full use of the space and facilities of the new building to create experiences that immersed the participants into what was essentially a theatrical experience. One such party was 'The Metal Party' in 1929 (see Figure 1.2). Originally planned as a bell party, it was (perhaps wisely) decided this would be too noisy; it was changed to the theme of metal, though many bells still made their appearance. The interior of the building, not just the canteen, was transformed using 'bent sheets of foil' and 'walls of silvered masks', ceilings studded with gleaming brass fruit bowls' and 'everywhere coloured metallic paper and the ever beautiful Christmas tree balls, some of enormous size' (Whitford 1992: 278). A gleaming metal slide propelled you into the main foyer. Of course everyone dressed appropriately using metal and silver. Schlemmer described how one girl coquettishly approached the men with a screwdriver attached to her wrist and asked if they would like to tighten up her loose screws (February 1929) (Schlemmer [1958] 1977: 110)! In short, the Bauhaus was touched with magic on that winter's night early in 1929; as Schlemmer recorded in his diary:

> The Bauhaus also looked attractive from outside, as it shone into the winter night. The windows, stuck on the inside with metallic paper; the white and coloured bulbs organized room by room; the view right through them which the great block of glass permitted: these, for one entire night, transformed the building, this workshop, into the 'University of United Form' (February 1929) (Schlemmer [1958] 1977: 110).

Schlemmer also describes a musical staircase ('every step gave out a different tone') allowing several musical 'virtuosos' to show off (109) in the course of the evening. Usually at the parties there were sketches on stage which were light hearted and amusing and Schlemmer (and not always at parties) opened up the theatre stage at the back exposing it to the canteen where most students and staff often gathered socially, and would give a short performance. Other memorable parties at Dessau were White Festival (1926), the Festival of Slogans (1927), Silent Night (1927) and Beards and Noses and Hearts Party (1928). What these parties actually represent is the 'unified work of art' which Gropius said was the aim of the Bauhaus, a total fusion of decorative art and social space, a cultural and ethical Gestalt or living form realised for one evening. The fact they took place in the new Bauhaus building was their inspiration and their strength since the new building was itself an intense and beautiful realisation of the design ideals of the Bauhaus, where harmonious design, integration of colour, minute attention to 'space shaping' replaced the need for decorative art to sit framed upon the walls as paintings, as it had been in the past. The parties added the complex element of humanity engaged in social intercourse, a necessary completion of the unified ethical/cultural Gestalt. The Bauhaus was indeed no legend, as Tut Schlemmer pointed out (T. Schlemmer in Neumann [1970] 1993: 164). It lived its ideals, usually on a day-to-day basis with strife, sorrow and power struggles; but for the party nights, the ideal was briefly, fragilely, ephemerally, realised. 'Tell me: how do you party? And I will tell you who you are' said Schlemmer (February 1929) (Schlemmer [1958] 1977: 109). Many students were still talking of the Bauhaus parties decades later.

After the successful but brief tour of Germany with the Bauhaus Dances in 1929, which was meticulously planned and organised by Schlemmer himself on a shoestring budget, he decided to accept another contract at Breslau, and in effect never really worked in an experimental stage space again.[39] His reasons for leaving centred on the turn that the Bauhaus had taken towards stronger functionalism under Meyer, and his keen sense that his theatre research was no longer understood or able to contribute to the new ethos in the Bauhaus. His strong ethical, social and aesthetic vision simply were incompatible with the strongly political Bauhaus that was rapidly emerging in opposition to a bullying right-wing local government. The Breslau Academy was prestigious and seemed to offer him new opportunities for stage research. His plans, however, were overtaken by political developments isolating him and making it impossible for him to work as an artist or teacher. His decision to leave Dessau was the beginning of a decade or more of unhappy times which would one feels have scarcely been avoided no matter what he did, given his fundamental opposition to the emerging regime in Germany. He found it increasingly difficult to get work as an artist and some of his works, including the murals at the old Weimar Bauhaus, were expunged. He was exhibited in the Degenerate Art (Entartete Kunst) Exhibition in 1937, then a mark of shame and distress to a man of integrity, but surely now a mark of pride. With a family to support, he was forced in the end to work in a lacquer factory in Wuppertal, miles from his family who stayed in internal exile in the South of Germany in a specially built family home he never really shared. He contracted a minor illness, and in the days before penicillin, died in a nursing home in April 1943.

And so the parties came to an end: not only for Schlemmer but also for the Bauhaus itself.[40] Under Hannes Meyer, who replaced Gropius in 1928, the Bauhaus took an overt lurch to the left and stood up in outright opposition to the right-wing local government that had taken over Dessau.

It ended with the Bauhaus, now under Mies van der Rohe, leaving its purpose-built home there and decamping to temporary and insecure buildings in Berlin. It could not last. It finally shut in 1933 with the arrest of the last of its students and masters and closure of the buildings. But by that time most of the leading teachers, the ones that added 'lustre' to the Bauhaus, had gone. And in subsequent years most were to flee to America, where they spread Bauhaus teaching via Harvard (Gropius), the New Bauhaus in Chicago (Maholy-Nagy) and Black Mountain College (Albers) in North Carolina. These are only the most famous names; there were innumerable others who influenced not only design and pedagogy but stimulated the growth of the avant-garde in the States and especially the push into performance (Pawelke 2005). Often the innovators had been at the Bauhaus or were taught by Bauhaus masters in the States.[41] The influence of the Bauhaus in performance terms has been recently traced not only by Pawelke (2005) but, interestingly, via music and sound, by Schoon (2006). It is not the task of this book to trace minutely instances of the impact of the Bauhaus stage on American avant-garde performance in the course of the twentieth century, though there will often be reason to mention specific instances of this; it is rather to claim the contemporary relevance and usefulness of Bauhaus thinking today, mainly in terms of the stage but more broadly recognising that its work is not yet complete, indeed has scarcely begun. The ideals and ideas of the Bauhaus need to be understood in broader focus than has yet been undertaken in any studies of the institution, where Bauhaus essentialism and idealism hitherto seems to dog its interpretation and cloud our ability to imitate their pragmatism and utilise those ideals. Accordingly, the next chapter concentrates on understanding this intellectual context from which the Bauhaus and its theatre emerged.

2 Modernism

It is May 2009 and I am visiting an exhibition: *Das Bauhaus kommt aus Weimar*. In the New Bauhaus Museum, Weimar, Goethe's exquisitely arranged blocks of colour, dissections of leaves and pulverisations of natural materials are gathered in glass cases displayed amidst the copious artifacts, paintings, design drawings and photographs of the Weimar Bauhaus. Goethe's 'exercises' are scarcely distinguishable from those of Johannes Itten and his pupils on the Foundation Course of the Weimar Bauhaus over a hundred years later, which lie beside them. Bauhaus masters and students alike had access to Goethe's work, these very same startling combinations of textures and colours, these robust forms and their often fragile reality, their freshness, their scientific precision and their aesthetic beauty. The parallels are extraordinarily exact. Once more one senses the later impact of the new Dessau context on the pedagogical, aesthetic, ethical and social ideals of the earlier Weimar Bauhaus: the profound shift from a historically rooted Weimar idealism, whose gaze was ultimately directed heavenwards above the grinding machines of industry and the dusty factory floor, to the transformed faith in Dessau that determined to engage strongly with a modern Germany, an emerging economy and practical hopes for a better society. The teachers who guided this brave and ethical shift (for ethical it was) without the Bauhaus descending into utilitarianism and functionalism were only able to do so because of the prevailing ethos of the Weimar Bauhaus, a system in which the world was felt to be interconnected, formed, deliberate, purposeful, a belief system which continued to be held by its leader Walter Gropius, and the lecturers who taught there, László Maholy-Nagy, Joseph Albers, Wassily Kandinsky, Paul Klee: and above all Oskar Schlemmer who led the Theatre Workshop, the 'beating heart' of the Dessau Bauhaus (Goldberg 2003), and, as he put it, a 'force for order' (January 1926) (Schlemmer [1958] 1972: 189).

The prevailing canon of beliefs in regard to Modernism, particularly in relation to the Bauhaus, can alienate us from history, denying us access to past wisdom and past mistakes, and prevent us from advancing our understanding of ourselves. Hubert Hoffmann quotes Klemens Klotz: 'Modernity isn't even here yet, Modernity is yet to come' (Bogner 1997: 15). If

Gestalt thinking at the Bauhaus, and its development through the Dessau years, is properly understood, and if we realign the Bauhaus as an adaptation of early and late nineteenth-century thinking into the challenging contexts of the early twentieth century, contexts to which it was more than equal intellectually and practically, then we will understand its essentialist principles of creative form as flexible and expansive enough to speak to us at the start of the twenty-first century. Understanding the theatre enables us to do this. In terms of theatre itself and its history, Schlemmer's stage, his '(meta)physical' theatre, is only today being realised in the shifting and permeable spaces of the postmodern stage that forge communicated meaning in the absolute physicality of their *mise en scène*. The cutting-edge postmodern stage, often non-narrative, non-character based, but always rich in its application of the stage elements, eloquent in its articulation of space and uncompromising in its engagements with the quotidian and unrelenting question of how to live, lays bare our culture, politics, aesthetics and morals, not only as they are but as they might be. It exposes the bodying forth of our culture in all its complexity and demonstrates how it is in our power to influence, change and transform ourselves. The stages of Jan Fabre or Pina Bausch, Jan Lauwers or Robert Wilson catch us in the very act of living and shaping the milieu in which cultural meaning, impact and agency is forged, and insistently demand we engage actively in the process. Schlemmer's theatre of the Bauhaus did no less.

The theatre of the Bauhaus is impossible to understand if we rely on commonly held notions about the Bauhaus itself, that is, coming to terms with and embracing mechanisation, recognition of the importance of integrating the machine, responding to the pressure of increasing industrialisation and so on. These realities, undoubtedly present in the Bauhaus, and deriving from the crisis of the social and industrial milieu following the First World War and before, cause commentators, especially those not from a theatre background, to describe Schlemmer's stage figures as 'robotic', a tribute to 'man as machine', 'mechanised performers' and so on. Complex streams were interacting at the Bauhaus, especially in its early years, where hope in and concentration on the future was at least equally balanced with neo-Romantic Expressionist sensibilities. Social, industrial and scientific developments in the mid to late nineteenth century in Germany, France and the United Kingdom had done much to advance humanity in the name of progress on every front. Increasing numbers of the population were involved with industrial work in the cities, and manufacturing industry along with the population itself had grown very rapidly in a short space of time. Society was showing the signs of strain long before the First World War and the Wilhelminian regime was in many respects struggling to cope with the rapidity of change. The defeat suffered in the war was to prove its downfall.

German engineers and philosophers had joined forces to suppress the national yearning for metaphysics, but never quite defeated it. Philosophy, psychology, biology and aesthetics proved reluctant to let go of metaphysical mysteries. 'Lebensphilosophie' (vitalism) never lost its appeal, at least for artists, and enjoyed a renaissance in the early twentieth century. The French philosopher Henri Bergson, whose ideas on the creative evolution of man were translated into German in the early years of the twentieth century, fuelled the contemporary vitalist debate which touched scientists and mystics alike.[1] The division between disciplines in universities was still confused. Philosophers and the newly fledged psychologists rubbed shoulders in the same department. Psychologists were sneered at by their disparaging philosopher colleagues as 'scientific' in their approaches to the mind, but even professional psychologists frequently indulged in occult practices.[2] The result was an almighty conflict and confusion in early twentieth-century German Modernism between scientific rationalism and mystical yearnings, and this was faithfully reflected in the Bauhaus.

Schlemmer engaged in the contemporary debates on mechanistic versus holistic interpretations of the world. His own beliefs centred on the relationship between (and mutual interdependence of) 'Natur', 'Geist' and 'Seele'. In Schlemmer's system, largely derived from Ricarda Huch (Huch 1922), 'Natur' is the external material world including the body. 'Geist' is the mind, sometimes highly misleadingly translated only as 'spirit'; importantly, it is the seat of intellectual and rational thought, which he considered non-material and outside space and time.[3] 'Seele' or soul is primarily of this (material) world, and is the crucial link between 'Natur' and 'Geist'. Schlemmer termed art, including his theatre, 'Gebrauchsgegenstände der Seele' or 'utensils', useful tools, for the soul.[4] To understand the theatre of the Bauhaus, as Schlemmer shaped it, we have to understand its threefold rootedness in the material world, the soul and the non-material mind/spirit; and, more widely, to grasp the theatre's role in the Bauhaus as an institution, we need not to repeat the clichés about Bauhaus Modernism but to grasp its contradictions, hopes and aspirations.

As long ago as 1989, Alain Findeli argued for a reappraisal of the Bauhaus, seeing its ideals, particularly in architecture, as a possible 'unfinished project' that was only reaching its fruition in the postmodern era (Findeli 1989/1990: 58). These ideals, which were founded upon 'continuity and connectedness' with the past as much as upon a bold grasping and reshaping of the future, he saw as having been hijacked by the functionalism in architecture that dominated the 1960s and 1970s and which came to distort the vision of social, aesthetic, ethical and cultural unity that the Bauhaus in fact stood for. The historical rootedness of the Bauhaus has been ignored in favour of promoting its radicalism and newness. Galison exposes this process in an important article where he traces members of the Vienna Circle such as Herbert Feigl, Otto Neurath and Rudolf Carnap stepping into (literally and metaphorically) the Bauhaus, and virtually taking over the Bauhaus idea from 1929 onwards, applauding and promoting its functionalism over any holistic and essentially old German values that Gropius had held (Galison 1990). Bauhaus

Modernism was eventually synonymous with the highly influential International Style which by around 1980 was thoroughly discredited, and had in most people's minds degenerated into the notorious 'one size fits all' architectural Fordism, and later, in popular consciousness at least, even concrete 'Brutalism' during the 1960s and 1970s. The identification of the Bauhaus with what became the International Style began early during the period when the institution was lurching towards closure under the new director, the left wing and uncompromising Hannes Meyer, and was boosted in America within the New Bauhaus in Chicago. The process was aided and abetted by Gropius himself to some extent as early as 1930 (Overy 2004). The reason the holistic, Romantic and vitalist values of the Bauhaus were suppressed under Hannes Meyer is very understandable: the desire not to be associated with the National Socialists and Nazi ideology was very strong, and the Bauhaus ideals played into the hands of the enemy. [5] Later, in America, it was equally understandable that its distinguishing holistic, metaphysical and vitalist ethos, so peculiarly German in origin, and so alien to American culture, should have been conveniently forgotten in the educational curricula of the New World.

Many of the philosophical and aesthetic problems here identified and discussed were common intellectual currency around the turn of the century. Schlemmer himself was hugely well read, and so were his painter colleagues at the Bauhaus, and we can assume their general familiarity with contemporary aesthetics and the history of eighteenth- and nineteenth-century European (and in Schlemmer's case especially German) culture. Gestalt thinking was fundamental to the Bauhaus (Lupton and Abbott Miller 1993) and although it has a long history in German culture, it is most easily identified with Goethe.

In its simplest translation, 'Gestalt' means 'form' or 'creative form' or just 'design'. It is also true that the word today is commonly used in German simply to mean form or type and usually lacks the cultural ramifications that it once had in German culture, especially in the early twentieth century, and which dictionary definitions and colloquial use do not reveal. These revolve around the ancient German concept of 'Gestaltung'. The German suffix 'ung' normally is added to verbs (here 'gestalten', to shape or form) to denote the action of the verb.

Arthur Wensinger describes it thus in a note:

> Gestaltung was among the most fundamental terms in the language of the Bauhaus and is used many times by Schlemmer and Maholy-Nagy in their writing, both by itself and in its many compounds, such as Bühnengestaltung, Farbengestaltung, Theatergestaltung. T.Lux Feininger writes: 'if the term "Bauhaus" was a new adaptation of the medieval concept of the "Bauhütte", the headquarters of the cathedral builders, the term "Gestaltung" is old, meaningful and so nearly untranslatable that it has found its way into English usage. Beyond the significance

of shaping, forming, thinking through, it has the flavor of underlining the totality of such fashioning, whether of an artifact or of an idea. It forbids the nebulous and the diffuse. In its fullest philosophical meaning it expresses the Platonic eidolon, the Urbild, the pre-existing form' (Wensinger in Gropius and Wensinger [1961] 1996: 50).

This definition of a 'Gestaltung' towards the end of the quotation has already been given in this study in Chapter 1 where the mention of the 'Platonic eidolon' went unremarked. However, Feininger here equates the 'Gestaltung' or 'Urbild' with the Platonic pre-existing form[6], which can be very misleading, since the Bauhaus, and indeed all artists, explored *material* combinations and creations, hardly a Platonic meditation. The idea of 'fashioning' or creating new 'Gestaltungen' stresses the handling of and action on materials but guided by the precision of an idea, the simplest or 'Ur-'form. It is very hard not to equate the 'Urbild' or 'Ur-form' with a mental (Platonic) idea/ideal but this important caveat about its ultimate manifestation through the *material* world is worth noting if the complexities of the Gestalt concept are ever to be understood. It is surprising that few commentators on the Bauhaus (except Lupton and Abbott Miller 1993) have tackled the notion of 'Gestaltung', or traced its history, given Wensinger's comment about its fundamental importance to the Bauhaus. Schlemmer described his stage work as the process of discovering 'the primary meaning' of the stage through creating a 'Bühnengestaltung', which might be translated as 'shaping of the stage' but this loses the Gestalt overtones. Never before had the visionary found quite such a practical and material realisation as it did in the Bauhaus, and above all on the Bauhaus stage.

Although Feininger in the note quoted earlier describes the term 'Gestaltung' as ancient, its history is here traced from Goethe onwards, since Goethe is of direct relevance to much neo-Romantic thinking in the early part of the twentieth century, particularly his colour theory. Schlemmer not only read Goethe but also the work of Carl Gustav Carus in the 1840s, and later still the work of Ludwig Klages, both of whom developed their vitalist ideas from Goethe's theory of the 'Urpflanze'.[7]

In Keith Hartley's *The Romantic Spirit in German Art*, Werner Hoffmann explains:

'The eye above all, was the organ with which I [Goethe] laid hold of the world,' he recalls in Book 6 of his literary self-portrait 'Dichtung und Wahrheit' ('Poetry and Truth'). A few lines further on, we read: 'Wherever I looked I saw a picture.' Goethe relied on this eidetic faculty all his life; it was the source both of his metamorphic theory of the Urpflanze or archetypal plant—form as variable—and also of his personal Gestalt concept, based on 'inner necessity': form as definition (Hoffmann 1994: 19).

Goethe developed his theory of the 'Urbild' or ideal type, so that all advanced structures (plant or animal) were

> transformations from a single fundamental organism . . . He accounted for similarities among the members of a species by formal laws of self organization ultimately derived from an ideal type he called an Ur-bild . . . In Goethe's morphology, the term 'Gestalt' referred to the self-actualizing wholeness of organic forms . . . He introduced the Gestalt concept to nineteenth century German thought (Ash 1995: 85).

This is an organic not mechanistic theory and it takes into account the dynamism of life, while identifying universals and constants. Goethe's ideal morphotypes were both 'real' and 'nonmaterial'. This is a seemingly impossible paradox, but they are resolved in Gestalt thinking. It concerns the unity of material and non-material worlds, especially the mind. Ash offers Goethe's colour theory as the prime example of this belief in the 'fundamental unity of material and nonmaterial reality' (Ash 1995: 86). Without here fully explaining the differences between Goethe's approach to colour and that of Newton, Goethe claimed colour as a *property of objects themselves* rather than of the refrangible light that hit them; this places the structures or 'Gestalten' into the material world. This is very much in tune with Gestalt thinking but has never been scientifically accepted. However, his descriptions of colour and its behaviour in different circumstances and combinations resulting from this belief have always rung truer for artists than Newton's descriptions of colour optics. In the early twentieth century, Goethe's colour theory formed the basis of Itten's system as taught at the Weimar Bauhaus and developed by his successors, including Kandinsky.

In the latter half of the nineteenth century, especially in Germany, Romantic ideas from the late eighteenth and early nineteenth centuries, and Goethe's theories of basic morphologies, had almost completely died in the face of huge advances in science and growth of materialist think-ing. Gustav Fechner, for example, developed a scientific and systematis-ing approach to psychology (especially the measurement of sensation from around 1860) and so did his pupil Wilhelm Wundt. Psychology was at that time part of philosophy departments in German universities. However, in the 1890s, with the experimental observations of Ehrenfels, more holistic Gestalt psychological thinking began to develop within philosophy, albeit still taking an experiment based, scientific approach (and this always dis-tinguished psychology from philosophy) to the problems of perception and the nature of the mind (Henle 1961: 1–13). Since Ehrenfels was observ-ing 'Gestalten' or unexplained structures in the world around him, there was a historical link with Goethe's thinking, his idealism and his holistic attitudes. In the words of Kohler, 'There was a great wave of relief—as though we were escaping from a prison': that is, an escape from mechanistic approaches to the mind, to qualitative not purely quantitative evidence (Henle

1961: 4). Later called 'Gestalt Psychology', developed around 1912 through the work of Max Wertheimer, and his pupils Wolfgang Kohler and Kurt Koffka, the discipline remained within philosophy departments in German universities until well into the twentieth century, and caused much friction with pure philosophers who eschewed scientific experiment. The philosopher and founder of phenomenology, Edmund Husserl, was closely associated with these men and their Gestalt thinking, but broke from them and their experiments in 1912 and went on to develop his ideas within pure philosophy. Needless to say there was also friction between experimental psychology and natural scientists, since Gestalt Psychology was considered by many scientists to be a kind of absurd neo-vitalism masquerading as science: that is, a vague, almost mystical, unifying life force supposed to be found in matter, was being subjected to dubious 'scientific' perceptual experiments. This mix of science and mystical aspirations is typical of conflicts within early Modernism, though the bifurcated approach had presented no problems to Goethe. By 1928, when a series of lectures were given and well received at the Bauhaus, Gestalt Psychology was quite well respected, and Kandinsky and Klee found it accorded with their own theories of art which had developed largely independently of these developments in psychology and philosophy (Lupton and Abbott Miller 1993: 30).[8] Kandinsky in 1912 in *On the Spiritual in Art* (Kandinsky [1912] [1982] 1994) had described whole forms in Gestalt terms, without, so far as we know, being aware of the contemporaneous experimental research on these matters by Wertheimer and others:

> With reference to form, purely pictorial composition has two tasks before it:
> 1. the composition of the whole picture.
> 2. the creation of the individual forms that are related to each other in various combinations, while remaining subordinate to the whole composition. Thus many objects (real, or possibly abstract) are subordinated within the picture to a single overall form altered to make them compatible with this form, which they comprise. In this case, the individual form, which mainly serves the overall form of the composition, can retain little of its personal sound and should be regarded principally as an element of that form. The individual form is shaped in this particular way not because its own inner sound [regarded as separate from the overall composition] necessarily requires it, but mainly because it is called upon to serve as a building block for this composition. Here the first task—the composition of the whole picture—is pursued as a definite goal.
>
> In this way, the abstract element in art gradually has become increasingly to the fore (Kandinsky [1912] 1982: 167–8).

This is Gestalt thinking. Wertheimer explains in a 1925 essay:

The fundamental 'formula' of Gestalt theory might be expressed in this way: There are wholes, the behaviour of which is not determined by that of their individual elements, but where part processes are themselves determined by the intrinsic nature of the whole. It is the hope of Gestalt theory to determine the nature of such wholes (Ellis 1938: 2).

Later, Wertheimer says:

Advancing another step we come to the question whether perhaps any part depends upon the particular whole in which it occurs. Experiments, largely on vision, have answered this question in the affirmative. Among other things they demand that the traditional theory of visual contrast be replaced by a theory which takes account of whole part conditions (Ellis 1938: 5).

This was written over ten years after Kandinsky had produced such a theory in *On the Spiritual in Art*. And in 1922 Wertheimer wrote: 'Empirical enquiry discloses not a construction of primary pieces, but gradations of giveness "in broad strokes" (relative to more inclusive whole-properties), and varying articulation'; he goes on in abstract terms virtually to paraphrase Kandinsky's words on colour in a painting (Ellis 1938: 14).

Kandinsky was writing just before World War I, when painters (including Schlemmer) were experimenting or about to experiment with abstraction where such ideas on 'essences', in relation to form and colour, could be realised on the canvas composition or 'whole'. Kandinsky's thought was widely read, and Schlemmer himself described *The Blue Rider Almanac* (*Der Blaue Reiter Almanach*) (Lindsay and Vergo 1982: 229–283) (though this did not include *On the Spiritual in Art*) at the time of its publication in 1912 as 'sehr gut' (Maur 1979a: 38). There is a clear desire by artists, manifested in the Blue Rider group and its adherents before the First World War, to identify transcendent concepts, absolutes that can be identified, while demonstrating them through painting as existing dynamically in the material world, and not deriving from the mind alone.

The notion of Gestalt is largely out of favour within psychology now (Ash 1995: 405–12) because of its fundamentally essentialist approach, claiming structures in the mind, that fails to take sufficient account of physical, cultural and social environments. And this is true: Gestalt thinking aims to understand fundamental form and structure, to unravel the mystery of the raw moment of perception in these terms. Husserl's phenomenology sought to do the same within the discipline of philosophy. Both disciplines came from the same roots, namely the early researches into intentionality by Franz Clemens Brentano in the 1870s, concerning the relationship between the perceiving mind and the matter it encountered.

Karin von Maur describes Schlemmer's 'artistic phenomenology' (Maur 1979a: 330). This term, from one of the most distinguished commentators on Schlemmer's paintings and sculptures, is more than a turn of phrase, even though she does not expand much upon it, except by linking this sensibility to an Expressionist aesthetic *circa* 1913, the year Edmund Husserl conceived 'Ideas on a Pure Phenomenology'. She describes Expressionist artists using an 'eidetic' reduction process, step-by-step going from 'the visible to invariable outlines and to the very contours of being' (Maur 1979a: 330). All this suggests the actively seeking eye of the artist, putting the artist in touch with an underlying form and order. The 'actively seeking eye' could describe the 'eye' demanded in the pedagogical approach of Paul Klee in his teaching, laid out in the Bauhaus book *Pedagogical Sketchbook* (*Pädagogisches Skizzenbuch*) (Klee [1925] 1953, 1968) and most fully in his *Notebooks*, especially *The Thinking Eye* (*Das bildnerische Denken*) ([1956] 1961). What is most apparent in Klee's design theory is his stress not only on the discovery of form but its *active creation* too. This idea will emerge strongly in this chapter as a fundamental Bauhaus idea within design, photography and on the stage.

Brentano's original notion of intentionality in perception identified that the mind always 'intends' something (i.e. it does not operate in a 'vacuum'). Nor does the mind passively absorb information. Intentionality puts the mind back 'in touch' with the known world we experience. Previous to this, philosophy seemed to have reached an impasse, lost in idealistic morasses of uncertainty and rapidly losing ground to scientific thinking (Spiegelberg 1982: 28–31). Brentano was, in fact, in the face of this, attempting to tie philosophy down to a more secure and analytical basis in order to begin understanding the nature of consciousness. His ideas were the keenest blow to dualist thinking, endemic in Platonic-based systems of thought which separated mind and body, that had yet been delivered in Western philosophy, because he claimed that perception does not take place in the mind but is a *relation* between a perceiver and what is perceived (Kern [1983] 2003: 7). This is the first fissure in idealist, essentialist thinking, opening up some years before its full implications were recognised. Brentano's desire to nail down uncertainties, to be more 'scientific', was the same as that of Edmund Husserl, founder of phenomenology, and contemporary to Schlemmer and the Bauhaus. Husserl absorbed Brentano's teachings via Carl Strumpf, and he argued that despite our uncertainty as to what constitutes knowledge, we can at least be sure of what presents itself to our consciousness, and it is this that we need to study if we are to know the phenomenon itself. It is worth looking ahead at this point to later in the twentieth century. Whilst Husserl remained steeped in Germanic sensibilities, the phenomenological attitude, as it came to be called, ultimately tried to cut out God altogether. In the mid-twentieth century, the French philosopher Maurice Merleau-Ponty argues for a full-blown existentialist phenomenology even as he talks about the 'haloes of being' which he saw conjured in Cezanne's painting (Merleau-Ponty 1974a: 285); as his commentator Monika Langer puts it, 'we must guard against the temptation [i.e. in Merleau-Ponty's writing] to reduce the object's essential nature to a Kantian noumenon. The perceptual synthesis which accompanies the unification of our sensory experiences is fundamentally different from an intellectual synthesis and must not be regarded as merely a step along the way to the latter' (M. Langer 1989: 78). Even Kant had left room for God, the 'noumena', the unknowables outside our consciousness. Increasing the status of the material world, and drawing attention to our making of that world through the differing perceptions of our bodies, makes it hard to maintain a faith in the sublime and the unknowable, and opens the door to full-blown existentialism.[9]

However, Husserl's early phenomenology was still called 'transcendental' because it aimed at absolutes—'*eidetic* abstractions', or universals, the essences that consciousness grasps or 'intends' despite the variations of individual circumstances.[10] The '*eideos*' is what is *in* the mind when consciousness is aware *of* something; and according to Husserl the mind always 'intends' an object—consciousness is not isolated from the material world. This is the concept of 'intentionality'. To get at this '*eideos*' or essence(s) in consciousness, Husserl identified a way of looking at phenomena that engaged with our consciousness alone, and not our *thinking about* the objects. This involved a state of non-thinking, a 'bracketing off' of everything we know about the object and only being open to the phenomenon itself: this was a Husserlian '*epoche*'. The phenomenological attitude attempts to look at the phenomenon shorn of any social, political, historical or cultural context, and to simply embed consciousness in physical reality. In the following quotation, Kandinsky describes the 'inner sound' of an individual element, one of the 'parts', in this case, the colour red, when it is not part of a material whole (or Gestalt). The similarity with a Husserlian essence, or 'epoche' or '*eideos*' is remarkable:

> This red [in the imagination] which one does not see materially, but imagines in the abstract, awakens on the other hand a certain precise, yet imprecise, representation ['Vorstellung'] having a purely internal, psychological sound. This red, echoing from the word ['red'], has of itself no particularly pronounced tendency towards warm or cold. This must also be imagined, as fine gradations of the shade of red. For this reason I have described this way of seeing as mentally imprecise. It is however at the same time precise, since the inner sound is left bare, without particularities arising from an accidental tendency towards warm or cold, etc. This inner sound resembles the sound of a trumpet, or of the instrument one pictures in one's mind when one hears the word trumpet, etc., where all particularities are excluded (Kandinsky [1912] 1982: 162).

The 'eideos' corresponds to the universal form or Goethian 'Urbild' which all Expressionist painters and poets believed to be lurking beneath the surface of the visible world; hence Maur's reference to their 'eidetic' reduction in abstract work (Maur 1979a: 330).

Whilst this desire persisted in the Bauhaus, at Dessau the Romantic Gestalt idealism began to be transformed, particularly under Maholy-Nagy. Maholy-Nagy, as a Hungarian, was free from the German heritage which had weighed heavily on the Bauhaus at Weimar but nor was he the hard-headed utilitarian Constructivist he has been too often made out to be. His restless creativity and impatience with the worst excesses of Itten and Grunow ensured a practical and forceful change in direction towards new design prototypes, but his attitude was grafted on to the deep held and enduring Gestalt thinking in the Bauhaus. Joseph Albers had come through Itten's Preliminary Course and instead of taking students down to the Goethe House in Weimar took them on factory tours in Dessau. T. Lux Feininger remembers 'his leading us through a cardboard box factory with the kind of religious conviction one would expect from a lecturer in the Louvre' (T. Lux Feininger in Neumann [1970] 1993: 191). His exercises with paper are an excellent example of the transmutation in Dessau of Weimar ideals, i.e. work on basic forms: he too investigated the basic properties of objects but in this case chose paper, a manufactured substance, and even as it was being reduced to its basic elements (strength, tensile qualities, texture and so on) it was being forged into new 'Gestalten', such as making a structure from cutting paper that was strong enough for a man to stand on. The paradox is apparent in T. Lux Feininger's description:

> The criteria for the evaluation of the works were structural invention and static and tensile strength. Aesthetic values were not sought, and were condemned as a point of departure. The absence of any 'purpose' in these exercises strengthened the functional feeling: another paradox! The function was, to be as much wood, metal, paper, as possible, to be paper at the top of one's bent so to speak (T. Lux Feininger in Neumann [1970] 1993: 191).

At the same time Schlemmer began to develop new forms for a new German theatre on his stage: the 'Bühnengestaltung' Wensinger mentions. The work as a whole at the Dessau Bauhaus is grafted on to the Romantic Gestalt thinking of the Weimar Bauhaus into new syntheses of (new) materials, time and motion and above all, in Schlemmer's case, the body.

Photography within the Bauhaus will serve as a useful practical introduction to the development of Goethe's 'laws' that took place at Dessau, here led by Maholy-Nagy, and faithfully reflected in Schlemmer's own attitude to photography.

Jeannine Fiedler in her book *Photography at the Bauhaus* (Fiedler 1990) makes the point that photography gradually emerges as an important design medium within the Bauhaus, initially under the influence of Maholy-Nagy from 1923. Photography is developed not merely to reproduce reality but to produce new images, provoke new ways of seeing. Andreas Haus cautions against photography being seen in the early Bauhaus as a new art form, at least at first (Haus 1978). The difference is hard to grasp, but it is initially seen more as a pedagogical and learning tool, illustrative to the students of basic Gestalt principles underlying Bauhaus thinking, here in relation to light. However, Maholy had his own agenda: 'Maholy tried to accustom the traditional natural manner of perception to a new *productive* mastery of *secondary* nature: i.e. that of a technological and urban environment. He wanted therefore to seize upon its functioning and manifestations in an *elemental* way in order to gain from it *material* for a reconstruction of perception' (Haus 1978: 13).

Maholy-Nagy entitles his essay 'Fotografie ist Lichtgestaltung' in the Bauhaus magazine (Haus 1978: 47–8). Haus translates this as 'photography as the pure manipulation [Gestaltung] of light' (Haus 1978: 11) but this as ever loses the proper Gestalt overtones. Maholy-Nagy's photographs challenge the eye by using new perspectives and odd angles as well as strong shadows and light contrasts. Maholy-Nagy is not only using the 'manipulation' of light but deliberately seeking and producing new creative forms or 'Gestalten', as Haus says, to 'extend the sense of reality in a fantastic way—especially through *the irritation of biologically founded and culturally conventional conceptions of space and perspective*' [my italics] (Haus 1990: 16). In other words, he pushed the Gestalt idea into new areas of creativity away from mysticism but without subscribing to any mechanistic view of mankind. Andreas Haus in the same essay (Haus 1990: 17) refers to 'Produktion-Reproduktion' written in German by Lucia Maholy and her husband in *De Stijl 5*, the journal for Constructivist aesthetics.[11] Maholy-Nagy at that time could not speak very good German and as Rolf Sachsse demonstrates in his 'Notes on Lucia Maholy' (Fiedler 1990: 25–7) one is inevitably led to the conclusion that many of the ideas in it are strongly led by his wife Lucia. Lucia Maholy, née Schulz, had encountered the embodied thinking of Ernst Mach and others around 1914.[12] Mach had described our mental grasp of geometry as issuing from our bodily encounters with the world. Sachsse notes that whilst the Maholy-Nagy essay does establish a 'biomechanical knowledge model' it constitutes 'the unusual turn away from bio-functional determination of human beings to stress their independent creative activity'; it was an attempt to 'break out of the recently established biological model' or mechanistic approach to the body developed in the nineteenth century. This biological or mechanistic approach had established itself within the discipline of psychology/philosophy via Gustav Fechner and later the hugely influential Wilhelm Wundt. Broadly speaking and without doing justice to the subtleties of their approaches, both these men and their pupils established a scientific experimental approach within psychology that tended to encourage deterministic thinking. It was this, we remember, that the Gestalt Psychologists rejected.[13] In a similar mode of non-mechanistic thinking, which pays homage to the Gestalt thinking developed at the Bauhaus in Weimar, the Maholy-Nagy essay pleads for creative 'Produktion' not 'Reproduktion' in photography.

Schlemmer too pursued this creative 'Produktion' not 'Reproduktion'. Gisela Barche analyses photographs of the Bauhaus stage, pointing out that Schlemmer kept careful control over the images, setting them up, and he touched up and collaged images to produce the final photograph (Barche 1990: 239). This is true, but this idea can be pushed much further than she does, by connecting it with Schlemmer's creation of the 'Bühnengestaltung' or stage Gestalt form(s). (Naess's definition of Gestalt thinking as 'wholes that are perceived to have an organic identifiable unity in themselves, as a network of relations that can move as one' (Naess 1989: 6) remains useful here.) Schlemmer constantly collaged photos and drew upon them in pursuit of the new 'Gestalten'. T. Lux Feininger's photograph of the white figure standing in centre stage with the diagonal ropes stretched from roof to floor to articulate the space is usually re-printed in books as it was taken, frontal view, the block at 90° angles. Schlemmer however worked on a large copy of this photograph and put a black triangular card piece in at the top and bottom, thereby tilting the photo to the right. The effect is disturbing and far from straightforward reproduction of (stage) space: it is rather a re-creation of it or 'Produktion'. It also pushes the juxtaposed 'Gestalten', or attempted stage 'Ur-forms' (the shape of man in contrast to the geometry of the ropes/space) further, into a suggestion of added tension, motion, energy, i.e. the possibility of new 'Gestalten'.[14] Another example is the photograph collage of the *The Triadic Ballet* (see Figure 2.1). Here there is a play with scale and geometric pattern on the floor which creates a virtual space that impacts upon the viewer. This is surely a good example of what Haus describes as 'Nietzschean coloured activism which pays homage to the new and to the so far non existent' (Haus 1990: 17). It is clearly not reproduction of an existing space. Barche contrasts these photographs with the very different ones of Naftali Rubinstein, Robert Binnemann and Charlotte Rudolf, which deliberately reproduce and capture to some extent the actual dynamic movement in the Bauhaus dances. 'Schlemmer remained unmoved by this development in the reproduction of movement' (Barche 1990: 243).

As an a exact parallel to his stage work, there was no interest in reproducing reality in photographs as accurately as a medium would allow, but absolute focus on the creation of new forms, new combinations, complicated Gestalt forms. In the Bauhaus, this is as much a discovery, an uncovering, as it is a creative act. In the word of Maholy-Nagy: '[C]reations are valuable only when they produce new, previously unknown relationships' (Haus 1978: 46).[15] This latter phrase could equally describe the best of postmodern stages, the theatre of Robert Wilson, for example, whose juxtapositions and visual acrobatics continually surprises us. Both Maholy-Nagy and Schlemmer were in fact pushing into new territory beyond Goethe's 'Ur-forms', Schlemmer himself exploring new combinations of light, scenery, the body, motion, objects, sound and time. Moreover, the viewer is clearly implicated in the creative act by 'the irritation of biologically founded and

Figure 2.1   Oskar Schlemmer, *The Triadic Ballet, Figures in Space* [*Das Triadis-che Ballet, Figuren im Raum*], around 1924. Photo Archive, C. Raman Schlemmer, IT-288824 Oggebbio (VB) Italy.

culturally conventional conceptions of space and perspective' (Haus 1990: 16). And we remember that the implication of the viewer is what distinguishes a phenomenological approach.

Without suggesting direct influence, Husserl's phenomenological attitude of open looking, being open to the phenomenon itself, without cognitive thought, corresponds with several statements by Schlemmer in the 1920s; here, for example, urging his imaginary companion to lay himself open to the 'visual play' ('Schauspiel') alone and not try to understand it or, in other words, think about it rationally:

> I have simply let them make their effect on me, without any precon- ceived idea, and I believe that you ought to have as little prejudice as possible when dealing with the new, especially new artistic things (Schlemmer 1928: 1062).

And soon afterwards:

> To be sure, these things [in the 'Schauspiel'] have their own sense. They are not devoid of sense, of course not; in the end, they have more sense than many other things presented in theatre. They have sense in a fun- damental way, that is to say, that in each case they take you to the basis of things, and lay bare the roots in order to seize hold of the primary sense, the actual first cause of the event (Schlemmer 1928: 1063).

A phenomenological reduction does not start in ignorance of contexts but involves a gradual stripping way of this knowledge to reveal the 'eidetic' (universal) essence. This is Schlemmer speaking of simplicity in very phe- nomenological terms:

> Simplicity, understood as the fundamental and the typical elements from which the organically varied and singular develops, simplicity understood as a tabula rasa, completely clean of the eclecticist accesso- ries of all periods and styles; simplicity must surely guarantee the way, and the way is the future! (April 1926) (Schlemmer [1958] 1977: 87)

And now speaking of abstraction:

> What is it, what does it mean, 'abstract'? To be brief, and to generalize, it signifies simplification, reduction to essentials, elements, first prin- ciples, to pit the one against the many. It signifies and consists of the uncovering of the common denominator, the counterpoint (not only in music), the law of art (Schlemmer [1927e] 1961: 27).

And of creating theatre:

> The recipe the Bauhaus Theater follows is very simple: one should be as free of preconceptions as possible: one should act as if the world had just been created; one should not analyze a thing to death, but rather let it unfold gradually and without interference. One should be simple but not puritanical. ('Simplicity is a noble concept!') One should rather be

primitive than over-elaborate or pompous: one should not be sentimental; one should be sensitive and intelligent. That says everything—and nothing! (May 1929) (Schlemmer [1958] 1977: 243)

However, like Diogenes and his barrel, his was a practical philosophy: he actually worked with these Husserlian concepts on stage, using the material forms of the stage elements. As a result, he developed what was in effect idealist phenomenology into living embodied forms on stage.

Whilst Schlemmer devotes much energy at Dessau to identifying and isolating the most basic and simple forms of the stage as his starting points, he then builds on this purity of form, this 'basic stage' or 'Typenbühne' (Schlemmer [1958] 1977: 84), developing a 'metaphysical theatre' that would be peculiarly German and revive the stage as a valued aesthetic form. What we find is that Schlemmer persistently couches his 'Gestalten' in idealistic terms, even though he is dealing with material matter in relation to the body: the body of the performer and spectator. For example, his stage illusions are seen as glimpses of the immortal and the transcendent: 'and, not least, it [the stage] serves the desire for the metaphysical in humanity, in that it sets up an illusory world and creates the transcendental on the basis of the rational' (Schlemmer 1927c: 1). This tension between the transcendental and the rational (or 'real') on Schlemmer's stage is a tension carried through to the postmodern stage where interest in the live body as a performative tool is balanced at least equally by a persistent hope to escape existential bleakness and purely solipsistic reference points. Certain performance artists too, such as Marina Abramović, present their audience with profoundly disturbing material (metaphorically and literally) that nevertheless communicates an indefinable sense of its rootedness in human experience, and that offers comfort and succour and even a sense of order to the human spirit in what Zuckerkandl designates as 'wholly flux' (Zuckerkandl 1956: 241).

Early in Chapter 1, the methodology of this book was itself characterised as phenomenological, peeling away 'layers' even as Schlemmer did, but in our case these 'layers' are the ideological 1920s background, the Romantic Gestalt thinking, the idealism and the search for 'Ur-forms', and this gives us direct access to the lived experience of Schlemmer's stage; it will reveal to us the instability of space, the shifting and permeable borders of the body, and the meanings that emerge from the relationship of body and object. His answers will prove extraordinarily potent to artists who seek meaningful engagement with the world amidst the absolute impermanence and instability of being. A systematic analysis offered here of his 'basic stage' in terms of the singular elements within it and their deployment will gradually, naturally and inexorably give place to the imaginative release of these stage elements within the postmodern stage.

3   Space
Light and Scenery

In this chapter we concentrate on two tools that Schlemmer used to create his painterly spaces on stage: light and scenery. Both were used to conjure a fluid and transformative space in constant flux, which was the essential distinguishing feature of live performance as Schlemmer recognised (Schlemmer [1931] 1990). Towards the end, the case is made for Schlemmer's stage work being rooted in human actions and life and ultimately society and by no means the remote, abstract, dry geometric stage postures that visual sources and popular cliché may suggest.

Space is the supreme concern of all Schlemmer's work as painter, sculptor, choreographer, designer, performer. Yet space is the ultimate absence in presence. Schlemmer says as much: 'What is space? You cannot get hold of it, its essence, except through what is tangible' (Schlemmer [1929] 1965: 8). Material form, motion and sound all articulate or 'make visible' space. Even the human body is a form of plasticity in itself, a space 'creator'. As Schlemmer observes, without material form there is only the void. 'Space, like architecture, being primarily a thing of dimensions and proportions, is an abstraction in the sense of a contradiction against nature, if not a protest against it' (Schlemmer [1926] 1969: 118).

Schlemmer's manipulation of stage space derives from his skills as a visual artist. Schlemmer's paintings and sculptures were created in direct relation to the space in which they were (ideally) to be shown and experienced. The 'real' contextual space always formed part of the Gestalt and inevitably takes into account, indeed emphasises, the experience of the viewer, and this experience is not only visual but, as in architecture, haptic and even aural. The word 'haptic' is originally defined by James Gibson (Gibson 1966). Bloomer and Moore (1977) usefully gloss Gibson's extensive analysis of the haptic sense as 'the sense of touch reconsidered to include the entire body rather than merely the instruments of touch, such as the hands' (34). It is the whole body sense of feeling in a space, and can be illustrated by Bloomer and Moore's example that to sense a mountain haptically is to climb it not just stare at it (34). Schlemmer's haptic awareness enables him to deploy an entirely new and painterly inspired handling of (stage) space for the twentieth century and beyond with purposeful and deliberate manipulation of its constituent elements, which the Symbolists, early modern dance and Dada never even came near. Whilst his approach needs to be historically placed and understood in its Modernist context, it nevertheless forms the roots of later performance art and the highly visual and sophisticated stages of today. Schlemmer opened up controlled 3-D space experienced in time as a new dimension of art which he considered potentially more powerful than any other medium. In contrast to many of the other great theorists of the visual stage such as Appia, Craig, Kandinsky and Artaud (except, arguably, Appia at Hellerau), he had the opportunity to put his ideas into practice in a concentrated period of research between about 1926 and 1929. Schlemmer, stripping the complexity of space down to its constituent elements, provides us with a practical handbook for understanding the basic medium in which performance operates—space— and demonstrates simple techniques for sophisticated transformations of that medium. More importantly, he gives us an ethical and cultural under- standing of why we might want to undertake such a curious yet apparently so compelling task.

Although he differed considerably from his German contemporaries in his formal style (which derived from an incisive and analytical approach), Schlemmer shared the common early Expressionist impulse to reach a transcendent and idealist plane, which was a neo-Romantic urge entirely in keeping with that of Kandinsky, Klee, Itten, Macke, and almost every painter active in the German art scene in the years before World War I. All these painters strove to experience and communicate what is in effect the Kantian 'noumena', or unknowable plane of existence, but they did it via the material means of this world—the application of pigment on to can- vas, and the consequent manipulation of the space the viewer experienced. Schlemmer insisted on nature and the 'real' world, objects and the flesh, as a starting point. Like Maeterlinck and Craig he was suspicious of the actorly sensibility that got in the way of communicating this poetic transformation on stage, but like them refused to resort to the mechanical theatre and pup- pets evident in the student work in the 1925 theatre of the Bauhaus book. Craig's Übermarionette shares many characteristics of Schlemmer's live 'Kunstfigur' or 'Art Figure', and both have affinities with the way Robert Wilson treats his performers as plastic elements within the stage composi- tion. Schlemmer has been called a 'figurative' Constructivist (Paz 1996: 191) because of the admixture of spiritual (Expressionist) longing, classical yearning towards form, and straightforward analysis of means. Construc- tivist analysis forms an important part of his ostensible approach at Dessau, but the visionary in him was always the dominant force.

The momentous shift from Schlemmer manipulating the space of a paint- ing to the space of the stage came about because Schlemmer was both painter and dancer. His investigations complement the work (and the theories) of his contemporaries— Adolphe Appia, Gordon Craig and Antonin Artaud— but push their ideas much further. All four understood the potential of stage space to be as powerful an aesthetic experience as any other art form, if not more so. This claim needed fighting for. Theatre in its popular forms did not have much status as art at the turn of the century and, although there were art theatres that commanded respect, from Russia for example,[1] to the citizen on the street, theatre certainly did not command the same respect as painting. If we pause to consider Schlemmer's pre-war influences, we can appreciate how his treatment of space on the canvas developed and changed in the 1910s and early 1920s, preparing him by 1925 to launch on the Bauhaus stage his serious investigations into the expressive—and indeed explosive—potential of 'real' space.

Following Schlemmer's exposure to French Cubism during his year in Berlin in 1911 (where he encountered a range of contemporary European paintings, styles and movements) he began in the pre-war period before 1914 to develop a Cubist style (Maur 1979a: 40–9). Maur points out that Schlemmer's Cubism was far more influenced by Cézanne than it was by the extreme multiple viewpoints of Picasso and Braque, and she analyses how he was drawn to the abstracting of form from the natural landscape and buildings, using both line and colour. It was the formalism of this approach that appealed to him, a quality of coolness and objectivity, which he sought to overlay with his Germanic Gestalt sensibilities. In direct contrast to the formally driven French Cubist style, many German painters were developing an Expressionist style which was in effect much freer and looser than Schlemmer wanted. Schlemmer continued to develop his own ideas, taking what he saw was valuable from the French, as he enriched his thinking via extensive reading and study of the early Romantic thinkers, aestheticians and philosophers, including Goethe, Novalis and Schiller, along with later thinkers Friedrich Nietzsche and William Worringer. He acquired an easy familiarity with the history of art but especially the history of painting within his own beloved north European tradition. The result was that his personal philosophy of art put as much emphasis on the discipline of form (abstraction) as the 'empathy' of (Expressionist) feeling. This bifurcation of terms derives directly from William Worringer's *Abstraction and Empathy: A Contribution to the Psychology of Style* (*Abstraktion und Einfuhlun: ein Beitrag zur Stilpsychologie*) (Worringer [1908] [1948] 1953), a key text on the state of contemporary art at that time, and which Schlemmer read in the early 1910s. Unlike Schlemmer's German contemporary artist colleagues who (as he saw it) concentrated on Expressionist empathy, and the French abstract painters who stressed the discipline of form, Schlemmer wanted both: 'I would like to present the most romantic idea in the most objective form' ('in der abgeklärtesten Form') (September 1915) (Schlemmer [1958] 1977: 21). In the war years, whenever he was able to paint, he moved on from Cubism and produced a largely flat and restrained surface of pure abstraction in *Picture K* (*Bild K*) 1915/6, and, significantly, he began to present the human form (his lifelong subject), albeit at first abstracted and smoothed out into virtually limbless creatures floating in a flat 2-D space of pale colour (the embryonic yet sublime *Composition on Pink Ground* (*Komposition auf Rosa*) (1915/6). This shift into figurative work parallels his experimentation with transforming the human figure on stage using costume, *The Triadic Ballet*, a version of which was first performed in 1916 in a necessarily short performance in wartime using three costumes. As the war ended, the space in his paintings started to deepen so that by the early 1920s (e.g. *Companions at the Table* (*Tischgesellschaft*) in 1923 and

Figure 3.1 Oskar Schlemmer, *Lounge* [*Ruheraum*], 1925. Photo Archive, C. Raman Schlemmer, IT-288824 Oggebbio (VB) Italy.

Lounge (*Ruheraum*) in 1925) (see Figure 3.1)[2] he was presenting a tightly controlled experience of an interior 3-D space peopled by human figures devoid of personal traits, individual physiognomy and unique facial features, but often deeply human in their activities and moving through and engaging with the space they occupied (sitting at table, climbing stairs, resting together in a spa room). These paintings hint at work to come on the stage at Dessau.

Schlemmer believed in a form and order underlying the world of external appearances, a holy precision that lay beneath the outward profusion, diffusion and confusion of the external world. He saw this order above all in the shape, motion and function of the organic human body. This order was founded, as he believed, on mathematics and geometric forms, not in a rigid and simplistic sense, but rather in the kind of 'artistic, metaphysical mathematics ... where everything begins with a feeling that slowly becomes form and where the unconscious and the subconscious enter the clarity of consciousness' (Schlemmer [1926] 1969: 118). He revealed geometric forms in his paintings and drawings with endless variations on the mathematics/geometry of the structure of the human body and its physiognomy. His subject—the human body—is the ultimate Gestalt, providing endless forms, each unique yet all interconnected—a dynamic perfection. That his holistic and essentially vitalist view included all the functions of the human body is clear from his course 'Man' which he gave at the Bauhaus in 1928 (Schlemmer [1969] 1971). His ultimate vision, more in hope than expectation, was a German cultural Gestalt where aesthetics, ethics and politics co-existed in harmony and to the benefit of all.

He applies mathematics as the 'ultimate, the most refined, the most delicate form' (Schlemmer [1926] 1969: 118) to space, in order to create 'Bühnengestaltung' or stage form—a stage space that is not 'nature or the illusion of it' (Schlemmer 1925: 13). His initial tool both in the costumes for *The Triadic Ballet* and at Dessau is indeed geometry. In 'Stage Elements', a little known but invaluable essay from 1929 on scenography, he describes how, because space itself is only realised through what is tangible, he uses 'the line' and 'exploration of its palpable limits' (Schlemmer [1929] 1965: 7) to articulate this 'non-imitative' space. In practice this meant initially drawing the geometry of the stage surface, that is, making visible its centre point, and the axes, diagonals and curves.

Schlemmer did this literally on the Dessau stage space by stretching ropes across the stage from its central point high above the white clad performer standing in the centre, and drew lines upon the floor, a huge circle, with diagonals radiating out from the centre point of the floor. His performers played with geometric forms setting them in motion alongside the Gestalt of the human body smoothed into a universal or uniform shape. The held sticks and hoops, the angular lines and triangles, necessarily frozen in the photographs, seem a little heavy-handed today and may, misleadingly, appear the most dated aspect of his visual stage. But in developing his images, Schlemmer also used a number of other dynamic and subtle forms that we relate to instantly, such as light, colour, sound and the body, and the examination of these material and aural forms in this and the next three chapters will take us into shifting and permeable space, fluid places imbued with the magic of illusion, the warmth of human contact and the mystery of motion, and not the apparently rigid boxes defined by circles, squares and lines which we see in photographs and sketches of the Bauhaus stage.

As a painter and sculptor, Schlemmer was keenly aware of the function of light in transforming the shape, volume or texture of the object it illuminates. Light, of course, plays a vital part in all Schlemmer's paintings and sculptures. For example *Abstract Figure, free sculpture* (*Abstrakte Figur, Freiplastik*), 1921–3 shows a white plaster human figure made up of abstract forms, deeply indented with hollows and shadows which change as the viewer circles 360° around it.[3] His wall paintings and decorations equally play with the light source. For example, in the wall paintings for the Workshop Building in the Weimar Bauhaus, the light from the staircase roof, among other windows in this building, played a significant part in the reception of this work.[4] (That the viewing of these murals also involved motion goes without saying but is reserved for the next chapter.) Indeed light is such an obvious part of a visual artist's awareness and repertoire it seems almost foolish to point it out; however, not everyone notices how light operates its magical transformations in our lived experience of the world. Light has a continuous sculptural function on all surface/edge information fed to us and this enables a lighting designer to transform what we see on stage. This stage process is commonly known as illusion, and it is part of the purpose here to tease out the meaning and significance of stage illusion, not just on the stage of the Bauhaus but on all stages that set up 'illusions' with a deeply serious intent.

'Illusion' is a problematic term. Its unspoken gloss is 'delusion'. Understanding of stage illusion impacts upon understanding of performance art where illusion is often spurned in favour of so-called 'real' experience. It will gradually emerge that in Schlemmer's work, at this crucial juncture in the development of live art forms, 'real' experience and 'illusion' fuse into one and the same experience. This will enable us to side step the sterile dispute between the 'real' and the 'unreal', sometimes couched as performance art 'versus' theatre, and instead identify some common aesthetic threads between (apparently) very different works of live art. In Schlemmer's case and for many artists who followed, from Joseph Beuys right through to performance in the early twenty-first century, the desire for a transformative experience actually given live in performance (often but not always on a stage) remained and remains a driving force. In Schlemmer's theorising it was linked to essentially romantic and idealistic notions of art derived from the early nineteenth century. In later avant-garde performance, the experiential element—the desire for the authentically 'real' and live—is equally forceful. The live art work may suggest metaphysical longing, or it may stress the critique of cultural and aesthetic norms: it may do both. In every case, however, the authenticity of the live 'bodied' experience is paramount. In the case of light, Schlemmer was aware of its power upon an audience to induce such an experience.

Schlemmer, despite relatively primitive electric stage lighting, ranked stage light as a vital 'plastic' form:

> Non-rigid and intangible form occurs as light; the geometric shape of the light beams and of the pyrotechnics steadily realises, in the appearance of the light, three dimensional objects as well as the space itself (Schlemmer 1925: 11).

Note the light articulates objects or solids, at the same time realising the space itself. The light on the Bauhaus stage functioned, as Schlemmer described it, 'for what it is' ('als das was es ist'), namely yellow, blue, red, green, violet etc. (Schlemmer 1927c: 3). He eschews using light mimetically to imitate 'sunlight and moonlight, morning, noon, evening and night . . .' declaring the illusion he deals with refers to an illusion in a different or 'higher' sense ('eine illusion in höherem sinne')[5] (3). This is the Expressionist yearning again, where illusions are serving, as he said, the need or desire for the metaphysical (Schlemmer 1927c: 1), that is, they conjure up the unseen, the beyond, the Kantian 'noumena'. Gropius articulated this in 1922:

> the stage derives from an ardent religious desire of the human soul (theatre = show for the gods). It serves, then, to manifest a transcendental idea. The power of its effect on the soul of the spectator and auditor is therefore dependent on the success of the transformation of the idea into (visually and acoustically) perceivable space. The phenomenon of space is conditioned by finite limitation within infinite free space, by the movement of mechanical and organic bodies within this limited space, and the oscillations of light and sound within it (Gropius in Wingler 1969: 58).

These 'illusions' are new 'Gestalten', as described in the previous chapter, and are actually experienced and felt: metaphysics meets science. 'Let us open our eyes and our senses to the pure strength of colour and light. Furthermore, we will recognise with surprise that the laws of colour—and changing colours through coloured light—cannot be proved more convincingly than on the stage, which is a physical and chemical laboratory. As a result, through pure illumination, we will perceive fantastic possibilities in the simple changing of colours' (Schlemmer 1927c: 3). Despite the technological dreams encapsulated in Gropius's Total Theatre (Gropius and Wensinger [1925] [1961] 1996: 11–14), simple means were the only ones that were available on the Bauhaus stage at Dessau to make illusions, and we do not even know if he had any kind of dimming system.[6] He had no cyclorama with which to experiment, and the development of more sophisticated lanterns in German theatres (Baugh 2005: 127) (which Schlemmer as a practising scenic designer was probably aware of) were not available to him at Dessau. Indeed students spent hours experimenting with simple lighting to get special effects for their light plays, and were forced to be inventive.[7] The limited resources had the effect, not out of keeping with his instincts anyway, of forcing Schlemmer to strip down his stage elements, including light, to their most simple and basic applications, since sophisticated lights were not available to him. Whilst the stage was the perfect forum for the new unity of art and technology, a vision that Gropius and others such as Maholy-Nagy and Farkas Molnár (Gropius and Wensinger [1961] 1996) bear witness to, Schlemmer played with the most basic characteristics of light—and darkness.[8]

There are two types of light, radiant and ambient, and we can be certain Schlemmer, as a painter, appreciated the difference. Whilst ambient light surrounds us, diffused through the sky and reflected off surfaces into our eyes, radiant light originates in an energy source and enters the eye directly, such as the light of fireworks, a bonfire, a bulb. In the Old Masters of course it is the effulgent light issuing forth from holy visions.

Light is continually reflected off the surfaces of objects. James Gibson points out: 'Terrestrial airspaces are thus 'filled' with light; they contain a flux of interlocking reflected rays in all directions at all points' (Gibson 1966: 12). Gibson describes how radiant light hits a surface and creates the 'scatter information' so that one ray becomes many. These rays in turn hit surfaces making a network of convergence and divergence. Convergence points are all over the space we are in and it is these convergence points that enter the eye. A mirror's surface is of course so smooth that all rays bouncing off from an object or person onto its surface rebound into the eye with no 'scatter' and thus produce a reflection. Boundaries are also crucial; these are where rays hit adjacent surfaces differently:

> The reason for boundaries in an array is that faces of a room reflect different amounts and colours of light to a convergence point. No two adjacent faces (or facets) will project the same intensity if they are at different angles of inclination to the source (Gibson 1966: 193–4).

Schlemmer was surely aware that theatre lighting attempts to control the information that the light rays give to the eye, modifying both the amount of ambient rays and their direction (and, often, their colour). With the light sculpting the plastic form in the stage space, it is these controlled boundaries and surfaces that shape our perception.

Evidence of ambient light in Schlemmer's live performances is hard to recover as it may be distorted in the available photographic evidence. The light sometimes had to be increased in order to take the photograph, and there was a danger of flooding the original effect, as in many photographs of *Stick Dance*, where one assumes in performance the body would have receded and the light caught the sticks.[9] On the other hand, Schlemmer preferred to use a photograph not as a record of the performance but to create a new Gestalt. His careful manipulation of the image can hint of the actual use of ambient light on stage, or at least what he aspired to if only he had had the facilities to do so; one assumes such luxury was probably rarely the case and may explain his apparent preference for radiant light as easier to achieve and to control.[10] 'The Abstract One' ('Der Abstrakte') in one photograph is lit so that parts of the figure recede into the darkness and are invisible, and other parts protrude into the visible space and the asymmetries of the figure are fully articulated (see Figure 3.2). Whether this was actually achieved with ambient light *on stage* is another matter. A photograph of all the costumes from *The Triadic Ballet* gathered on stage, that was taken in Berlin when Schlemmer had hired them out as a desperate financial ploy to a revue, sometimes still appears in publications.[11] Here there is no attempt to control the lighting and sculptural effect of the costumes, and Schlemmer wrote 'bad photograph' on the back, for exactly this reason.[12]

Radiant light is much more rarely experienced in the world around us, and on the stage, than ambient light. Nevertheless, it is an important stage device and for Schlemmer especially so. In contrast to other members of the Bauhaus theatre, with their mechanical theatre productions, radiant light in performance was an essential tool for him and him alone at the Bauhaus, because of its capacity to transform the space, blur its edges and play with the perception of the audience. *Metal Dance* is an example of obvious radiant light: it flashed the light source into the audience (rays travelled to the metal surface of costume and set, then entered the watching eye without reflecting off any further surfaces) and, more subtly, so did *Glass Dance*. His choice of reflective materials was always deliberate. The smoothed out full head masks of the performer in *Space Dance*, *Form Dance* and *Gesture Dance* were metallic silver, copper and gold. The costumes in the Third, Black 'metaphysical' section of *The Triadic Ballet* were all reflective: the Spiral Dancer (*Die Spirale*), the Dancers of the Gold Spheres (*Goldkugeln*), Wire Costume (*Drahtkostüm*) and parts of the Abstract One's costume. The spiral dancer spun round as she advanced across the darkened stage; her shiny costume picked up the lights and, depending on the level/sophistication of the lighting and speed of the spinning, the spiral may have lingered on the retina momentarily in live performance. Schlemmer's use of radiant light complements the basic built-up body-costume shapes of (motion and) the 'metaphysical forms of expression . . . *dematerialisation*' [my italics] (Schlemmer 1925: 17) , which he sketched in his essay 'Man and Art Figure'. Whilst his theory about built-up costume is entirely his own, the universal effect of reflective light brooks no argument. It is a timeless device for 'dematerialisation'. Schlemmer knew that radiance deliberately blurs

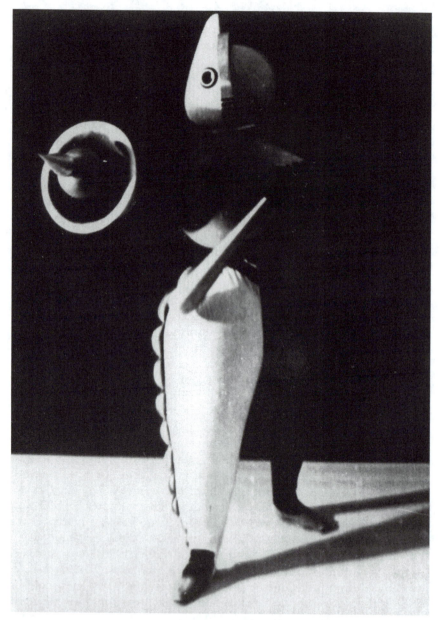

Figure 3.2   Oskar Schlemmer, *The Triadic Ballet*, 'The Abstract One', figure from the Black Section [*Das Triadische Ballet*, Der Abstrakte, Figurine aus der schwarzen Reihe], 1922. Photo Archive, C. Raman Schlemmer, IT-288824 Oggebbio (VB) Italy.

spatial boundaries. It bursts open the physical boundaries of the (costumed) body and the delimitation of the space it occupies, either momentarily and repeatedly. The Metal Party of 1929 immersed the participants both in a social situation and in the perfect Gestalt of the Bauhaus architecture; the radiance offered a simultaneous, continuous and physically experienced dissolution of the defining boundaries of the building into an infinitude of new 'Gestalten', as they were reflected on the shimmering surfaces hung within, attached to, or moving through the space (see Figure 1.2). Here, through the use of light, Schlemmer created in effect a grand, immersive 'illusion' that consisted of the flux of physical space and social exchange.

Used in live performance, radiant light can be hugely powerful in shifting the boundaries of our accustomed space. Turning the lights round to shine into the audience makes a shocking ending to the clown Slava Polunin's *SnowShow* (Edinburgh 1996 and still touring at the time of writing). A wind machine, activated at the same time as a hugely bright light shines into the audience, simultaneously blows thousands of small paper pieces into the audience's faces. Most audiences are disconcerted by having a bright light shone upon them so that they suddenly consciously become the (visual) centre that they had until that moment been projecting, unconsciously, on the stage ahead of them. The pieces of paper that rain upon them in this example moreover emphasise the haptic or whole body dimension and further add to the shock of the sudden 'reversal' of two spaces.

Polunin's trick can be considered a technical parallel with Schlemmer's use of radiant light to disrupt our habitual sense of space. Over used, such tricks become vaguely unsatisfying, offering a surfeit of visual trickery and a paucity of content. Whilst the clown Polunin reminds us of the 'holiness' that Schlemmer insisted imbues popular theatre, where there is consistent and structured manipulation of radiant light the impact is of a different order, and this feeds into Schlemmer's more integrated and ambitious vision of stage space in his serious pieces at Dessau: pieces located in the central category 'Theatre' in his schematic grid, 'Schema für Bühne, Kult und Volksfest, unterschieden nach Ortsform, Mensch . . . Sprache, Musik, Tanz' ('Scheme for Stage, Cult and Popular Entertainment, divided according to Place, Person . . . Speech, Music and Dance') (Schlemmer 1925: 9). Schlemmer locates theatre as a central part of the total cultural Gestalt that he envisioned for Germany. The next five chapters will re-interpret and re-orientate this neo-Romantic and idealistic vision in terms of contemporary theatre today within our own cultural 'Gestalt' at the start of the twenty-first century. This is possible by stripping away the cultural specifics of the Bauhaus context—for example, the lines and the spheres and the squares—and accessing the shared embodied experience of space and the meanings that emerge from such an encounter, particularly in this chapter in terms of stage illusion. Ultimately it will be clear, in the words of Findeli who was arguing for a new design education for the new millennium, that rather than Utopian fixed ideals '[t]he process requires that the archetype be reconstructed and experienced anew, as many times as necessary' (Findeli 1999/2000: 39). Moreover, '[t]he comprehension of this archetype cannot be reached by logical, discursive, and rational means: it must be re-created anew, it must, so to speak, be brought down to earth and embedded, involved, experienced in a specific context'(Findeli 1999/2000: 39).

Robert Wilson offers us such a context. Like Schlemmer, Wilson has a consistent and intelligent application of light, and, like his contemporary Robert Lepage, it builds as part of a considered fabric of the whole piece, not a one-off trick or effect. He offers us an embodied experience of a space that resonates beyond intellectual understanding, a space continually reinforced by his manipulation of all the spatial elements. Although it is light that is here analysed, it is the total social, ethical and aesthetic space (Findeli's 'context') he creates that concerns us. For example, Wilson treats Strindberg's *A Dream Play* (Barbican Centre, London BITE01) largely as a spatial realisation of text. His controlled use of radiant light is a finely honed tool throughout the fabric of the performance; it is a space creator that is modulated with infinite care throughout. Individual touches can be quite subtle but all are an intimate and integral part of the 'build' in the whole fabric of the piece. For example, the 'Stage Door' appears in scenes 3 and 12. The first time we see this door it is shut and set in a huge and overwhelming grey wall along with a small door and a window, not unlike some of the openings through to another space in Schlemmer's paintings, such as *Five Figures in Space (Romanesque) (Fünf Figuren im Raum (Römisches))* (1925) or *Lounge* (1925) (see Figure 3.1).[13] The scene depicts the officer waiting in vain for his lover Victoria. The large door remains firmly shut but the smaller door opens to let people out and from it and the window pours a bright, radiant (effect) orange light. The second time, when we are approaching the end of Agnes's earthly journey, this scene appears again, the door is opened at the officer's demand, and there is nothing behind it, a palpable emptiness. Throughout this piece, light behind the set (that is, on the cyclorama) consistently irradiates a seemingly boundless envelope for the human activities depicted, underpinned by the grey and muted tones of the set, alongside the apparent continual 'shutting down' (metaphorically but also as a physical/visual effect) of that infinity by materiality and human actions—for example, the geometry of interior spaces furnished with long tables and angular chairs, contrasted with inaccessible towers with lit windows. The tower is an ancient symbol of metaphysical thought but seems to gain physical impact beyond its symbolic value through its integration into a 3-D 'lived' stage space. This theatre consists of metaphysical ideas translated into physical reality, from the opening scene of watching a lone female figure (Agnes) descending a diagonal path to earth that cut across the space (see Figure 3.3), to the mirror reversal of that image in the final scene as she abandons this world. Wilson builds up his visual language in this carefully sustained, purposeful and controlled way, so that we absorb the information not as a thought, but as a carefully structured experience.

Figure 3.3   A Dream Play directed by Robert Wilson, Stockholms Stadsteater, 2001. Photograph courtesy Lesley Leslie-Spinks.

Similarly, Lepage's use of light creates a fluid and endlessly permutating space that rediscovers and reconstructs Findeli's 'archetype' for our times (1999/2000: 39). The use of light, including projection, is very much more sophisticated than that of Schlemmer, so much so that we tend to forget the simple shared techniques on which it rests: radiant and ambient light. For example, in *The Dragon's Trilogy* (Barbican Centre, London, 2005), the idea of a toy sandbox is conjured by the gravel covering the huge and shallow stage surface below us in traverse staging, and the opening image is of two girls playing with boxes in it. But later the gravel is scraped away to reveal radiant light snaking out beneath its glass surface, a potential radiance that lies just under the feet which tread on the dirt that hides it. The reflective glass ball, the present given to the ill and abandoned child Stella, is a performance artifact whose light has a palpable effect upon the viewer, a source of radiance that taps into the theme of stars in this section, picked up in innumerable images of radiant light, especially pinpoints of light, for example the light bulbs in the art installation by the young man at the end. Lepage is also a master at using ambient light—for example, in depicting distorted psychological states. In the opium den in *The Dragons' Trilogy* he simply projects an uneven red shape upon the sandbox, using a moving filter to shift the spatial boundaries. Here the light reflects off the horizontal surface suggesting not only a shifting floor below but the imagined walls and ceiling morphing and shifting. The space becomes so much more than the four walls and a ceiling of an opium den. It is the space of the mind and also a boundless space. The difference between a sustained integration of 'illusion' and meaning, and its use as theatrical trickery (however entertaining and competently done) distinguishes Lepage's theatre, and that of Schlemmer's, with a totality of vision: in short, with ethical, social and moral intent.

Both Wilson and Lepage make clear that illusion does not always have to refer mimetically to everyday reality outside the theatre, but puts us in touch with other experiences, other possibilities. In this they are at one with Schlemmer, who eschewed the use of light to imitate, for example, moonlight. Schlemmer's 'illusions' explicitly attempted to touch the Expressionist transcendent 'beyond', but, lacking his frameworks, we are less sure of the resonant and suggestive spaces of Wilson and Lepage. To what can their non-mimetic stage spaces be referring? In addressing this, the analysis offered here develops our non-logical, phenomenological experience of space.

Light works in ways we do not cognitively comprehend. An example of this is using ambient light to create a radiant effect, by isolating a lit up object in the surrounding blackness of stage space. To achieve this is quite easy. Spotlights set at a low level behind side curtains do not reveal themselves as the light source, only the object/figure it strikes on stage.[14] Either this or something like it appears to have been used in several Bauhaus pieces such as *Black and White Trio* (*Schwarz-Weiß-Trio*) (1928/9) and *Illusion Dance* (*Illusionstanz*) (1928). In the latter piece he isolates white clad limbs and reflective full head masks of three performers to create a play of disembodied hands, legs and heads, an image first seen in version two of *The Figural Cabinet*, namely the dancing demon (Gropius and Wensinger [1961] 1996: 39). Schlemmer was concurrently teaching his course 'Man' at the time of *Illusion Dance* and a glance at his sketches for this course which continually divide and 'slice up' the human body to discover the relationship of organic form to geometric volumes, reveals these dances as a live exploration of the same ideas (Schlemmer [1969] 1971). *Black and White Trio* appears to have been his humorous version of the same dance using costume pieces such as hats. The transformation of metaphysics into humour was very characteristic of Schlemmer and the Bauhaus stage and it is an important dimension of his work often largely lost to us. It is arguable that there is a level of response to this use of radiant light that remains time and era specific, centring on Schlemmer's concerns about the beautiful Gestalt of the body and its protruding limbs; but on another deeper level there is a shared embodied response and it centres on light and dark.

The simple device of an illuminated body (part) isolated in the black surrounding stage space taps into our strong response to (radiant) light, i.e. we latch on to a source of light, even an apparent one, with a certain sense of relief (Arnheim 1972: 309). The light/dark contrast is utterly basic to human perception. It is so much part of our 'gearing into' the world that we cease to notice it. Live performance can re-vivify this basic sense even if we do not stop to think why it is powerful. Wole Soyinka in 'Drama and the African World View' (Drain 1995: 326) describes a light/dark contrast in relation to the conception of theatre as one arena 'in which man has attempted to come to terms with the spatial phenomenon of his being'. Using the example of a lone figure illuminated in the stage space, Soyinka claims that the stage space can become an image of the unseen, an impulse from what is normally not thought about or considered, a visualisation of the 'cosmic envelope' that is ignored. Why? The practical reality is that a totally isolated object/person illuminated by ambient light on a blacked out stage at once looks and feels softly 'radiant'. In witnessing this we do not think about the 'real' light source actually originating in 'our' blacked out space but, phenomenologically speaking rather than logically, we *experience* the illuminated figure/object, to a greater or lesser extent, as the source or (only possible) origin of the light. This is a two-edged sword: directors have used it to communicate both the sublime and the terrifying, and even the most prosaic example of someone on stage in a spotlight echoes this basic light/dark contrast 'programmed' into us. Samuel Beckett used light/dark contrasts to communicate the fear of an existential universe but also to reveal the indomitable presence, often irresistibly strong, of the human. Billie Whitelaw's continuously labile mouth in Beckett's *Not I* (Oxford Playhouse 1974) punctured the stage curtain high above the audience, a pinpoint of living flesh in unbreachable loneliness; the close ups on video (Beckett 1973) read rather differently, like a live body sealed in a grave, faintly obscene with its wriggling fleshly opening: in both cases, however, the mouth is the only source of light indeed, deeply ambiguous in its effect, by turns comforting, uplifting and also a tiny isolated circle of living pain.

Schlemmer like Beckett was seeking to expose 'meanings' that are not to do with reproducing (as he said) sunlight or moonlight (Schlemmer 1927c: 3): 'we will rather let light work for what it is . . . Let us open our eyes and our senses to the pure strength of colour and light' (3). Although Schlemmer cast his search in idealistic and metaphysical terms (aiming for 'eine illusion in höherem sinne' or an illusion, in other words, that touched the metaphysical (3)) he was in fact exposing his audience to the phenomenological power of light just as Beckett did in *Not I*. Whereas Beckett used this power of light within a strongly structured text, there are instances on the contemporary stage that are very close to reproducing Schlemmer's 'pure power of colour and light' divorced from any text, narrative or character. In *More or Less Infinity* (*Plus ou moins l'infini*), directed by Phil Solnatoff with Compagnie 111 (Queen Elizabeth Hall 2006), several images are riveting to watch but very hard to make logical sense of: as Soltanoff said in the after show discussion there was no one meaning that they wanted to tell but rather 'this thing and this thing together make sense . . .'[15]. Two previous shows explored the cube (*IJK*) and the plane

(*Plan B*). In *More or Less Infinity* he explores the line: hundreds of them, in the form of actual sticks, poles, horizontal slots and sometimes projection. The performance is more of an experience than an idea, a physical release and exhilaration of spirit whilst seemingly tied ultimately to the restrictions of bodily weight and gravity. What he does particularly well is to combine the dynamic of the line with the organic 'lines' and flow of the human flexible body. The title of the piece encapsulates its metaphysics: the line with its inexorable basic form is explored through illusion and whole body contact (see Figure 3.4). The light continually transforms the sticks: for example, at one point three poles rise up through the floor slots and a data projector is used at the front to texture both them and the space with wavy lines so that we become unsure of their position in the space. He also lights the held sticks so that we do not always recognise the hand that holds them as living flesh: the sudden realisation that we are watching a human operator rather than a mechanical device gives a sudden frisson. For example, the flexible sticks are lined up across the stage and the performers behind grip each stick around the centre and their hands are lit from the front. The hands are at first still, held as fists, and then suddenly the hands open. The image is very simple and yet the sudden fleshly presence is startling and arresting. Elsewhere there is a single upright stick lit so that the top looks thicker than its base. Then something alive seems to appear at its base, looking almost like a puppet as it seems to stand up, but then we realise with a shock that it is, again, flesh and is a hand grasping the stick from below, through a slot in the stage. Elsewhere upright white sticks are held in formation across the stage, in four rows. They twist and turn yet somehow maintain a form, so that the space appears to morph, expanding and contracting. Throughout the piece Soltanoff uses Schlemmeresque devices: large shadows, and a play with scale and mathematical ideas such as doubling and halving the image. Communication to the audience during the magical illusions they present is not semiotically transparent; they communicate (like so much of Wilson and Lepage and Schlemmer) through the phenomenological directness of the effect: in this case, poles and bodies, a juxtaposition of form and motion, sticks and the fleshly reality that grasps them. The space expands and contracts and is in constant motion, a theme that the next chapter will pick up.

It is worth trying to push further the exact effect on the audience when such illusions 'practise to deceive'. We have established that light plays a vital part in creating stage illusions, though of course it is only one tool of many. Light can change the space because light realises plastic form; it sculpts and moulds plasticity, whether actively to deceive the eye or simply to make the eye see plastic form in varied, unexpected or strange ways.

In considering the sculptural capacities of light and its 'illusory' effects, the distinction between making an audience see differently and 'deceit' becomes hard to maintain: for what is the 'true' view of anything?

Figure 3.4 *Plus ou moins l'infini* Cie 111-Aurélien Bory and Phil Soltanoff, photograph Aglaé Bory, 2005. © Aglaé Bory.

In connection with the idea of a 'true' or 'normal' view of something, the philosopher and phenomenologist Maurice Merleau-Ponty claims that when we see something in a different or unusual light (literally not figuratively) we do not cognitively hold the 'correct' or 'true' colour in our minds and memories and actively compare the 'new' colour with it. On the contrary, we live in the moment, as it were, and accept what is offered to us (Merleau-Ponty 1974b: 199). At the same time he makes an interesting point about our normal perception of light:

> In the same way it is not true that I *deduce* the true colour of an object on the basis of the colour of the setting or of the lighting, which most of the time is not perceived [my italics] (Merleau-Ponty 1974b: 199).

Merleau-Ponty here does seem to capture a truth about an aspect of our perception of light; certainly, in everyday life one normally accepts the colours one sees and the quality of the ambient light without necessarily noticing the light or making a mental calculation as to the 'correct' colour. We are immersed in the world, geared into it, continually experience it without the intervention of thought. Schlemmer instinctively understood this and the artistic vision that naturally and continually circumvents thought.

> What is it, if I stand spellbound in front of an impression in nature? Like a medium, trembling like a divining rod, electrified, excited to the core of my being? My feeling for a nuance of nature decides it, or nature as I see it and experience it, the form in which it makes the greatest impression on me (April 1915) (Schlemmer [1958] 1977: 19–20).

If the act of perception is normally unnoticed, it is also true that in certain instances one does (go on to) make a calculation, when for example one is choosing a particular shade of colour, or if a colour of something familiar looks particularly odd or merely different. Merleau-Ponty does not talk about the possibility of oscillation of attention between phenomenological, non-cognitive perception and cognitive attention and thought. I suggest that this oscillation between rational and irrational perception is very common and more extreme in an audience, especially one watching continual illusions and visual acrobatics such as Polunin's *SnowShow* described earlier. At one point a massive 'cobweb' is dropped from an overhead bar on the heads of the audience with a sudden shock, and they spend much of the interval disentangling themselves; or in *More or Less Infinity* the strangeness of some perceptions almost demand you stop and work them out. The director's crucial task is perhaps to prolong the moment of wonder and acceptance and the phenomenological, embodied impact of the illusion as long and as strongly as possible. This may merely delay the audience member who through curiosity eventually tries to work it out rationally; or preferably (as often in Wilson) the audience member may not recognise the spatial manipulation as an 'illusion' (i.e. 'false') but absorbs it as part of the fabric of meaning being communicated. The more they are unwilling to dissect, the greater the impact, the stronger the effect. The audience for *Illusion Dance* knew rationally that limbs do not separate and dance independently, but almost certainly here Schlemmer's intention, using light and dark, was for the shape of the limbs in isolation to impact upon the perceiver with a bodily felt directness that he was (as stated earlier) concurrently exploring in his lecture course 'Man', and which his lectures and paintings could not achieve in the same embodied and direct way.

The word 'illusion' traditionally devalues and limits such an experience in theatre and indeed in performance art such a word is avoided in principle. They demand we approach it as a 'real' experience. But illusions in theatre are not necessarily any less 'real' in their phenomenological impact. It is worth recalling that the German director and designer Achim Freyer, who derived so much from the legacy of the early moderns, especially Craig, Schlemmer and Kandinsky (Brinkmeier 1997: 54–6, 120–3), states that his own visually driven work is 'not a play with appearances, it does not represent, it is what it is' (Freyer in Schober 1997: 137).

Long before Grotowski and Brook, Schlemmer claimed for the illusions of popular theatre a 'holiness', an unconsidered and precious dimension of the human spirit.[16] Today this dimension of popular entertainment, amazement in the face of the ostensibly impossible, is largely lost to us, since live performance as popular entertainment is much rarer. Today we do not witness (or only rarely and moreover with a cynical rather than enchanted eye) the sleight of hand practised by a stage magician in popular theatre, who saws the lady in half, or pierces the flesh and blood body in the box by swords, and defies our logic and undermines our knowledge of how the world operates, and its physical laws which we cannot transgress. Digital transformations have blunted our sense of wonder but not entirely extinguished it.[17] Such fantastical illusion on stage may be a far richer and more mysterious source of meaning than popular theatre itself ever laid claim to in that it gave a live experience of magic: no more, no less.[18] Polunin, in competition with instantly gratifying digital illusions of the most sophisticated nature, still attempts to access this magic, and against all the odds, succeeds.

In both Schlemmer and in the visual stages of the twenty-first century, an illusory experience is an essential part of the 'authentic'. Bonnie Marranca, whose book *The Ecology of Theatre* (Marranca 1996) extends and updates her fascination with 'theatre of images' (Marranca 1977), places the shifting 'ecologies' of theatre firmly in the visionary Modernist tradition of which Schlemmer was so much a part.

> The history of modernism and the avant-garde is rooted in the striving toward the transformation of human thought and society, that led artists to recognise the possibilities of art, opening it up to abstraction, conceptual performance, and revolutionary perceptions of time and space (Marranca 1996: xix).

There is scarcely a page of Marranca's book that does not echo this faith in the transformative and essentially healing powers of the stage. Schlemmer too believed in the power of the stage to transform and heal. In his letters and diaries he reveals his hopes that theatre will save the Bauhaus from what he considered to be the excesses of Constructivism.

> For my theatre must do more than mirror chaos and shadow box with itself. It must—if only it would succeed—offer 'enchanting pedagogy' and be founded on Schillerian principles. Oh for success with the setting, the proposition, the language, the speakers, and the audience! A stage thought out like this could become a powerful force for order at the Bauhaus (January 1926) (Schlemmer [1958] 1977: 86).

Illusion demonstrates the differing configurations of space, its shifting and unpredictable nature, its permeable boundaries and promise of infinity. It remains as much part of the experience of contemporary performance as it was on Schlemmer's stage, and mirrors too Schlemmer's strong desire to utilise the phenomenologically direct experience in its service.

Since the mid to late 1990s it is hard to find any commentary on live performance that does not subscribe to the power of the phenomenological lived experience of the event, as opposed to its 'representational' or symbolic intentions. The inauguration of *Performance Research* in the UK opened up this approach and perhaps David George's seminal article in that journal in 1996 was one of its clearest articulations: 'Performance is never a representation of anything except itself' (George 1996: 20). Such attitudes have a direct link with the early 'phenomenological' sensibilities of Schlemmer and his artistic circle. We are ideally placed today to understand what Itten was doing in his preliminary course at the Bauhaus when he emphasised the lived experience of a painting and promoted understanding via physical engagement with the materials the students handled, alongside breathing exercises and bodily workouts. As Will Grohmann, student at the Bauhaus, says, 'Space was not explained but rather experienced on biological grounds of experiencing space' (Grohmann in Neumann [1970] 1993: 178). There is no anachronism here in designating these beliefs as 'phenomenological' and even 'embodied'. The modification of Husserl's transcendent phenomenology in the 1920s by Heidegger, away from the notion of the mindful 'epoche' into the 'lived', handled and worn material object, and developed much later by Maurice Merleau-Ponty into embodiment theory, was anticipated a good many years before in Germany both in art and in pedagogical theory and practice, even if its full anti-idealist implications were not. This includes the artists of the Bauhaus, who whilst paralleling the idealism of Husserl stressed the importance of engagement with material form in their teaching and their work; and so did the key German educationalists from the nineteenth century, mainly Froebel but also Steiner and others, who placed bodily experience at the heart of their pedagogical method for training the mind (Lupton and Abbott Miller 1993). Schlemmer, sharing this common German heritage that emerges in the course of the twentieth century as Gestalt Psychology, Gestalt aesthetics and ultimately phenomenology and embodiment, pushes in his practice the ideas of intentionality beyond a mutual dependency of mind and matter into a creative relationship, a synthesis of the two, engaging with material form in the shifting context of motion, time and space.

In order to research such ideas within a non-mimetic, non-narrative performance space, Schlemmer, in addition to light, also used larger 'space dividers' or scenery ('Mobiliar').[19] Schlemmer was an accomplished stage designer who worked throughout the 1920s on productions mainly in Berlin, developing a flexible stage space, harnessing scale, perspective, line, colour and contrasts to conjure the mimetic spaces required. He had undertaken several stage designs, collaborating with Paul Hindemith in Kokoschka's *Murder, the Hope of Women* (*Mörder, Hoffnung der Frauen*) and Franz Blei's *The Thing-a-majig* (*Das Nusch-Nuschi*), Landsestheater, Stuttgart, 1921; and as mentioned in Chapter 1, Hauptmann's *The Disloyal Tsar*, Berlin Volksbühne, 1923, and Leonid Andrejew's *King Hunger*, Berlin Volksbühne, 1924. All these sets, and two in particular, *Murder, the Hope of Women* and *The Disloyal Tsar* reveal a Constructivist approach to design, and one which is also reminiscent of Adolphe Appia's stripped down staging at Hellerau, and indeed this was a style more widely spread in its use in Germany by the 1920s than is generally realised.[20] In it, the stage is divided by bold and simple shapes, flats, steps and structures capable of various mimetic interpretations as demanded by the text. Yet the stage design work, good as it was, constituted no more than one of the compromises for the 'creator of the stage today' which he described in 'Man and Art Figure': the 'creator' ('Bildner', deriving from 'das Bild', a picture, hence a 'picture maker') 'may seek fulfilment within the given situation' (Schlemmer 1925: 20) which he did as a scene designer giving visual form to the work of the poet and player, but as he said, it is only luck when intentions coincide (20). More satisfying was to work as a designer in ballet, pantomime and variety where the visual had more status. Best of all however are those areas free of the constraints of both writer and actor, where the artist can play with anonymous and mechanical moving forms, colours and human figures. He in effect describes here his vision for the stage workshop at the Dessau Bauhaus, an experience and opportunity which no theatre at that time was able to offer him but which he found, in modest proportions, at the Dessau Bauhaus.

Schlemmer had a fascination with the floor geometry of the stage (for example, the angular shapes of the actual rectangular edges), and other floor patterns which he could clearly see and sense. At Dessau, enjoying his freedom to experiment, he made these visible, such as the diagonal interstices drawn right across the floor surface, and the stage centre made visible with a large circle drawn round it. As a dancer himself, he also felt as palpable form the geometry traced by the motion of the dancer's body across the stage. (Motion itself will be dealt with more fully in the next chapter.) He regretted that the frontal view of the audience did not permit the floor patterns of the performer's movements to be seen properly from above (i.e. in tension with the ever present fixed spatial geometry).[21] At Dessau, he develops a new approach using stage flats. They are never used as background or backdrops but, placed within the playing space and actively engaged with, they are intended to be upright 3-D extensions of the geometry of the floor. They make smaller spaces within the larger space of the stage, against, around, beside and behind which the organic body moves. Schlemmer wanted at Dessau a four row track system for the moveable walls or flats, and this was almost the only technical resource he had, apart from some lamps, cloth, costumes and skeletal staging rostra—minimal means for Gropius's 'fifth wheel' on the Bauhaus wagon, as he ruefully described his theatre workshop to his friend Willi Baumeister (December 1926) (Schlemmer [1958] 1977: 90); but in truth, for Schlemmer, the simpler, the better. As far as we know, the four tracks on the ceiling were used to move 'space dividers' or flats smoothly around the larger space of the stage (though we do not know how well they worked in practice). In coming up with this practical device, he was also probably influenced by the earlier work in Weimar that had used large cut outs (such as *The Figural Cabinet*) and which would have been immeasurably easier with ceiling tracks. The Dessau work is a momentous shift in Schlemmer's thinking from *The Triadic Ballet* in that it opens up the space in which the figure is situated and explores fluidity of form,[22] whereas in his ballet the form is somewhat rigid and affixed to the body via built-up costume, albeit in motion.

In his workshop he set out deliberately to isolate and investigate the dramaturgy of placing spatial structures and space dividers (as he called them) in the space, these structures being one of the 'stage elements' which he expounds in his essay of that name (Schlemmer [1929] 1965). In that essay he lays out the stage elements as form and colour, space, light and movement. But what is actually analysed in this essay is the figure of man as performer, simple movements, scenery, held objects, masks and costumes. The way he describes the 'Mobiliar' ('furnishings') or scenery demonstrates his clear affinities with his contemporary Gordon Craig in recognising the dynamic possibilities of moveable stage screens or flats. He describes the scenery as a tool of transformation, 'displacing the spatial structure', and it does so through the 'idea of a wall'. The walls on stage build, he says, 'small spatial structures' in the larger space, but like Craig he recognises the energies which such structures generate, inviting human movement:

> The secret of a wall is what is behind it. From it is born corridors and passages, as well as energies that cross them, go along them, in front of them . . . The corridor sees its very essence uprooted, its dramaturgy laid bare (Schlemmer [1929]1965: 8–13).

He also recognises the dividing stage curtain as a kind of wall, a wall that divides audience and performers, with its own energies, some of which were explored by Schlemmer in the short performance piece *Curtain Play* (*Vorhangspiel*) which formed part of his pre-performance lecture demonstration, during the tour of the *Bauhaus Dances* in 1929. Schlemmer goes on to point out that variations on the idea of the 'wall' on stage depend crucially on the materials out of which it is made, whether the wall is transparent or opaque, dull or reflective. He describes the walls as the stage's 'mirror' which allows fantastical illusion to appear, using lights, projection, translucence and so on.[23] At the end of his essay Schlemmer parallels architecture and stage space: they are spaces that impact upon both those within and those 'without' who view it.[24] Scenery does not articulate the space in isolation from the human figure moving around it. The mechanical theatre experiments beloved by the students and Joost Schmidt did not interest Schlemmer in the long run. It was the (moving) geometry of the human body—a feeling, sensible creature—that was rich for transmutation, by entering into a relationship with the static geometry of the stage.

Much of what Schlemmer says here is directly relevant to the staging of Robert Wilson, already cited in connection with light, who creates a carefully constructed yet sensual and emotional relationship with the space. Wilson claims that it is the space behind that gives power to the performer, like a stretched bow. 'The figure will never be as strong as the space behind' (Wilson 2004). Schlemmer sought to understand this 'space behind' and how it functions in relation to the figure. He knew that the power of plastic structures, both on the stage and in architecture, derives from its human 'use' and that the human is and should be embedded in that space but in ways that complemented the visual Gestalt built up. He knew the relationship was and is reciprocal, embodied, alive: in this, in the way he paralleled architecture and the stage, he anticipated much of the criticism levelled in later years at the 'International Style'. This was his 'force for order' at the Dessau Bauhaus: man, always man. He demonstrated the way the body is fully implicated with and embedded into the space with an insight that in practice anticipates Heidegger's 'Dasein' or embeddedness in the world, and much later Merleau-Ponty's embodiment. At Dessau, Schlemmer researched the dramaturgy of scenery, its presence, its dynamism and its changing energies. It also acted as a prompt to stage action and remained an integral part of the stage 'business' that emerged.

Schlemmer's development of stage action is an aspect of his work that has been little recognised.[25] It connects him with his contemporaries, such as Meyerhold, Craig and Appia, and with our contemporary stages, belying the interpretation of his work as cold and abstract, geometric and dehumanised. In *Flats Dance, Curtain Play, Equilibristics (Equilibristik)* and *Light Play* the human engaged with playful behaviour with hoops, sticks, light, shadows, flats, stairs and rostra: it was behaviour that derived directly from the presence of the 3-D stage structures and would have not been possible without them. *Flats Dance* used the three flats to structure the action of the performance which lasted about five minutes. It consisted of the actors playing with notions of appearance and disappearance, actions that sprang entirely from play with the three uprights and the gaps between them, which altered as the flats were moved around. At one point it used the old musical hall joke of impossibly expanded arms and legs appearing at either end of the single wide wall of flats; at another point separating the three flats prompted a 'Keystone Cops' type chase.[26] *Gesture Dance* derives its elementary plot lines, human behaviours and comedic content partly from the character 'types' originating in Kandinsky's theorising on colour and shape (for example, perceiving blue always as 'slow' but yellow as 'lively') which Schlemmer develops into stage business, and partly from the interplay of figure and furniture; *Box Play* derives its content from the action of building (and dismantling) a wall of blocks by the three actors, and was no doubt much more humorous than Hastings' reconstruction appears to be (Hastings 1968). In this way it is a comment on human co-operation (and its opposite) in building/architecture and indeed in more mundane tasks at the Bauhaus encountered day by day. *Three Women* is nothing less than a hilarious scene of three women, all men dressed up, attempting to arrange themselves before a camera for a photograph.[27] *Curtain Play* demonstrated the 'dramaturgy' of the front stage curtain, with Werner Seidhoff developing a little humorous scene of hide and reveal purely by engaging with it as a material object. Through play, the intention is to fuse mind, material and body in a unified sequence of action: creating the perfect, and simple, stage Gestalt, usually laced with laughter.

In his essay 'Stage Elements' ('Bühnenelemente') ([1929] 1965), Schlemmer gives a humorous example of this unity of plastic form and human behaviour: his Musical Clown (Der Musikalische Clown) (see Figure 3.5). This clown, played often by Schlemmer on the Bauhaus stage, and inspirational to Weininger's version of the same character, had a costume covered with instruments that made noises when he moved but he never played them as such; instead he reacted with terror at the noises he produced, for example running away and then creeping back before being terrorised once more, unable to work out what had made them (Flocon 1994). It was very funny to watch. Schlemmer says the clown was a 'sacrifice' to musicality because he did not actually create music himself but only reacted to everything he played with (Schlemmer [1929] 1965: 21). The parallel with the scenery is clear. The performer is not *imposing* upon the space/objects/scenery but playing in conjunction with them. In this Schlemmer takes a dancerly approach to space and revolutionises theatre, moving beyond both Gordon Craig and Adolphe Appia in his radical thinking about what theatre could be. The question is not so much what the actor can bring to the space as what can the space offer the actor?[28] In *Treppenwitz* (*Staircase Joke*), Seidhoff engaged with the dynamics of a small set of stairs. This piece made a verbal joke, which puns on the name given in German to the witty reply we remember too late (on our way out going down the stairs? See page 25, this volume) into a physical joke, and is a good example of translating thought into spatial realisation. Schlemmer understood that stage design (and architecture) is haptic in essence, that is, it is a felt, bodily and three-dimensional experience, and not a purely visual event: it is both visceral and corporeal.

Scheper quotes Schlemmer in 1929 laying out plans for stage work at the Breslau Academy (sadly never realised):

> We feel the space by dint of the feeling and co-operation of our senses, especially those of the face, through the eyes scanning the space in time . . . Furthermore equally depending on time is the sensing of space like that of a blind man: and lastly by walking through space, aiming at physical feeling and bodily confirmation of it (Schlemmer in Scheper 1988: 255).

Figure 3.5 Members of the Bauhaus stage class with Musical Clown on the roof terrace of the Bauhaus Building [Bauhaustanz mit Musikalischem Clown und grosser Maske], 1927. Photo Archive, C. Raman Schlemmer, IT-288824 Oggebbio (VB) Italy.

This 'sensing of space' is haptic. His insistence on his students playing and engaging with the 'Mobiliar' or scenery within this space remind us today of the absolute necessity of designers consciously resisting the pull of the purely visual, and entering into haptic contact and bodily play with the materials they use. Schlemmer distinguishes 'Mobiliar' from three elements of materials on stage that can actually be held ('Formen, Gegenständen, Requisiten' or 'forms, objects and props') (Schlemmer [1929] 1965: 13). He says there is no immediate bodily contact with 'Mobiliar', the stage 'furnishings' or scenery because it is not 'held' (obviously) but it is clear from his exercises on the Bauhaus stage that he demands bodily contact or interplay nevertheless. As a performer he knew it is fatal to separate 'stage design' from the experience of being on stage and directing. In the case of stage design, whole body engagement as performers is needed to understand fully the construction of the stage in conjunction with the communication of meaning. This needs to be taken into account in training stage designers—and architects—today.

Schlemmer synthesised his space with ordinary human behaviours, and insisted on their mutual creation together in attempt to unify the simple stage elements in new 'Gestalten'; and he at one point attempted to push his ideas much further in a piece that used words, the *House of Pi or The Home of the Stars* in May 1927. This slight but unique piece has already been recognised by Thomas Schober as an important forerunner of postmodern theatre techniques (Schober 1997). This experiment pushed Schlemmer's metaphysical stage the furthest into 'dramatic' action and words that it ever went, and had to be prematurely jettisoned (Schlemmer by now had his eye on the Dance Congress at Magdeburg, and wanted to concentrate on it).[29] The piece is an important landmark.

The central 'character' was the Astrologer whose telescope reached towards the stars from the roof of the house. The number 'Pi' in Greek is of course a mysterious number relating to the ratio of a circle's circumference to its diameter. A fragment of script remains alongside a sketch by Schlemmer of the set: 'The action took place as a waking dream, between reality and unreality' (Scheper 1988: 156). Schober describes the action so far as he can make it out as Fate unfolding but with no through story line: singular destinies were brought together (as Scheper also notes) by the structure of the building itself (the large 'set', consisting of a flat roofed house built over several levels) which allowed the different playing areas. The action took place over a single night.

> The 'objective calculations' of the Astrologer formed the starting point as he worked on the roof of the house. On the left balcony stood the dancer Hyacinth who was bewitched by the words of love whispered by a 'fancy man'. In the focal point, the centre, of the house slept the family. In the front of the house was the acting area for three thieves, a mysterious figure and a passer by. The spatial setting, which was only broken up by the vertical movement of the Astrologer's lift, allowed for simultaneity of actions, which gave rise to complex time relations between events (Schober 1997: 129–30).

The key point here is the way Schlemmer mixes metaphysics with ordinary actions in ordinary lives, as Wilson did in *The Dream Play*. The house itself bears a resemblance to the Masters' Houses built near the Dessau Bauhaus, one of which was occupied by the Schlemmer family. Schober points out that the everyday actions in and around the house seem to emerge from the mutterings and actions of the (metaphysically 'in touch') astrologer on the roof. The Greek number 'Pi' of course is the 'transcendental, irrational' number (Scheper 1988: 156), connector between the circle's diameter and the circle's circumference. The roof of the house has a half circle or dome rising above it with the Astrologer's telescope protruding like a radius reaching out to the stars. The plot seems to hinge on the seemingly disconnected fates of the other characters below, in, around and in front of the 'House of Pi', being brought into a particular connection with each other by the Astrologer. As in the *Figural Cabinet*, to use Schlemmer's own words, 'meta' is made physical. Schober quotes the opening words of the Astrologer: they consist of strings of numbers and murmurings about weddings and stock broking, internal systems of the body and body parts, i.e. random items of 'real' life both visible and hidden, mixed with what sound like mathematical calculations and the plotting of planetary positions and the stars: there are no complete sentences, only phrases strung together. The words fused with the unfolding actions below, a simultaneity of viewpoint which was only made possible through the physical structure of the house holding it all together. The words in a sense dynamically fused with both the physical action and the plastic structure or set. They enter into a new stage Gestalt that includes language. In this piece, Schlemmer, rather than cut out language, displaced the then usual predominance of word and/or music on stage and forged a new synthesis of human actions in a simultaneous rather than linear structure, and demonstrated that simultaneity through set, movement and language; as Schober claims, he discovers and lays bare in effect the ABCs of the postdramatic stage, particularly, as Schober demonstrates, the stage of Robert Wilson and Achim Freyer (Schober 1997).

On postmodern stages, as in *House of Pi*, the 'story' is often either non-linear or minimal or even nonexistent, and the spaces conjured slip out of a defined place and time. The resonant and motile 'places' utilise human behaviours and actions, ordinary life and objects, but the scenery and figures are released from straight mimetic function. They create new 'Gestalten' of space and time often using language: the kind of performance spaces in fact that Kantor first conjured over fifty years ago. Such a space is his school room in, for example, *Wielopole Wielopole*.

Kantor, like Schlemmer, makes physical an idea. It is helpful to look upon Kantor as someone in a direct line of development from Schlemmer, since his spaces, more obviously than Schlemmer's, combine Schlemmer's 'abstraction' with human action. Kantor talks of the geometric elements of abstraction as 'a rare phenomenon in theatre . . . fully realized in the Bauhaus in the theatre of Oskar Schlemmer' (Kantor in Kobialka 1993: 209) and these elements are all 'elements of drama'. He recognised that Schlemmer's work, even in its utilisation of the primordial geometric structures of space, was not disconnected from life. Kantor's space transforms itself on a continual basis, oscillating between past, present and future, the dead and the living, memory and experience. Kantor's 'memory room' for example is built from these elements.

> No doubt we will have to extend the boundaries of our idea of THE REAL to encompass a territory as yet not grasped materially, MEMORY . . . Which means we must construct a real model of MEMORY. Its workings and its expressive resources (Kobialka 1993: 159).

And this physical room, built (materially on stage) and perpetually changed (through objects and human interaction with those objects on stage) is 'the room I keep reconstructing again and again/And that keeps dying again and again'. It is no longer a staged representation of a fixed place but staged memory itself, [30] which is a 'new type of "SPACE"' (Kobialka 1993: 158). In one sense Kantor's memory room is a series of staged memory 'Gestalten', and elements of them connect to the audience who in turn make their own memory 'Gestalten' in a continual process of forming and re-forming. In *The Milano Lessons* he specifically refers to space as 'Ur-matter' in Gestalt terms, without using that word: 'I am fascinated by a mystical or utopian idea and a supposition that in every work of art, there exists some kind of UR-MATTER that is independent of an artist, that shapes itself, and that grounds all possible, infinite variants of life . . . It seems that the autonomy of an image is born in this remote layer of the creative process. I believe in this SIMULTANEITY and this EQUALITY of actions—in my individual actions and the action of this primordial matter . . .' and he goes on to describe the Ur-matter of space as endlessly forming and re-forming into infinite changing states or 'Gestalten' (though he does not use this word). Kantor is explicit that the aesthetic problem that his theatre wrestles with is one of the separation of object and mind, the Cartesian split between mind and matter, and he sees Schlemmer similarly wrestling with this conundrum: for example, in his Schlemmeresque exercise 'The Object's Immobility' he states, "A representation of a real object in a painting is a naïve cognitive belief in the possibility of being able to know the attributes of a real object by imitating it' (Kantor in Kobialka 1993: 214).[31]

The constant physical 'play' on stage that Schlemmer engaged in during his researches far exceeds analysis of 'spatial organisation' (Scheper 1988: 190) in a Constructivist mode. In Russia, artists had engaged with analysis of materials and the dynamics of space in the 1910s: for example, Rodchenko, with his spiralling spatial structures which folded down or his boxes that fitted together; or Tatlin's fascination from around 1914 onwards with abstract sculptures protruding from larger structures such as corners, splicing shapes together in an attempt to pin down the dynamics of plane and point and line in 3-D. Such work meant Russian Constructivist artists were then well placed to work for the Revolution on folding chairs and space saving tables.[32] But Schlemmer's definitions of and continual play with space on the Dessau stage move beyond abstract play with the dynamics of space, into human action and drama itself, however simple the (mainly comic) pieces were that emerged. This dimension of his work, the dramatic, is not at all obvious from just studying the photographs where his approach can seem reductive and confined to abstract, geometrical forms and shapes, albeit in conjunction with the human figure. Schlemmer's approach in fact derives from a truly holistic vision of action, drama and staging. This is especially obvious when comparing the Bauhaus stage at Dessau with the contemporary Constructivist stages of Popova, Meyerhold and Stepanova, which largely concerned themselves with designing after the event of the text, however new and flexible the scenography. Schlemmer, because of his working method, and using simple and limited means, prefigured the harnessing of all the stage elements from the very inception of idea through the entire production process that we find on the stages of Tadeusz Kantor, Robert Wilson, Robert Lepage, Laurie Anderson, Kirsten Denholm, Pina Bausch or Simon McBurney (to name but a few highly visual directors) as no other director succeeded in doing in the 1920s.

Schlemmer describes the unity of elements on stage as fusing the 'transcendent' dimension of space (mathematical, mysterious and resonant) and the richly tragi-comic space we inhabit in our daily lives. As always, the Romantic basis of his theorising, with his stress on the metaphysical transcendent experience that has to be physically realised and shared on stage, risks alienating us and disguises his affinities with us. Stage space transforms the ordinary if structured purposefully. The actor becomes transformed in behaviour by the surrounding physicality and ordinary actions become purposeful.[33] He saw this 'transformation' of the everyday as having reached its height in the past on the stage of Shakespeare and later Schiller, but he aspired towards it for a new German 'metaphysical' theatre. The notion of the extraordinary import of the ordinary has affinity with Eastern disciplines of performance, particularly Butoh. In 'Man and Art Figure' towards the end (Schlemmer 1925: 20) this is exactly what Schlemmer means by the new theatre forms that still awaited their creation, a fusion of human content and spatial metaphysics, an alchemy for the ordinary. In one sense this is the Romantic aspiration, bridging the gap between life and transcendency; and in another, freed from the transcendent imperative and from logic, linear narrative and mimesis, it is the transformative space of the postmodern theatre.

4 Body and Motion

The human body was central to Schlemmer's intellectual belief and pivotal to his cultural, aesthetic and ethical system; research into the body in motion takes his thinking to a new level, embodying as it does the force and dynamism of its organicism. Movement admits change, flux and impermanence. Within Schlemmer's mature aesthetic, motion always forms part of the Gestalt, to a greater or lesser extent—less obviously in his paintings, more so in his reliefs, sculptures and wall paintings and majorly so in his stage work. Schlemmer's interest lay not so much in speed and motion as manifested in the modern world of cars and trains and clock time (Kern [1983] 2003: 109–130, Hughes 1991: 9–56) as in the deeper ramifications of motion, flux, change and impermanence within philosophy, metaphysics and ethics. Whilst some early twentieth-century artists offer a somewhat limited attempt to incorporate movement in their work—as in, for example, Futurist paintings that resemble a series of film stills—other artists pushed notions around movement and change much further, and their work as a result retains a charge and resonance that still reverberates in the twenty-first century. Duchamp's kinetic art, for example, offers a meditation upon flux and instability, and his work often manifests his more esoteric reading on new models of the universe that emerged in the early twentieth century, models which depend on abandoning Euclidean geometry and substituting new paradigms for understanding space.[1] Schlemmer's awareness of these new radical structurings of the universe, time and space was probably limited: his profound awareness of motion as a mysterious phenomenon that the logic and proofs of Euclidean geometry could not fully explain emerged not only from his readings in philosophy but above all from his embodied experience as a dancer moving through space. Interest in motion within the Bauhaus was widespread—manifested, for example, in photography, the *Reflected Light Plays* of Hirschfeld Mack and in Maholy-Nagy's kinetic work. It is also fundamental to the pedagogical design theory of Paul Klee and Kandinsky that emerged from their Bauhaus teaching (see Klee [1925] 1953, 1968; Klee [1956] 1961; Kandinsky [1947] 1979): a line was always described, for example, as a point in motion.[2] Schlemmer's approach to motion using performance offered a radical way forward that painting and the now largely extinct art of kinetic light shows and kinetic sculptures did not.[3]

Schlemmer's attitude to the body was rooted in his neo-Romantic thinking in which the body demonstrates both perfect abstract mathematics in its movements, the 'mechanics' of its joints ('Gelenkmechanik') (Schlemmer 1927c: 3), *and* the mysterious life force that linked the mind ('Geist') with nature ('Natur').[4] Ricarda Huch, in *Vom Wesen des Menschen* (*On Man's Being*), which Schlemmer acquired soon after publication in 1922, expresses similar ideas (Huch 1922). It originates in earlier Romantic theory as explained by Karin von Maur:

> Schelling was also a man who understood the human form as a symbolic analogue of universals, and a perfect unity of 'soul and reason', when he interpreted the human upright stance as a 'pulling upwards and away from the earth', man's symmetrical physique, with its limbs protruding, as two such complete halves in unity, and the head as the unifier of both systems (Maur 1979a: 330).

These ideas are also connected to Schlemmer's belief in the world as a microcosm of the macrocosm, an ancient idea familiar to Schlemmer from his readings of the medieval doctor and philosopher Paracelsus, so that the body itself is a (geometric) analogue of perfection—but one that is organic, living and in motion, a constantly changing Gestalt which provided him with a lifetime's inspiration.

The distinction that Alwin Nikolais makes between motion and movement is useful for our purposes:

> Basic dance—and I should emphasise the word basic—is primarily concerned with motion. So immediately you will say but the basketball player is concerned with motion. That is so—but he is not concerned with it primarily. His action is a means towards an end beyond motion. In basic dance the motion is its own end—that is, concerned with nothing beyond itself . . . As art—dance is the art of motion not movement . . . the manner in which the action takes place is motion (Nikolais 1971: 19).

Following Nikolais's lead here, let us say 'movement' as he defines it (as in that of the basketball player) is purposeful; motion is not.[5] This chapter accordingly refers to 'motion' rather than movement, since it is the motion itself, 'the manner in which the action takes place', which drives Schlemmer. Motion on his stage is not a function connected to mimesis or a 'means to an end beyond motion' but a function in itself, powerful and mysterious.

> Furthermore: the starting point is the fundamentals . . . One should start with one's physicality, with being, with standing and moving,

leaving jumping and dancing for much later. For taking a step is a tre-
mendous event, and no less so is raising a hand, moving a finger (May
1929) (Schlemmer [1958] 1977: 113).

Nikolais identifies a seismic shift in the history of dance in the twentieth
century towards the isolation of motion as a phenomenon in itself (despite
him saying *all* basic dance is concerned with motion), attempting to strip
it of semiotic significance, and tear away the frame of mimesis, focusing
on the moment of reception itself: the shift originated in this early Modern period, percolated into the happenings of the 1960s, is fundamental
to postmodern dance, and ultimately is found in the 'postdramatic' stages
identified by Lehmann (Lehmann 2006), whereby action itself (not mimetic
action) becomes the main interest, the focal content of a piece.[6] This shift
away from mimetic action continually marks out twentieth-century avant-
garde performance work. The concentration on action rather than mimetic
action is rooted in philosophical concerns, namely phenomenology, but, to
steal Schlemmer's own words in relation to mathematics, not the sort of
philosophy we 'sweat over in school' but an embodied philosophy 'where
everything begins with a feeling that slowly becomes form and where
the unconscious and the subconscious enter the clarity of consciousness'
(Schlemmer [1926] 1969: 118). In other words, ideas take form and substance before our eyes and are actively experienced. Motion is a difficult
philosophical problem and perhaps holds the key to metaphysical riddles
that engage the mystically inclined artist and thinker.

> You should have a deep respect for every single action performed by the
> human body, especially on the stage, that special realm of life and of
> illusion, that second reality in which everything is surrounded with the
> radiance of magic (May 1929) (Schlemmer [1958] 1977: 113).

Concentrating on simple actions on stage (taking a step, raising a hand,
moving a finger) might mean, he claimed in his diary in May 1929, that the
keyhole (but presumably not the key!) to the riddle of the Bauhaus Theatre
might at least be (nearly) found (Schlemmer [1958] 1977: 113): a modest
claim indeed—but offered by Schlemmer here ruefully and without irony.

In virtually all Schlemmer's Bauhaus stage work, motion derives from or
is explored in relation to the human body. His work contrasts fundamentally to that of his students and colleagues who spent many happy hours
engineering the relatively simple and straightforward motion of mechanical
objects: simple in Schlemmer's estimation, since no matter how complex
the mechanics for moving objects, none compared, he believed, to the complexity of the effect on stage of a human body taking a single step.

In his paintings and drawings, which are ostensibly 'static' visual work,
his interest in the body develops via his figurative work from around
1916, and this date unsurprisingly coincides with the first performance of

The Triadic Ballet. Not only do human figures appear in his paintings in the late 1910s, and moreover figures engaged in human activities, but as Karin von Maur points out, they begin to engage with objects that invite movement—staircases, corridors, bannisters. Scheper is clear that Schlemmer's own development was not from 'point and line to plane' (Kandinsky [1947] 1979), but rather 'point and line to curve', and rightly sees the development of the curved line in Schlemmer's 2-D work as evidence of the pull towards movement (Scheper 1988: 242). He sees this reflected in all Schlemmer's paintings, sculptures, wall reliefs and wall paintings, as well as of course the curving lines of the costumes of *The Triadic Ballet.* This is clear in Schlemmer's illustrations for the essay *Man and Art Figure* where the stereometric straight lines of the rectilinear space are envisioned as infused with the flowing lines of the organic body. Performance by the living 'Kunstfigur' or 'art figure'[7] is a radical advance upon the Cubism that Schlemmer manifested in the early 1910s, and one which took him ten years to realise fully. As in a Cubist painting, there is discipline and concentration upon form (in Worringer's terms, abstraction rather than empathy), manifesting an intellectual ordering and planning in order to embed and implicate the viewer in a multitude of perceptual viewpoints; but the experience unfolds in time.[8] Stage work became the physical realisation and development of Cubist ideas within perceptual flux, where the line becomes sinuous and sensuous, motion and change is actively experienced and 'symbols' have a perceptual complexity and fleshly reality. The experience of motion actually originates in Schlemmer's 'static' visual work.

All Schlemmer's sculptures are meant to be walked around, to appreciate fully the play of light and shadow in the changing 'Gestalten' of their mass (R. Schlemmer 2001: 25). Schlemmer's wire wall reliefs of human figures (e.g. *Homo* (1916)) are designed to be placed on the wall of a room, where the surface wall can be seen behind it and shadows change as the human occupant/viewer moves around the room, making a total Gestalt in which the curved geometry of the human figure (sculpture and viewer) harmonises with the geometry of the walls and surfaces.[9] His full engagement with stage work between 1925 and 1929 was his attempt to extend the necessarily limited 'motion' of his paintings and sculpture into real motion in real space. He strongly refuted the criticism of an ex-student of his, Ernst Kállai, about the split, as Kállai saw it, between plastic form and figure on stage in the Bauhaus Dances, creating static tableaux (Kállai 1990). Schlemmer repeated his published riposte in his diary: 'I readily acknowledge that I came to the dance from painting and sculpture, and as a result I am bound to appreciate dance's essential element, movement, more keenly, because the expressive range of painting and sculpture by their nature is restricted to the static and rigid, to "movement captured in a fixed moment"' (Schlemmer [1958] 1977:131).

Wall painting functions as a particularly useful paradigm model of Gestalt thought in relation to space, body and motion, and elements of his total vision look ahead to immersive installation art later in the century. Wall painting was one of the workshops in Weimar alongside stone, book binding, ceramics and so on. We may be confused as to why 'murals', that old-fashioned decorative art, should have found a place at the Bauhaus. But wall paintings are central to understanding the Bauhaus concept of architectural space; and in relation to Schlemmer, architectural space is a scaling up of the space of the stage. Both involve motion though the space so that architecture is not only a visual art but something immersive, physically experienced, volumatic, energetic. Gropius says in his manifesto which opened the Bauhaus:

> The ultimate, if distant, aim of the Bauhaus is the unified work of art—the great structure—in which there is no distinction between monumental and decorative art. The Bauhaus wants to educate architects, painters, and sculptors of all levels, according to their capabilities, to become competent craftsmen or independent creative artists and to form a working community of leading and future crafts men. These men, of kindred spirit, will know how to design buildings harmoniously in their entirety—structure, finishing, ornamentation and furnishing (Gropius [1919] 1969: 32).

Note the stress here on designing the totality of a building including the decoration: this harmony was arguably actually achieved later in Gropius's design for the new Bauhaus at Dessau, a building that remains stunning in its combination of subtle detail and simplicity of total impact. Paintings *per se*, to be hung upon the wall, were not encouraged at the Bauhaus despite many of the teachers there continuing to produce them. The problem was that too often a 'framed' image (itself a 'virtual' space of course) was stuck in the middle of the wall and destroyed the architectural spatial Gestalt instead of being conceived and experienced as part it. The Bauhaus ideal was that the walls would incorporate colour[10], shape, designs/images/objects in aesthetic harmony with the room/space as a whole; 'images', if any, were painted directly onto the walls, or presented as wall reliefs in wire or plaster, hung strategically in relation to the space (and Schlemmer worked in all these media).

Ideally, the wall painting/design was conceived as a whole from the start in the planning stage, or more pragmatically, sometimes their site was carefully chosen and the design composed accordingly. Schlemmer undertook this latter task several times: in Cologne, Weimar, and in the Folkgang museum at Essen. Wall painting could fill the surfaces completely as they did in Schlemmer's wall paintings in the Workshop Building at Weimar, or could be smaller scale, such as single reliefs on a wall. Schlemmer of course also favoured easel painting and saw no disharmony between his works and the Gestalt of a building space, because they were carefully put together 'Gestalten' of structured space themselves, with human figures smoothed into mathematical perfection, and the overall Gestalt harmonised absolutely with, and became part of, the Gestalt of the room.[11]

This is what Schlemmer meant by 'necessity':

> What do I want? To create a style in painting which denotes a necessity over and above fashion and aesthetic form, which can hold its ground against the functional necessity of purely practical objects and machines (November 1922) (Schlemmer [1958] 1977: 63).

This style is therefore by necessity an 'ethical kind' (64): a representation of a style of life in order to 'heighten self consciousness' (64). He wanted to achieve this in works of art which while altogether self-sufficient, naturally 'demand and shape' ('fordern, gestalten') their appropriate environment, especially architecture (64). Similarly, Klee and Kandinsky never abandoned painting either. Schlemmer's comment in 1919 on his own easel paintings uses Gestalt thinking, whereby the Gestalt of the painting allies itself with the larger Gestalt of the wall and of the architecture itself: in effect, he describes his paintings here as 'Gestalten' that are complete in themselves, a compression of form, but which also form part of other 'wholes' in which they are set.

> As to my pictures: 'pictures' in the usual sense they are not, that is, canvases on which a piece of nature, or the world, is captured using all the illusions of space and light in order they might live out their particular existence in salons and museums, compressed into their gold frames. Rather, they are surfaces which break open the frame and join to the wall becoming part of a larger surface, part of a larger space than themselves, an actual part of the envisioned architecture we aspire to. Compressed in them, reduced in miniature, is what should constitute the laws and form of their surroundings. So they are pictures in this sense: they are the Tablets of the Law. The representation of man will always constitute the greatest parable for the artist (November 1919) (Schlemmer [1958] 1977: 36).

Note here that man is the most important Gestalt of all; in German, the sentence reads: 'Die Darstellung des Menschen wird immer das große *Gleichnis* für den Künstler bilden' [my italics]. 'Gleichnis' is often translated as 'symbol' but this fails to communicate the full biblical impact of the word in German which may be better sometimes rendered as parable (as above) or allegory, but even this is unsatisfactory. In Western thinking, the term 'symbol' has often been used to distance us from lived, embodied experience and the possibility of transformative experience.[12] Schlemmer's 'symbols' do not remain cognitive signs worked out in the mind alone; they are embodied and felt and lived and experienced. Above all, they are not divorced from motion. In the wall paintings in Weimar, the observer walks amongst and experiences the reciprocal flow of form between body, space, architecture and image. In November 1930, Schlemmer, aware that his Weimar reliefs have been destroyed, and devastated by the blow, says that Van de Velde's building (with its vestibule, walls, niches, stairs and corridors) was one chosen in order to create a unified and unifying work, consisting of wall paintings and reliefs, and his work was acknowledged as an important attempt to revive the lost but close bond between architecture, painting, and sculpture (Schlemmer [1958] 1977: 123).

Schlemmer executed these large scale wall decorations in the existing entrance hall and stairwell of the workshop building of the Weimar Art School for the Bauhaus Exhibition in 1923, consisting of plaster wall reliefs of abstracted human forms and painted designs. He was helped in this by students who made sections to his design, and by Joost Schmidt. The walls are only partially restored (at the entrance) and restoration is slowly ongoing, denying all access to the building at the time of writing, so that one is currently forced to imagine the total work through sketches and poor photographs. Herzogenrath's account of the Weimar wall paintings is illuminating and unique in its commentary upon their innate and integral motion. This means not only the dynamism and tensions in the figures and designs themselves, but also that the decoration was conceived as part of the architectural space that one moves through and up (via the stairs); and the shape, colour and scale deliberately enhanced the viewer's sense of motion. Wall painting is thought of as a plastic art that is meant to be haptically experienced and immersive, like architecture itself, and indeed theatre.

Schlemmer often paints or moulds a human figure that is abstracted, but contains a horizontal pull (the upper arm) and a vertical pull (the whole body slant, thrusting diagonally). The 'horizontal/vertical pull' figure is found as early as *Composition in Pink* (1915) and reappeared on a collaged curtain for *The Triadic Ballet* in 1922 and in sketches for *The Triadic Ballet* that year, and is developed in the Weimar wall reliefs of 1923. Herzogenrath says that the relief figures opposite each other in the entrance to Van de Velde's building seem to stand and hover, so that the dominant vertical and horizontal movement or tension is so strong that movement itself seems to be their primary subject. Continual denial of balance in the figure in this way sets up a tension and energy.[13] The frieze figure in the stairwell is divided into two lines of movement: one above hovering and one beneath plunging down; these lines both overlap a little bit into the first floor and disturb 'the full calm of the standing figure' (Herzogenrath 1973: 53). As a dancer, says Herzogenrath, Schlemmer was always interested in flights of steps as a motive for movement (Herzogenrath 1973: 53) with their horizontal and vertical forces at work; we encounter this again in his paintings and in the Dessau stage work. He also used shading to get a 3-D effect above the staircase. Topping the round stairwell with its three-quarter turn staircase is a square skylight window. He put three concentric circles on the roof in colours round the square window, using grey, light yellow and white, and surviving photos do not show the resulting relief or 'shadowing' effect.[14] As in the stage photo described in Chapter 2, which he mounted and tilted, Schlemmer seems always to push the space for unexpected 'Gestalten' and haptic experiences. We see Schlemmer here projecting himself into the experience of the 'audience', so that his wall painting is only one step removed from performance itself.

Schlemmer had to devise ways of shaping and presenting the living bodies that form part of his moving spatial 'Gestalten' on stage. In Schlemmer's stage work, the body is always a plastic form, a space shaper alongside light and scenery. Even in his comic and more content driven pieces, this abstract rather than empathetic approach is co-present: it is a crucial aspect of the total Gestalt he presents. Nothing is casually placed; every physical element, no matter how tiny, in his stage 'frame', even the movement of a finger, is purposeful. The body is always a plastic form, a 'space shaper'. The danger is to misinterpret this approach as mechanistic, or thinking Schlemmer is treating the performer like a puppet. Properly understood, there is nothing mechanistic about a puppet, as the next chapter will argue; and 'space shaping' for Schlemmer, as demonstrated in the previous chapter, has more to do with metaphysics than mechanics. Craig misleadingly and surely mischievously suggested the live performer would have to be all together excluded from his harmonious visual stage, but in truth his desire for an ideal live performer was close to that of Schlemmer.[15] Schlemmer refused any bifurcation of aesthetics and the live body, and fully incorporated the human figure. Whilst the last chapter exposed an unrecognised use of dramatic business in much of Schlemmer's work, in certain pieces Schlemmer's aim was to cut out human quotidian actions and semiotic content altogether and expose motion itself to our scrutiny.[16] These pieces include the opening dances in his touring repertoire: *Space Dance* and *Form Dance*, and also *Stick Dance*, *Glass Dance* and *Metal Dance*. In all these pieces the body also engages with material form, held and/or worn, and this has further important resonances, explored in the next chapter. These pieces are simple (but not simplistic) meditations on the reception and perception of space that anticipate subsequent experiment in dance in the United States in the 1950s and 1960s.[17] This process in fact began with his first dance piece *The Triadic Ballet* which developed over a ten-year period of planning and making up to 1922, but in the 1910s he advanced his stage practice so far that the ideas behind the ballet and his subsequent work at Dessau that built on it are closer to our own century than to those of his contemporaries. But it did not begin that way. Schlemmer began with the idea rather than its embodiment (the first and greatest problem of performance) and struggled at first to create a powerful dance piece.

The Triadic Ballet came about after he met Albert Burger and Else Hötzel in Stuttgart, in late 1912. Both were professional dancers; Burger was a pupil of the painter Hölzel, as was Schlemmer himself. Albert Burger and

Else Hötzel had visited Hellerau that summer and seen the pared down staging of Adolphe Appia, using neutral steps and platforms, which boldly and strongly carved out the open stage space, with no proscenium arch and no naturalistic settings/backdrops: Appia also of course also used light to articulate the space. What seems at first, however, to have most impressed the couple was the emotional intensity of the dancers trained by Jaques Dalcroze and the unusual means of achieving this. The dancers were trained to move, so far as we can reconstruct this production of *Orfeo*, with repetitive actions, in what Christopher Innes describes as 'the abstraction of expression to universal shapes', that is using movements not immediately connected to human behaviours (as, for example, beckoning would be, or other mimetic gestures such as those expressing love) and so these abstract gestures could be somehow considered essentialist in nature, with 'eternal' meaning. The criteria for selecting such movements is less clear. In this way, the 'subjective' was translated into the so-called 'archetypal'—or at least, this was the theory (Innes 1993: 48). Moreover, the set, because it was abstract and not specific in its setting, seemed to offer the possibility of harmonising the plastic elements of the stage with the more abstract movement and the music: a harmony, it was felt, which had never been seen before in opera, and the desire for it was of course very much in keeping with the Expressionist sensibilities of early Modernism (see Chapter 2), finding essentialist connections between two entirely different disciplines (as they did between painting and music). It profoundly affected Diaghilev, Reinhardt and other leading directors of the avant-garde who saw it. Its impact was novel and powerful, tuned into the essentialist ideas of the era, and we might speculate that Appia achieved here the discipline of the stage elements he sought and which he saw lacking in conventional theatres of whatever type at that time. In any case, Burger and Hötzel communicated their enthusiasm to Schlemmer, who had recently trained himself as a dancer and had little desire to indulge in the narrative school of classical narrative ballet. The three collaborated in creating a 'modern' ballet which Burger apparently called *The Courtship* (Troy 1986: 128).

A description of this dance, or at least an early draft of key ideas, can be found in Schlemmer's diary entry of December 1912. He describes it as 'development from the old dance to the new' (Schlemmer [1958] 1977: 10). It is very expressionistic in form. Colour symbolism is still used but in a highly controlled way using criteria which do not read strongly to us today. For example, he describes the 'conventional' dance to open the piece as predominantly grey; then 'yellow-orange colour' bursts into the space with the demon's appearance (creating Dionysian chaos). After a period of confusion behind a dark brown gauze (with similarly 'dark' or 'brown' music!) the demon enters again and red and orange now dominate, all breaking into an erotic frenzy of dancing. With the degeneration into loss of control, yellow light mixes with shrill music, before the descent again into darkness. A violet dot of light, a circle, appears, which develops into a blue square: this blue comes to dominate the stage, getting larger with splendid, majestic music. With the arrival of an angel, silver and white saturate the stage to symbolise (in the excellent commentary by Troy) the progression from the intial grey of 'unconscious purity' to 'conscious purity' (Troy 1986: 128), which presumably reconciles 'Geist' and 'Natur' (mind and matter), and is a vision of total harmony. This use of colour symbolism is very crude in its attempt to match material form with Expressionistic yearnings but such beliefs in the essential unity of the material world and the metaphysical beyond were common at that time, as explored in Chapter 2, and demonstrated in the Expressionist Bible, Kandinsky's *On the Spiritual in Art*. Scheper, however, gives evidence as to how Schlemmer's thought was developing at this time in a highly original direction, away from the freely expressive body of this early dance, *The Courtship*, towards a dance that places the body in direct contact with material form. Scheper quotes a diary entry, 5 November 1913, on what Schlemmer calls the 'Duncan School' where the use of the mask, a plastic form worn by the body, is specifically described as speaking 'a strange, universal language' (Scheper 1988: 22). Importantly, Scheper also draws attention to a sketch of 1913 that depicts a dance costume where the costume is actually formed of triangular shapes (i.e. not just a pattern printed on to the costume) and sees this as a turning point in the development of ideas which led eventually to *The Triadic Ballet* (Scheper 1988: 23). It is this physical material form (i.e. the triangles) which comes to restrict and shape the bodily movement in *The Triadic Ballet*, rather than (as in *The Courtship*) conceptual ideas (on ecstasy versus order) that guide the choreography of the unrestricted moving body.

By 1916, when Schlemmer had an extraordinary opportunity as a soldier off duty to realise some of his new ideas on stage by building three costumes for a performance in Stuttgart, the form of the dance had changed completely. In some ways it now looked the opposite (as Scheper says) of Expressionist dance, but arguably the idealistic intentions were similar even if the method had changed completely. Motion had ceased to be an outpouring or a quasi-ritual invoking of metaphysical ecstasy. Motion now animated matter and form within what were actually attempts at costume 'Gestalten', and in this way motion becomes the focus for Schlemmer's most 'Romantic' (mystical) expression within 'objective' (or disciplined) form (September 1915) (Schlemmer [1958] 1977: 21).

We know little about this early, and necessarily small scale, presentation in war time but it formed the basis for developing and building the rest of *The Triadic Ballet* costumes after the war, and forging a choreography from them. No longer for Schlemmer was the stage a 'symbolic' space, which is looked into rather than felt, where colour and light joined with the expressive movements of a dancer to create a highly charged atmosphere. Now the physical contact with material form was central, engaging the body with the rigid, padded, heavy and built-up materials of the costumes, whose resticting shapes dictated movements (see Figure 2.1). The dancers moved in the costume through the stage space, showing off all 360° of their shape[18], often as it turned out, with a great deal of difficulty and grumbling by the uncomfortable dancers. They moved as mobile sculptures made up of more or less geometric shapes, predominantly circular (Michaud 1979: 74). Some of the figures were startling and extraordinary such as the huge toy-like Diver in scene 1 (predominantly yellow in colour, and intended to be lighthearted) which is designed to be seen spinning round, all striped leg(s) and round head, with a 'tentacle' skirt flying up from the shoulders: static renditions in exhibitions of these costumes do them no favours. The spinning dolls of this section and harlequin figures owe their origin to Schlemmer's love of tin toys and clockwork mechanisms from his childhood (Kunz 1991: 19–20). Schlemmer's later grid 'Scheme' showing all types of possible performance (Schlemmer 1925: 9, Gropius and Wensinger [1925] [1961] 1996: 19) in fact mirrors the three sections of the ballet so that the yellow section falls into the popular entertainment area, the second or 'rose' coloured section falls into the central area 'theatre' and the third and final black (metaphysical) section falls into 'Consecrated Stage', and it presents the most challenging costumes of all.

As Michaud rightly says, *The Triadic Ballet*, especially the Black 'metaphysical' section, has nothing to do with the machine *per se* and everything to do with the organic 'technology' or 'mechanic' of the body (Michaud 1978a: 74) as it is lived and experienced and felt. Unfortunately, the figures both of *The Triadic Ballet* and the Dessau stage are frequently interpreted as robotic, as if they were quasi Futurist or Constructivist stage creations. Often, contemporary Constructivist or Futurist productions employed the visual motifs of Modernism (such as the costumes by Alexandra Exter for the 1924 Constructivist film *Aelita*) but had no 'bodily fulfilment' ('körperliche Erfühlung').[19] Schlemmer's Constructivism was peculiar to himself in that he retained much of Itten's Expressionistic sensibility and sensitivity alongside an incisive and analytical approach to the body. Schlemmer's belief in the inherent mathematics of the body is not the mathematics which, as Schlemmer said, 'we sweat over in school' (Schlemmer [1926] 1969: 118). Schlemmer's mathematics are an orderly but infinitely creative and mysterious system, a cipher for the order inherent in the flux of the material world.[20] In his course on 'Man' (Schlemmer: [1969] 1971), Schlemmer continually reduces the body to simplified elements using geometric shapes and forms (simple mathematics) and builds these up again into the organic human form (a complex Gestalt). In the course he includes biology, philosophy and psychology alongside drawing and stage work (this included 'movement itself, the mechanical movement of forms and the organic movement of man in dance and pantomime' (27)).

Schlemmer himself valued *The Triadic Ballet* above all his other work. To him it was his most complete attempt to fuse motion and material form. In reality it was a work that was designed on paper and realised physically with a great deal of difficulty: the ideas struggled towards their embodiment. In 1922 he wrote following the first performance: 'I wore costumes for example in performance for the first time, which hindered the movement so much that they needed a complete rethink' (October 1922) (Schlemmer [1958] 1977: 61). The piece nevertheless remains one of the most original contributions to the changing semiotics of stage space in the early years of the century. Schlemmer wanted to cut out expressive 'hand-wavings' in dance (Schlemmer [1929] 1965: 13) and restricting the body draws the attention of the performer to the actual functioning of their limbs, the planar and mathematically related movements of the joints (Schlemmer 1927c: 3) they unthinkingly rely on. Once again Schlemmer can be seen anticipating an approach to the performing body that has only been realised in the later years of the twentieth century and today: it is a highly philosophic statement about movement, divorced from story and emotion, that starts with the experience of the performer rather than the image seen by the spectator. In 'Man and Art Figure' (Schlemmer 1925: 16–7), the four costume drawings provide the theory underlying the built-up costumes of *The Triadic Ballet*, which he boldly claims, represent the decisive ideas for all (in his opinion) 'true' theatrical costumes: that is, costumes that are not aiming to represent a character to tell a story, but striving for expression of eternal and transcendent truth. What is important here is not so much the detail of the theory[21] (though it does provide the clue for understanding these extraordinary creations) but an emerging blue print for the underlying 'Ur' costume he was about to create for the stage at Dessau less than a year later: the simple padded full body suit and plain head mask. In the original 1924 essay, the four drawings were placed together, centre double page, with the explanatory writing on the outside of the pages; the drawings' separation in the 1961 edition to the outer edges of the pages (Gropius and Wensinger [1961] 1996: 26–7) spoils visually the overall emergent and unifying 'Ur-form' of the human body, which is clearly perceived through the four different 'body casts' as the eye runs over them. This unifying Gestalt or bodily 'Ur-form' Schlemmer attempted to realise in the padded body suits on the stage at Dessau.

At Dessau in 1925 therefore he extracted the human body and let it move freely in space, releasing it from rigid attachment to the 'significant' plastic forms that dictated its motion, though they would still be in free contact with these 'space shapers' in the form of held spheres, sticks, cubes and so on (Figure 1.1). At the same time, he cut out all distracting and individual features of the performer. The main costume was a padded body suit, and a full head mask with geometric features which denied expression. This pushed the body towards the universal and ideal image in an attempt to start with a 'tabula rasa' from which to build up the stage 'Gestalten' item by item. Or at least, this was the starting theory.

Treating the body in this way invites criticism of Schlemmer's supposed naivety and body neutrality. Michaud, for example, in the 1970s recognised his body '*nu*' as a 'universal' surface on which Schlemmer's own material shapes could be imprinted (Michaud 1978a: 127–8). The intention was to restore 'the variations, the differences, but founded on an objective and natural basis' (Michaud 1978a: 128). The padded costumes of Dessau, in this reading, were 'elemental'—'it was essential to wipe out the differences between the bodies'. As a result, Michaud maintains here and elsewhere that Schlemmer's 'symbolic'[22] approach to the body is historically limited and locked within the mind set of his time, and that his work was not and can never be developed. Similarly for many contemporary theorists and practitioners today the body is not at all neutral, and can never be neutral, but is always deeply encoded, and readings on stage spring from its cultural and social inscribing. Feminist and Marxist critics are especially loathe to concede any points to essentialist thinking around body neutrality.

Philip Auslander maintains the performing body is always doubly encoded; that is, it is defined by the codes of a particular performance, and it has always been inscribed, in its material aspect, by social discourses (e.g. science, medicine, hygiene, law, etc.) (Auslander 1997: 90).

Arguably it is impossible by definition to throw off the first coding, despite the conscious attempts of 'Happeners' (such as Allan Kaprow in 'Calling' (Kaprow [1965] 1995) and many Fluxus artists) to throw off the frame of performance (Quick 1996: 12–22). The postmodern stage manifests a continuous awareness of the codes clustering around the frame of performance and frequently deliberately attempts to unravel them, such as in Forced Entertainment's *First Night* (2002).[23] This unravelling, however, actually began on the Bauhaus stage with Schlemmer: the effect of his minimalist stripped down body was to draw attention to the effects and demands it makes upon its audience. Michael Fried noticed this effect years later in connection with minimalist art (Fried 1967). In researching the building blocks of the stage act Schlemmer also turned his attention to the experience of the performer which fatally undermined the binary opposition of stage and audience. The resulting implosion of performer/ audience, framed space/viewing space was fully realised in the happenings of the United States and Europe over thirty years later, and the performed act has been endlessly deconstructed since. In other words, Schlemmer's essentialist, neutral figures, simply because they were live and carrying out actions in real time, were far more subversive of the Modernist ideal than any minimalist work of art later excoriated by Michael Fried.

Auslander's second social encoding of the body is more complex.[24] In some postmodern performances there is an acute awareness of the inscribing of the body and these inscriptions are often deconstructed. Auslander describes Acconci doing this, but he could equally have chosen body artists as Franko B, Ron Athey, Orlan or Annie Sprinkle who subvert and unravel the taboos, traditions and customs around the body. In the work of Wilson, Bausch, Castellucci, Fabre and many others the focus is often as much or more on the phenomenological presence of the body as its social encoding.

Adrian Heathfield has argued forcefully that the 'live' presence is itself the focus of much contemporary performance work (Heathfield 2004). However, concentration on one aspect does not eliminate the other. Moreover, as Gardner lucidly explains, the focus on phenomenal, physical presence which I shall equate with the 'neutral body' approach of Schlemmer, whilst always failing in the Grotowskian aim of 'transcendental self possession' (Gardner 1994: 30) (where this is intended), nevertheless still presents the body as an *irreducible presence in space* over and above any semiotic or representational codings. Whenever the performing body exists and moves on stage, including the Dessau stage, a corporeal reality is *also* present, a body which communicates its theatrical meaning through a phenomenological reality that co-exists with, but is very different to, the body on stage as 'representational' or 'symbolic': it is exactly this presence which much contemporary performance, visual theatre, performance art and postmodern dance obsessively explore and play with, and it is a presence starkly, arguably for the first time, exposed and exploited on the Bauhaus stage. Gardner describes this kind of corporeal presence as a more complex phenomenon than a Husserlian 'idealistic' pure presence: he calls the body a potential 'field of action', a 'play of actuality', rather than a 'stable essence' as Schlemmer (or indeed Appia, Copeau, Artaud and Grotowski) might have done (Gardner 1994: 9–13, 43, 45). This shift from modern (body as pure presence) to postmodern (body as field of action) is more a question of historical and intellectual mind cast: embodied performed actions on stage are always subject to this play of actuality.

In this regard, Schlemmer was right in 'Mathematics of the Dance' when he observed that using mathematical principles to measure space necessarily involves treating space as abstract, stable and Euclidean, whereas when the body in motion enters space it is no longer a simple measurable phenomenon (Schlemmer [1926] 1969). Stereometric measurements become insufficient to describe the phenomenon. Whilst geometrical principles can be used to project spatial ideas logically onto a piece of paper using circles, shapes, angles, lines and points, translation of Euclidean ideas of space into a three-dimensional place reveals their limitations. Points, for example, are problematic because they are an abstract concept: as soon as a point on a graph is translated from the abstract into (stage) space, perfection vanishes and the point is transformed into a place (however small) with height, breadth and length; on stage, the bulk of someone or something is standing there to articulate it. Schlemmer's pasted collage of images from *The Triadic Ballet* placing bulky figures balancing on point like legs (his favoured way of representing a dancer) on to a grid floor illustrates this well (see Figure 2.1). The main figure in this collage is similar to his archetypal stage costume, 'The laws of motion of the human body in space' (Schlemmer 1925: 17) that appears in action to spin around on a point. Schlemmer well understood the crucial distinction, the difference between Euclidean space abstractly realised on a piece of paper, i.e. in theory, and the lived experience of space, and it is on this that Schlemmer built his theories about the human body, its mathematic and its dynamism. Without necessarily endorsing Schlemmer's neo-Romantic interpretations, the mystery of the dynamism, motion and force of the body on stage, which he identifies, is a palpable reality and source of theatrical power and meaning. Schlemmer used them as stage elements isolated from representational function. In seeking to understand bodily motion in space, and why it should generate meaning on stage, it is illuminating to turn away from Schlemmer's own theories to the root of the mystery of motion, first identified in the ancient world, in the paradox of Zeno. The philosopher Henri Bergson, whom we shall return to shortly, uses this paradox to illustrate the inadequacy of logic to explain our existence in the world. The problem is that of time and change in relation to fixed form.

Ever since Zeno of Elea managed to prove through logical analysis that Achilles could never catch up with the tortoise, even though experience tells us Achilles always would catch up with the tortoise, logic has seemed at odds with life. If motion is analysed in the same terms as we analyse Euclidean space, this is the nonsense (Achilles never catching up with the tortoise) that results, where logic defies experience. Logic considers the smallest possible distance or space interval (as if one were cutting the travelled distance down into smaller and smaller units) and then asks what is the smallest possible time unit conceivable in the journey of both Achilles and the tortoise? The answer for both journeys has, of course, to be the same. Thus, logically, the answer to the question 'How far does each travel in this time interval?' has to be 'The same distance'. As Zuckerkandl puts it, the 'in between' vanishes, that is, the distance between points on the journey, if one were to mark them: 'And without a between in which it can develop, no motion is possible' (Zuckerkandl 1969: 127). Mathematics was addressing this problem when it developed Calculus to take account of movement (Whitrow 1961: 157). In this case 'X' has to tend towards zero, but not be zero—or nothing would ever move.

> These are not logical tricks, intended to confuse the mind. Things move in space. Space has no gaps. The course a moving thing follows is a line in space, a continuous series of places. Motion thus actually takes place through such shortest conceivable and, so to speak, 'betweenless' distances. How are we to understand that motion can develop at all; that space does not nip it in the bud? (Zuckerkandl 1969: 127)

Zuckerkandl is using these ideas to develop his theory of music as an 'alternative' auditory space, where ordinary spatial rules do not apply, and Zuckerkandl is returned to in the chapter on time. What is vital here to understand is rather the way logic is in just this way insufficient to explain the power of stage space; and the experience of motion, isolated on stage in a non-narrative and non-mimetic context, is close to the heart of its mysterious nature, and reveals to us the 'lived spatiality' we inhabit. In contrast to lived spatiality, Merleau-Ponty in 'Eye and Mind' describes Marey's photographs, the Cubists' analyses and even Duchamp's *La Mariée* as giving a 'Zenonian reverie' on movement: the body does not 'go', it is merely depicted in different places. This could apply more obviously to Duchamp's *Nude Descending a Staircase* (*Nu descendant un escalier*) (1912) and several Futurist paintings too (Merleau-Ponty 1974a: 306).

Pursuing this idea of going beyond a 'Zenonian' reverie into understanding the philosophical problem of motion, we remember that the concept of a Gestalt (as traced in Chapter 2) contains an in-built dynamism. It incorporates permanence and change, and it was appealing to early German Modernists for that reason. The desire to incorporate time, change and movement, as well as idealised forms, into visual art was one impetus behind the development of abstract art in Germany early in the twentieth century. Gestalt thinking, as demonstrated earlier through Kandinsky's theories, could be harnessed to this. Artists took inspiration from musical structures and this will be returned to in the chapter on sound.

The first part of 'Stage Elements' by Schlemmer gives insight into these mysteries as he understood them, and gives a historical context to these ideas (Schlemmer [1929]1965: 1–27).[25] In this essay, Schlemmer begins by declaring his purpose to be an attempt to discover what it is that unites, and what differentiates, the art forms, but he actually limits his discussion to painting and the stage. He says that he approaches the stage from the point of view of a painter. It is evident that he is describing the creation of images on stage in the same terms as he believes apply to the creation of images in a painting; that is to say, these images are not imitative of the space of life, but create a *new* space. This theory is derived from Adolf von Hildebrand in his book *The Problem of Form in Painting and Sculpture* (*Das Problem der Form in der bildenden Kunst*), which puts forward Gestalt concepts of form (Hildebrand 1907: 36–8). Schlemmer had read, studied and discussed this book in Stuttgart with, among others, Johannes Itten.[26] The basic tenet of this theory is that painting creates a 'virtual space' as Susanne Langer calls it (S. Langer 1953: 72–85). In this virtual space, presented to the eye alone, the painter has to supply substitutes for what is normally supplied by such things as touch, movement, memory and so on. Everything in the painting contributes to the creation of this space which is, of course, not the same composition as the space we inhabit—the purpose of a painting is the creation of this virtual space, and not the imitation of nature; its primary intention not to be mimetic or realistic, though clearly painters in the past have made these virtual spaces both imitative and realistic.[27] Painting creates space and does not re-create the space we move and live in. The purpose of this for Schlemmer lay in his Germanic neo-Romantic beliefs where the visible world is a microcosm of the macrocosm, a 'symbol' for the unknowable. It was in this sense that Goethe has Faust declare at the end of Part 2 of the tragedy: 'All that is transitory is but a symbol' (Goethe

1981: 236). Schlemmer's imaginary spaces in his paintings were created as new and better 'symbols' of that 'reality'—except that the 'symbol' also has a tangible and material existence, paint and pigment and canvas.

Karin von Maur describes the third phase of Schlemmer's painting in the early 1920s, the period when his stage work began in earnest, as 'The Magic of Space' (Maur 1986: 49). In this period, as she describes, he reintroduced depth perspective, and grouped figures to suggest spatial depth, and the figures were given 'tone and value' and thus volume. This is very different to his treatment of the figure in, say, *Composition on Pink Ground* originally called *Relationship of Three Figures* (*Verhältnis dreier Figuren*), a few years earlier in 1915/1916, where the figures (usually interpreted as body, soul and mind) float on a two-dimensional plane. Schlemmer said in 1922 in the midst of the 'Magic of Space' period: 'I should not direct myself toward building houses except the ideal house which is derived from and anticipated by my paintings' (November 1922) (Schlemmer [1958] 1977: 63). Von Maur examines in particular the painting *Lounge* (1925) (see Figure 3.1) which was one of his last paintings before he took up stage work full time in Dessau (Maur 1979: 160).

> Space, which in *Company at Table* still receded into infinite depths, is limited and defined by architectural motifs in the paintings after 1925, but in such a way that a prospect, an opening, is always retained. Interior space in the picture, suggested by architectural elements reminiscent of a stage set, and natural space, of which only a slice is visible, enter into a triadic relationship with the observer's empirical view of perception. Thus the space portrayed in the picture becomes an imaginary station between real space and a free space that can only be divined, so that the transition from reality to transcendent reality only occurs in stages, leading from the limited to the unlimited (Maur 1986: 55).

The space of *Lounge*, actually a room in a spa, is carefully constructed 'virtual' space and hints at his preoccupations as he is about to begin the Dessau stage work. He now abandoned painting, a medium where time and movement are excluded, for nearly three years, between 1925 and 1928 as he worked on the Dessau stage, thus substituting the creation of space on canvas for another 'created' space—that of the stage, where time and movement are essential constituents. Despite the obvious fact that the spatial medium here is real and not 'virtual', the terms in which Schlemmer in 'Stage Elements' describes the created stage space hark back to Hildebrand's ideas in regard to painting—the harnessing of all available physical elements, but economically and purposefully employed, for the creation of a *new* space, and this becomes the primary purpose of the artistic act of creation. The 'creator of images' uses form and colour, the stage uses man and space. He declares that space, light and movement are new tools for the stage (Schlemmer [1929] 1965: 6–7).

He talks of the excitement of a blank canvas to a painter as comparable to the excitement of the empty stage to a director, a white page to
a writer.

> The hour of creation begins! Nothing is there yet and everything
> is yet to be! The empty stage! You know with what impatience one
> awaits what will happen. The least little thing, a dot, a noise, are
> moved into a sphere where they become significant (Schlemmer
> [1929] 1965: 7).

Schlemmer describes the 'artist' poised to begin the creation of the stage
space, even as a painter faces a blank canvas. As far as he was concerned,
the task was no less complicated, no less noble. It is the notion of movement, of motion in space, that is unique to the stage and epitomises its
complexity; it is motion that reveals the gap between mathematics as logic,
and mathematics as 'artistic wisdom' (Schlemmer [1926] 1969: 118).

It is the transformation of space through embodied action which
Schlemmer was driving at when in both 'Man and Art Figure' and 'Mathematics of the Dance' he stressed the body in motion as bringing its own
power to the geometry of space and animating it. He knew stereometry
and logic in themselves were static formal abstractions and lacked the necessary dynamism and force of motion. It is the rigidity and lack of dynamism in Kandinsky's system of colour theory that Schlemmer was deeply
suspicious about, and which he refused to endorse. In *Gesture Dance* he
set Kandinsky's system in motion. Schlemmer identifies a *force* that is
palpable and demonstrable whenever a figure moves within the controlled
space of the stage: this force is not subject to scientific proof, anymore
than is Goethe's system of colours that struck so true for artists (see Chapter 2). It is perhaps comparable to the phenomenon of motion as a force
'identified' by the Gestalt Psychologist Wertheimer and his experiments
(Ash 1995: 125–31).

> We will perceive the appearance of the human body as an event[28] in
> itself and realise that at the moment when it becomes a part of the stage
> it will also enter an irresistible and as it were magical relationship with
> space. Each gesture and movement will, automatically and inevitably,
> become meaningful. (Even 'someone from the audience' removed from
> their sphere and placed on the stage would be clothed in this magical
> nimbus.) (Schlemmer 1927c: 3)

Gardner speaks of exactly this phenomenon—the body stepping on to
stage—as illustrative of the power of embodiment:

> As soon as an actor steps onto the stage and into this imagined the-
> ater scenario, a fundamental shift takes place with phenomenal

consequences, different for those artistic genres in which the body fails to make an actual appearance. With this appearance the phenomenal parameters of both stage and spectatorship undergo complicated reorientation. On stage what was orientated in relation to the gaze is now also orientated in relation to the body that inhabits its boundaries. Visual field now discloses, and must accomodate, a habitational field that constitutes a rival perceptual center (Gardner 1994: 46).

As Merleau-Ponty says, the body perceives and is perceived; there are no 'absolutes' in perception: 'Our body is both an object among objects and that which sees and touches them' (Merleau-Ponty 1964: xii) and it is exactly this recognition by Schlemmer of the audience's role in the 'magical nimbus' that moves him so close to our own century. Yet, despite the 'magical' energy engendered by the stage being subjected in this way to logical explanation by Gardner (and indeed before him Merleau-Ponty), the power and subtle accuracy of Schlemmer's phrase 'magical nimbus' persists. Pursuing this 'magic' pushes the implication of the viewer in the 'viewed' much further. This ultimately challenges Kantian ideas about the unreachable 'noumena', into an interpretation of theatrical 'magic' and illusion that is deeply metaphysical and batters down the endemic, chronic dualism of the Western mind and body. It implicates the postmodern stage in the transformative and idealistic processes that Schlemmer so firmly believed in.

In Chapter 2, a history was outlined of the solutions that philosophers and particularly metaphysicians have given to the problem of the relationship of the mind with the body and material world outside the mind. Transcendental philosophers struggled to maintain the existence of transcendent reality when no proof could be offered. Kant's theory was that the world is necessarily perceived in terms of time and space, and true reality, the 'thing itself' or the 'Ding an sich' can never truly be known, since this lies outside the boundaries of time and space. This was simply not accepted by a huge body of psychologists, academics, artists, spiritualists and, frankly, charlatans, many of whom engaged in paranormal investigations and séances in Germany in the late nineteenth century and early twentieth century (Treitel 2004). One thinker who also refused to accept this, and who tends even today unfairly to be placed alongside the company just listed, was the philosopher and metaphysician Henri Bergson, writing in the early twentieth century. His ideas on metaphysics suggest some insights into the difference between theoretical structure of space (geometry) and the lived experience of it (especially as exploited by Schlemmer). Bergson must always be handled with caution; he has been reviled as much as he has been loved and many would argue he does not deserve the name of a serious philosopher. But a Modernist visionary thinker he certainly was, widely read at the turn of the century, and he offers insights equally valid then or now. The correspondences between

Bergonsonian thought and the visionary postmodernism of Deleuze have been demonstrated by Paul Douglas (Douglas 1992: 368–88). Bergson demonstrates a lack of faith in intellect alone and an ultimate rejection of (logical) analysis, and in this he takes to an extreme ideas also found in Husserl.

In the words of Paul Douglas 'poststructuralism simply reenacts the vitalist controversy' (Douglas 1992: 380). Schlemmer's visual stage through its expression of metaphysics through physical means actively contributes to the vitalist debate, a struggle which (often unrecognised) continues to permeate Western philosophy (Bragg 2008). Bergson's 'creative consciousness' or 'élan vital', like vitalism itself, is the ultimate fusion of mind and matter, consciousness and what it is conscious of. Hildebrand's theories about the efficacious (lived) experience of 'virtual' space in a painting is similarly vitalistic in origin since the organic living creature infuses essentially dead matter with organic life by 'intending' the space. In essence, intentionality (core to all Gestalt thinking explored in Chapter 2) links mind and matter in an unending circle of perceiver and perceived. One of the most respected philosophers of our time, Colin Wilson, interprets Husserl's intentionality as an active, creative force so that the perceiver acts upon what is perceived: in this way the perceiver is not a passive recipient vessel but is, in effect, creative consciousness itself (Wilson 2006: 15–19).

By referring to Bergson's ideas on metaphysics, the suggestion is not that Schlemmer read or was influenced by him directly in any way. Even so, there are many synergies between Bergson's writings and the development of Gestalt and phenomenological thought at the end of the nineteenth and beginning of the twentieth century (Ash 1995: 69).[29] Whereas the transcendental idealists always placed the 'transcendent' reality (Kant's 'noumenon') beyond the things of this world, seeing the materiality around us as a barrier to full consciousness (an attitude rooted in Platonic idealism and dualistic thought), Bergson maintained that it was within the grasp of all of us. Like his contemporary Husserl, he recommends a 'plunge' back into 'things themselves' but, unlike Husserl, this is not so much to cut out what is 'known' intellectually about it and thus get closer to consciousness itself (though this is true too of Bergson) so much as to transform perception of it with visionary insight. Whereas Husserl's idealism is implicit in his system of thought, Bergson is openly visionary. Popular with artists, Bergson has been extremely unpopular with certain branches of twentieth-century Western philosophy, since he appears to be dealing with the types of experience for which no proof can be offered: intuitive insights into the human condition. His thinking is accused of being a vague and woolly branch of metaphysical thinking, neo-vitalism at its worst. For him, the 'transcendent' (literally beyond us) is actually the here and now, a transformative reality accessible to us. Like Goethe's colour theory a hundred years before, however, so-called 'unscientific' thinking has spoken loudly and strongly to artists. Susanne Langer and Victor Zuckerkandl both point to visual art and music as the living proof of much of what Bergson was identifying, and wonder why he did not turn more to art for illustration of his theories (S. Langer 1953: 112–9; Zuckerkandl 1969: 115, 244).[30]

In the major essays with which I am concerned, namely 'Introduction to Metaphysics' ('Introduction à la metaphysique') (first published in 1903) and the Oxford 1911 lectures 'The Perception of Change' ('La perception du changement') (Bergson [1946] 1968), Bergson primarily addressed himself to perception, opposing intuition to logical analysis (153–86 and 187–237). With the latter he associates immobility, logical constructs of 'clock' time, and conceptual thought. With the former, he associates mobility, timeless 'duration', and experience. 'Conceiving is a makeshift when perception is not granted us, and reasoning is done in order to fill up the gaps of perception or to extend its scope' (Bergson [1946] 1968: 155). This description of reasoning is very close to the earlier description in Chapter 3 (this volume) of audiences pausing to work out the illusion they have just directly experienced. He directly addresses the old philosophical problem of the inadequacy of analytical thought to explain our being in the world, presenting space, objects, motion and time in an entirely new way. In contrast to Kant, Bergson claimed we could perceive the 'unknowable' by using intuition rather than logical, analytical thought. He says most philosophers have run into problems because they try to rise above perception instead of trying to 'plunge into it' (Bergson [1946] 1968: 158). In other words, they try to take a position of immobility, rising 'above' it all, into logic and analysis, rather than realising that we should move much closer to what we perceive: and what we perceive is constantly changing. The key point to understand is that, as in a dance, we must stop perceiving change as a change from one immobile state to another:

> There are changes, but there are underneath the change no things which change: change has no need of a support. There are movements, but there is no inert or invariable object which moves: movement does not imply a mobile (Bergson [1946] 1968: 173).

In the words of the poet W.B. Yeats, 'How can we know the dancer from the dance?' (Yeats 1984: 215).

Our stable and fixed points for viewing are not fixed and stable at all; Bergson liberates us from the limits of logic and cognitive thought. In this way, Bergson destroys the validity of binary oppositions in theorising, metanarratives in cultural history and society and the stability of language in semiotics. In describing the nature of this reality in his 1903 essay 'Introduction to Metaphysics', he might be describing the space of the postmodern stage which is both exhilarating and disorienting:

This reality is mobility. There do not exist things made, but only things in the making, not states that remain fixed, but only states in the process of change. Rest is never anything but apparent, or rather, relative (Bergson [1946] 1968: 222).

That this 'rest is never anything but apparent, or rather, relative' was discovered by Schlemmer on his space stage. *Flats Dance*, *Curtain Play*, *Equilibristics* and *Light Play* all present a fluid and ever changing dynamic of space but the most extreme and resonant example of pure space in motion, using scenery, is *Hoops Dance* (see Figure 4.1), an extraordinary piece of performance for its time whose 'reality is mobility'. Again, this is not apparent from photographs. A reconstruction of the set, dating from 1994, with moving hanging 'puppet' figures in it gives some indication of the motile and unstable space this piece creates[31]; and in performance of course the dancer holding and moving yet more hoops gathered in her hands further adds to the kinetic sense of space in unceasing and complex motion. This set, consisting of white hoops lining the black box stage on all six sides, including the front giving visual access to the space, is comparable to kinetic art by Duchamp, or (as Doris Krystof points out) Action Painting of the 1950s (Krystof 1994: 56–7), or a Bridget Riley from the Pop Art era of the 1960s. Whilst we have the ability today for multiple set changes that take place before the eyes of the audience, and which change suddenly the dynamic of space of the stage,[32] this piece moves far beyond the idea of set change transforming the space. Space is here taken to an extreme of instability before our eyes in a single scene. Whilst the fluidity of the space can surely be felt in slick scene changes and in spectacular stagings, in the early twentieth century and now, that fully utilise light new materials, stage machinery and digital technology, transformative and mutating space on stage is of a different kind in *Hoop Dance* and resonates strongly with our embodied experience of space, and in Schlemmer's case hints at metaphysical levels of experience and at pure motion. This anticipates much later work especially in performance art and dance: Trisha Brown's *Man Walking down the Side of a Building* (1970) plays entirely with our perception of space, gravity and notions of up and down[33]. Theatre too harnesses the unknown dimensions of fluid space.

Robert Lepage uses the instability of space in the fiendishly complex machine set of *Elsinore*, finding a physical and haptic experience equivalent to the philosophical twists and turns of the mind in the central character. The machine sat on a central frame that could turn and spin, becoming a bed, a door, a window, even framing a hole down which Ophelia disappeared dragging a blue cloth with her as she drowned. In the fight scene Hamlet had a camera on a sword point and uses a mirror so that our sense of space is inextricably tied up with confusion of self and identity. In *The Anderson Project* (Barbican Centre, London BITE06), in contrast to his

Figure 4.1 Oskar Schlemmer, *Hoop Dance* [*Reifentanz*], 1927/1929. Photo Archive, C. Raman Schlemmer, IT-288824 Oggebbio (VB) Italy.

complex technology in *Elsinore*, he creates an empty space in the centre of the set, that acts as a fluid and ever changing immersive space, using projection to probe distance, time, motion, the mind and the outside world (see Figure 4.2). The use of an invisible shelf in this space was a simple device that enabled the human figure to be transported into other worlds very easily. A train, for example, was conjured by a few pieces of luggage and projection: space here seemed to be a tangible void. Recently, dance on the Internet using large screens has been possible linking spaces many thousands of miles apart so that dance is experienced in a multitude of places, virtual and real, and not in one single space. In this way, dance seeks to reveal fresh meanings emerging from our newly realised embodiment of technology, and its intrusion into the tried and tested and habitually experienced.[34]

In *Monsters of Grace* (Barbican Centre, London BITE98), Robert Wilson employed computer technology to plunge us into a new experience of space so that we experienced 'things in the making' and 'states in the process of change'. He did this by techniques such as prolonged distancing of an image (for example, the sublime image of the boy on a bike cycling endlessly towards us accompanied by Glass's inexorably repetitious music seemingly getting louder by infinitesimal degrees) and sudden close-ups that hovered above one's head as holograms that were

Figure 4.2 Robert Lepage, *The Anderson Project,* 2006. Photograph courtesy Erick Labbé.

both insubstantial as the ether and close enough to touch us, such as the white hand that then bled as the knife sliced it, and the polar bear's rough fur.

In seeking new 'Gestalten' of the body (involving performer and audience) Schlemmer first let the 'genie', motion, out of the bottle and applied it to space. Embodied stability simply did not and does not exist. But for Schlemmer, Gestalt notions of form and dynamism, unity in change, held the paradox together.

What is curious about Bergson himself is that the perceiving sensory body remains a vague presence. In 'Introduction to Metaphysics' (Bergson [1946] 1968), the effort to achieve breakthrough into creative consciousness is primarily made by the mind. In contrast, the body in theatre is never vague, whether it is the body of the live performer or the sensing body in the audience. Bergson's 'states in the process of change' (222) have a phenomenal reality on stage that theatre is uniquely able to offer. The stage gives a momentary yet experienced and lived example of what Bergson talks about in theory and the audience experiences a brief release from the normal theoretical 'Kantian' bounds of space through which this external reality is normally viewed. It is not mobility within an immobile space that we experience, but mobility within mobility. This knowledge of a different space is not dependent on cognitive processes or analytical thought, though both of these may operate in retrospect. Bergson becomes inadequate to explain it: it is a different kind of knowledge—experiential and bodily. However, the original and most eloquent exponent of embodiment theory, Maurice Merleau-Ponty, would ultimately assign the visionary uplift to a disturbance in the lived spatiality of the body. This is despite the fact that Merleau-Ponty himself is eloquent on the shimmering 'halos of being' (Merleau-Ponty 1974a: 285) which a recognition of the basis of perception in the anchor of the body releases. He sees Cézanne, for example, as a visionary painter for exactly his awareness of the shifting basis of bodily perception, his continual efforts to isolate the object's essential nature (280–311). Yet, as his commentator Monika Langer warns:

> We must guard against the temptation to reduce the object's essential nature to a Kantian noumenon. The perceptual synthesis which accomplishes the unification of our sensory experiences is fundamentally different from an intellectual synthesis and must not be regarded as merely a step along the way to the latter (M. Langer 1989: 78).

How existentialist embodied thinking like this can be married with idealism is a problem reserved until Chapter 5 on Objects, but the issues are opened up here and were touched on earlier in Chapter 2 (page 39 to 40).

We tend to think of the body as a fixed and stable point of perception; and indeed it is very good at quickly returning to stability if at all possible. Both Maurice Merleau-Ponty and James Gibson describe the body's ability to adapt quickly to new and disorientating physical environments if they are sustained over time—for example, after a short time in a room on a tilt, the body adjusts and we feel quite at home (Merleau-Ponty 2002: 249–50). But as Monika Langer explains, this reveals how the body is not a fixed and stable point of perception:

> Instead of a mechanistic, deterministic relationship of causality, we have an organic relation of motivation between subject and the world, such that the body possesses the world in a certain way while gearing itself to that world. In our normal daily experience, our actual body is at one with our virtual body—the latter being the one which the spectacle requires—and the actual spectacle is at one with the setting which our bodily attitude projects around it. Consequently, it is only when one term of the dialectic is upset that the part usually played by both terms becomes visible, revealing, simultaneously that direct power that the world holds over the body and the reciprocal power which the body has in anchoring itself in a world, in demanding 'certain preferential planes' (M. Langer 1989: 82–3).

This 'lived spatiality' as Monika Langer calls it, after Merleau-Ponty, reveals a discrepancy between the physical dimensions of space (intellectual constructs) and its lived reality (M. Langer 1989: 76). I suggest that theatre exploits this discrepancy; furthermore, this discrepancy is properly called 'theatrical illusion'. Whereas Merleau-Ponty invites us to re-discover the 'primordial' experience of the world (Merleau-Ponty 1974b: 209), theatre, as Schlemmer discovered, continually exploits this 'primordial' experience to theatrical effect.

Scenes by Phil Soltanoff and Compagnie 111 in *More or Less Infinity* (Queen Elizabeth Hall, South Bank Centre 2006) described in Chapter 3 illustrate clearly this discrepancy in their morphing stage space of theatrical illusion. The illusion is not mimetic of 'real' life in any sense. It is clearly not the 'stage of naturalistic illusionism' (Schlemmer 1925: 13). Illusion on stage does not of course always have to be identical to the reality it conjures to work as mimesis—a minimalist set can conjure 'reality'. The illusions in the Solnatoff piece on the other hand do not ostensibly make reference to reality outside the stage itself. Yet, to be illusions, they have to work in contrast to some normality present in the audience's minds—or bodies. Schlemmer identified non-mimetic illusion thus:

> The poet will arrive, as soon as these imaginary spaces and buildings are experienced, and new ideas and materials will necessarily come to him; being torn from his postcard representations where the old theatre kept him imprisoned, he will see that there is an abstract stage world made with valued means, and consisting of valued 'illusion', no less valued than the 'second nature' currently planted in the theatre (Schlemmer 1927a: 68).

It is very hard to isolate the moment of perception itself (Merleau-Ponty's 'primordial' experience) as a powerful theatrical moment from subsequent reflection upon it, the 'memorial experience' in the 'dispersing episode' (Beckerman 1979: 157).[35] After the event, a viewer puts a cognitive interpretation on the experience. Merleau-Ponty does not stress the continuous co-presence of these modes of perception in everyday life, but many artists are instinctively aware of this highly creative space of consciousness where thought is absent and everything is possible. Schiller describes the 'play impulse' as aiming at 'the extinction of time in time and the reconciliation of becoming with absolute being, of variation with identity' (Schiller 1954: 74). I suggest in contrast most of the time in our quotidian lives we oscillate between what is virtually a semi-conscious somnambulism and rational thought. But in theatre, we are far more alert: there is a continuous oscillation between the logical and illogical, thought and phenomenological perception, and this is fundamental to our experience as we watch any theatre piece. The oscillations in watching visual and spatial illusions are of a particular kind however. The audience does not *think* while the illusion grips them: it is *experienced*. Schlemmer said 'In the visible resides great power—the power of immediacy and the recognition of totality within one moment' (Schlemmer 1927a: 71).

'Meaning' interpreted in this way is extremely hard to describe ('die Erfassung der Totalität in einem Moment') since phenomenological directness cannot of course by definition be described; once described it is no longer experienced; or in Bergsonian terms it then becomes 'relative' and not 'absolute' experience (Bergson [1946] 1968: 187). As Bert O'States puts it, we are trying to describe the first four seconds of the 'Big Bang' of experience, but this implies we are studying the opening moments of a consecutive experience, whereas what we are talking about lies outside any concepts of consecutive time (O'States 1992: 370). It is the 'moment' before cognitive thought takes over, but the moment is *continually present* even if (except as now when we stop to 'catch' it) it is normally lost to our consciousness. Cognitive understanding or 'meaning' contributes little to the power of true theatricality, and theatre has the power to draw our attention to the lost 'moments' of our consciousness.

Music has an innate capacity through its abstraction to lose us in a 'new' space (Zuckerkandl 1969). To lose these constructs even for a moment is, it seems, intensely pleasurable, though also sometimes rather disturbing and powerful. Film and television are masters at deceiving us in this way; a classic example is the terrifying vision at the end of David Lynch's *Twin Peaks* (Lynch and Foster 1990/1991) when we are lost in a world of huge curtained rooms that do not seem to obey the laws of three-dimensional space. The absolute physicality of theatre and live experience of it perhaps shifts such imaginative articulations of space away from the terrifying towards the truly pleasurable; towards, even, *pace* Merleau-Ponty, the visionary in a Bergsonian sense.

Antonin Artaud wrote on the power of theatre's true language to reveal to us 'metaphysical' truths through absolutely physical means: using the example of the painting *Lot and his Daughters*, he described the physical means it uses to convey 'metaphysical ideas':

> I am sorry to have to use that word, but that is what they are called. And I might even say their poetic greatness, their tangible effect on us arises from the fact that they are metaphysical, that their mental profundity cannot be separated from the painting's formal, external symmetry (Artaud 1974: 26).

The link fusion between physical and mental effect here described is a hallmark of painting; and in the early years of the century this painterly sensibility began to be applied to the space of the stage. Artaud, passionate and wild with his 'poetry for the senses', and so different to Schlemmer in so many ways, nevertheless understood as he gazed at this picture in the Louvre how the great painters cast their thought in 'physical and tangible language' (26). At Dessau, Schlemmer began to explore and develop his own 'tangible language', that of space and motion, and discovered that it also invites an exploration of what can be touched, handled and grasped by and to the body: accordingly our focus now turns to objects.

5 Body and Objects

So far we have considered space as the primordial 'place' for action. Yet familiarity with this world as infants begins not with any formed sense of space, and certainly not with an appreciation of scenes, panoramas, landscapes: the prone body learns to stretch, push and roll using the resistance of the materiality on which it rests; later, as the body grasps, leans on and pulls against that materiality, connections with the material world develop through what Yi-fu Tuan describes as 'vivid, sharply defined objects in a weakly structured space' (Tuan 1974: 56). This chapter analyses physical engagement with plasticity and the meanings that emerge on stage from such contact.

Schlemmer usefully defined two types of plasticity on stage, one being 'scenery' ('Mobiliar'), and the other objects.

> If the relationship of the performer with the world that surrounds him, with the material which is placed around him, was up till now a 'disjunctive' one in so far as he had not got an immediate bodily link with this material [i.e.'Mobiliar'], another theme in contrast is that of the manipulation of forms, objects and accessories[1] to hold (Schlemmer [1929] 1965: 13).

Scenery as he here defines it has no direct bodily contact and is fundamental to the definition of the larger spaces of the stage; this was dealt with in Chapter 3. By contrast, it is manipulated 'forms, objects and accessories' ('Formen, Gegenstände, Requisiten') and the body which touches them that form the basis of this chapter.

Schlemmer goes on to make an important claim in relation to material form, here costume, in contact with the body. Costume and objects as material forms are normally differentiated, but for our initial purposes here, both are plastic, both are part of the material world and both are exterior to the body and the mind. He suggests that the 'meaning and basic nature' of costume is demonstrated in the following way, by placing a red glove on the hand of a totally white figure. He claims that 'Straightaway the emphasis has been moved, not only visually, but also as something felt:

the equilibrium of the body and mind is upset.' Moreover, since clothes 'express a part of our self' they heighten or disturb 'our equilibrium of mind and body' (Schlemmer [1929] 1965: 17). Schlemmer here claims psychic as well as physical changes in the performer when in touch (literally) with plasticity on stage. This exposes questions about the very nature of the experience of performing and opens fundamental difficulties about the relationship of mind, material world and the body.

The full import of Schlemmer exploiting the materiality of the stage, pushing the encounter of body and object to the fore of his research, must be seen within the continuing social and spiritual crisis before, during and especially after World War I. In Thomas Mann's *The Magic Mountain*, published in 1924, Settembrini, a Marxist and humanist thoroughly engaged with the world and its problems, fights to save the youthful Hans Castorp from the dangerous ensnarements of the idealist (and to Settembrini's mind, deadly and decadent) Jesuit, Naphta. He also sees Hans succumbing to the numbing (and liberating) delights of the life of an invalid in the hospital, on the 'Magic Mountain', removed from the hurly burly of the business of living. Transcendency or Platonic thought was, and indeed is, a dangerous doctrine. At its extreme, in its rejection of the material world, it distances us from the starving, the tortured and the needy. It is essentially an ethical problem that drew mystically inclined thinkers and artists in the early twentieth century, who loved and cared for the material world, towards vitalism as a way out of the dilemma. This was traced in Chapter 2. Schlemmer's approach to this problem was to create as he called it 'metaphysical theatre' (December 1925) (Schlemmer [1958] 1977: 85) that is also intensely physical, often involving sweating bodies literally struggling in heavy and oversized and/or restrictive costumes and continually pitting the body against material form(s). In this experiment, Schlemmer reached towards a subtle linkage of mind and matter that, I argue, live performance continually reveals but Western philosophy always struggles to articulate.[2]

Petra Halkes (1998) alerts us to the alluring and continuing fantasy of the puppet/cyborg as the image of the human freed from both materiality and consciousness.[3] This image was strong in the Romantic period and rediscovered by the early Moderns. Henrich von Kleist's essay 'On the Marionette Theatre' ('Über das Marionettentheater') remains a resonant and enigmatic statement epitomising the tangled thinking in Romanticism around the puppet or 'artificial man' (Kleist [1810] 1994). The puppet is an ambiguous image: either God-like (as Halkes explores) or a mere controlled mechanical being.[4] The latter image invited complex responses in the new machine age, and was used, dreamed about and abused by Futurists and others trying to find new stage languages. The dancing puppet that Kleist's narrator witnesses in the gardens, his interlocutor claims moves with absolute perfection since consciousness, the human capacity to think, which makes us both divine and 'Fallen', does not trouble the puppet. The important end section of the essay is often forgotten: the youth who lost his beauty because he became conscious of it and the bear who hit his adversary precisely because he did not think about it are less ambiguous images of the state of 'not-thinking'. Schlemmer was familiar with this essay and commentary deriving from it, including for example Gordon Craig, who advocated the 'Super-marionette' as the solution on stage for attaining a 'purity' of aesthetic that the stage seemed to deny and pollute.[5] Schlemmer places, so to speak, Kleist's unseen puppeteer at the fore of his research.[6] In Schlemmer's cosmic scheme, the soul was the link between spirit (Geist) and nature (i.e. between mind and material world), so that for him, the 'puppeteer' (essentially the human body) on stage performs the same job as the soul. This figure appears on stage in his work many times—the operator in the Figural Cabinet, the Clown Mr Eye, and Schlemmer/Walter Schoppe who is the 'Liebgeber' ('body giver') who dances in *The Triadic Ballet* (see his letter to Otto Meyer, October 1922) (Schlemmer [1958] 1977:62). The means of artistic expression Schlemmer employs in *The Triadic Ballet* and between 1925 and 1929 at Dessau are all essentially experiential and embodied; but the Dessau work represents a seismic shift in his research methods as the puppeteer becomes his focus equally with the puppet itself.

Schlemmer's 'art figure' ('Kunstfigur')[7] is an attempt to fuse the organic human body (the operator) with the 'purity' of a puppet (the material form of the costume) and is fully realised in *The Triadic Ballet*. However, in Dessau he separates the 'art' or material form from the 'figure'. We now are presented with a geometric artifact (e.g. a pole, a hoop) and its manipulator: essentially, as I shall argue, these are a puppet and puppeteer. Meike Wagner (2006) points out how the puppeteer as a separable figure viewed on stage rather than hidden from the audience's view only emerged strongly in post-World War II European theatre and she explores the complex meanings provoked by such a visible juxtaposition. Schlemmer anticipates such a separation in the mid-1920s. In doing so, he fatally undermines notions of the pure 'art figure', since, as Schlemmer admitted above on costume in 1929, the experience of the performer is implicated in the communicated meaning of the performed act. This experience is neither 'ideal' nor fixed in the way Schlemmer hoped: 'each of these [i.e. each object] has its own law guiding its manipulation' (Schlemmer [1929] 1965: 13). Later in the twentieth century, focus on the performers and their experience becomes a key preoccupation of performance art. I would like to argue that this shift from 'beautiful art figure' to performer and object neither (as the early Moderns feared) devalues the art of performance nor sullies the object. Indeed it opens the way to some of the most powerful experiences of the stage that we can have.

Schlemmer's aesthetic shift from autonomous art object (the art figure) to the erosion of that object's autonomy (at Dessau) anticipates the later alchemies of cross-disciplinary practices in the 1960s. These shifts evolve fundamentally from Western culture's troubled relationship with the material world. The 1950s American Abstract Expressionist paintings so praised by Clement Greenberg were evidence that art had perhaps 'refined' itself far beyond quotidian concerns and ordinary people's lives. The pattern is a familiar one in the West.

The opposing emphases (mind and matter) recur in Western philosophy since Plato was first opposed by Aristotle. Christopher Macann (2007) talks of the mind-based sense of unity, the creative insight, championed by Plato, as being countered inevitably and always by a succeeding philosopher who stresses physical awareness and the 'real' world. At the close of Chapter 2, Husserl's 'idealist' phenomenology was paralleled with Schlemmer's thinking. Despite Husserl's insistence on a return to objects themselves and on the reciprocal nature of perception between the mind and the world outside, he nevertheless maintained that there remained in the mind an area (a pure 'essence') into which one could 'retreat' to 'observe' this immediate ('phenomenological') perception. He devised a method for accessing this 'essence' or 'epoche' and it involved bracketing out everything we 'know' about the world and being open to the phenomenon itself: this state stands behind (as it were) consciousness and thought. It parallels the 'Ur-form' in Gestalt thinking. Heidegger, who was Husserl's pupil, went on to reject Husserl's idealistic pure 'essence' idea and recast the human as a 'being in the world' totally embedded in it, their situatedness being crucial to *any* perception. According to Heidegger, it was not possible to perceive isolated essences: 'the modes of being in the world . . . are not conscious structures but rather constitute the world *in which consciousness can function*' [my italics] (Stewert and Mickunas 1974: 70). We are always and inescapably entangled in our existence in the world. Broadly speaking, it is useful to see the Husserl v. Heidegger dispute within the Plato v. Aristotle binary opposition.[8]

Both Colin Wilson (2006) and Christopher Macann (2007) argue for a middle ground or fusion of these two extreme positions. Wilson evaluates those moments—often in art—when the two meet as the best moments we can experience on this earth. It is a philosophical tension played out on the Bauhaus stage. And theatre has a unique ability momentarily to realise this fusion.

This fusion, or sidestepping of the binary debate between the two positions (broadly, the mind v. the material world, thinking v. being) has been identified by a number of people as a valuable and rich and creative state of 'not-thinking' but a state nevertheless of acute consciousness. The Romantic poet John Keats called it 'Negative Capability' where there is no 'irritable reaching after fact and reason' (Gittings 1970: 43). Hans-Thies Lehmann identifies this state as one demanded of the spectator by the postmodern stage: 'in psychoanalytical hermeneutics the term "evenly hovering attention" ("Gleichschwebende Aufmerksamkeit") is used . . . here everything depends on not understanding immediately . . . meaning remains in principle postponed' (Lehmann 2006: 87). Even Heidegger himself talks of a state of 'Nachdenken' or 'thinking after'. '[T]he man who "thinks after" is a follower of, an attendant upon the object of his thought, which is Being' and 'his essential stance is one of expectation' (Steiner 1978: 130).[9]

Schlemmer himself was aware of this state of creative being and cultivated it on the Bauhaus stage. It emerges from the strong element of play in Schlemmer's new approach to form at Dessau as he develops his relatively rigid thinking about geometric form apparent in *The Triadic Ballet* into a more fluid experience of and play with form.[10] Although Schlemmer clearly planned out his approach carefully in theory (Schawinsky 1971: 40), the actual work appeared to emerge from performers engaging with objects, playing with them, discovering their properties, making up tricks with hoops and sticks and experimenting under various lights. This can clearly be seen in photos in the 1961 edition of *The Theater of the Bauhaus* (Gropius and Wensinger [1961] 1996: 96, 99), and juggling and circus workshops were a regular part of the Bauhaus stage. The notion of 'play' relates to the ideas of Friedrich von Schiller.[11] In his '*Letters on the Aesthetic Education of Man* (*Briefe Über die Ästhetische Erziehung*) which Schlemmer read and enjoyed and often referred to, Schiller says that the sensual (i.e. the body) and rational (i.e. the mind) in man are two mutually dependent faculties, both of which need cultivation, and that an excess of either is undesirable. This closely relates to the positions of Macann and Wilson referred to earlier, and of course to Kleist's essay. In the Fourteenth Letter, Schiller proposes 'Spiel' or 'play' as the situation where man can experience both impulses together and develop both in harmony to their fullest extent. 'Play' of course refers not only to exploratory aesthetic activity but to any activity where logical thought is suspended and there is no 'irritable reaching after fact and reason' (Gittings 1970: 43): '[T]his play impulse would aim at the extinction of time *in time* and the reconciliation of becoming with absolute being, of variation with identity' (Schiller 1954: 74). Kandinsky in his writings talked about his colour sensations being not a thought but an impulse. In rehearsal, a company creating a performance essentially plays to discover the moments that 'work', since rational planning can never on its own discover the performance or stage 'Gestalten'. Rather than eventually bodying forth 'absolute being' however, the 'play' on the Bauhaus stage opened up a fissure in the Bauhaus master plan and in Modernism itself, one that was never to be closed. This, however, proved to be no bad thing.

This fissure begins with two new elements—the body and time. (Time is returned to in the final chapter.) Using play that unfolds in time, Schlemmer made the live body an equal element in the struggle to find unified form. This transgression of the boundaries of the actual (art) object contributed to what Barry Schwabsky has described as the eventual 'dissolution' of the boundaries of the work (Schwabsky 1998: 43).[12] As Adrian Heathfield puts it, 'The physical entry of the artist's body into the artwork is a transgressive gesture that confuses the distinction between subject and object, life and art . . .' (Heathfield 2004: 11). Schwabsky's 'dissolution' of the boundaries of the work of art is seen at its most extreme in later body art where the body itself becomes the object of performance. Already on the Dessau stage we witness the profound shift from product to process that characterises much art of the twentieth century and which so appalled Clement Greenberg and Michael Fried thirty or so years later. Fried describes Minimalist or 'literalist' art of the 1960s (for example, Donald Judd's white cubes endlessly multiplied in a room) as objects which in their very blankness and apparent refusal of 'meaning' draw attention to their context and the audience's own reception of them and moreover continue this process over time: the object has 'duration' (Fried 1967). Fried identified this sort of object as 'theatrical', for him a pejorative term in relation to the art object since the object is no longer 'fixed' i.e. the artist no longer endeavours to fix meaning and 'contain' meaning within the object (fifty years of theory later, we would probably deny this is ever possible, but the basic concept/intention remains). Yet, it is this very condition of 'theatricality' on stage in relation to Bauhaus objects—the flux and possibility of change—that appeals to Schlemmer as deeply ethical. It works against any illusion of easy intellectual superiority and grasping of a final 'truth' which he saw as a pernicious threat within the Bauhaus after 1925. In this, Schlemmer was far ahead of his colleagues anticipating and defending against new directions within Modernism that emerged strongly later in 1950s America.

Commentary on the Bauhaus tends to stress its idealistic aims, and its Modernist beliefs in absolute forms, pointing to statements by Gropius and other members of the Bauhaus that describe their search for ultimate and unitary principles, a key for art and architecture that would guide the new age.[13] Gropius said in retrospect:

> Artists at the Bauhaus attempted to find an *objective common denominator of form*—in a way to develop a science of design; this has since been expanded in countless schools in various countries. Such a foundation of *general, superpersonal laws* provides an organic and unifying background for various talents. Personal expression then has reference in each individual creation *to the same, universally acknowledged basic concepts* [my italics] (Gropius in Neumann [1970] 1993: 21).

Lupton and Abbott Miller (1993) demonstrate that the Bauhaus grammar of design is actually a highly culturally specific one: 'universally acknowledged basic concepts' are never either universal or eternal. The arrogance of this attitude has been exaggerated and misunderstood, partly because of the prevalence in Europe in the twentieth century of the now discredited International Style of Modernist architecture which was largely associated with the Bauhaus. At Weimar, and especially under Itten, the process of finding the universal 'grammar' was very exploratory, gradually gaining in strength. Moreover, in the Bauhaus at Weimar there was an acute awareness, with some humility, that they were seeking guiding principles for their own late Western culture that was (in their eyes) seriously adrift. Spengler's *Decline of the West* ([1918] [1922] [1921–2] 1932), widely read in and out of the Bauhaus, laments the loss of a sense of direction in Western culture, which was irredeemably finished in his eyes, and actually evidences embodied and Gestalt thinking strongly, analysing cultures in terms of cultural artifacts being shaped by hugely different mindsets in previous civilisations. There is, however, of course an overriding essentialist assumption of *sub specie aeternis*. Worringer's *Abstraction and Empathy*, highly influential in aesthetic thinking at that time, showed similar sensibilities in evaluating cultural history. Nevertheless, by the late 1920s, there was a certain rigidity in thinking at the Bauhaus, a sense that the new forms for a new age had been found, reinforced when Gropius was replaced by Hannes Meyer and later Mies van der Rohe, champion of the new International Style that came to dominate ideas of Modernism. In 1978, Eric Michaud evaluated Schlemmer's stage work as trapped within Bauhaus visual concepts and fatally limited by them (Michaud 1978a: 134–9). I would argue on the contrary that it is precisely because Schlemmer translated these ideas on to the stage that he demonstrates his own freedom from them. He opened up the question of aesthetic form in visual art to an embodied approach, in effect building on Itten's early work, and even that of Gertrude Grunow, in the preliminary course (see Chapter 1) and retaining an absolute openness to possibilities and never fixing on one answer.

The meanings that emerge from such contact of body/object on the Dessau stage are far more complex than Gropius's words suggest. Not only must they be taken in the context of the Bauhaus concepts of 'Gestaltungen' explored in Chapter 2, that is, the belief in a system of form with in-built dynamism and changes, but Schlemmer himself was very wary of rigid systems of thought, and on stage took a more sceptical and questioning approach to form than the other Bauhaus masters. Stripping it down to basics, he took nothing for granted, even the Holy Gospel tenets of the Bauhaus. He totally disagreed with Kandinsky's unchanging 'rules' about shape and colour—not that they were necessarily wrong but his insistence that they were *always* true: 'Kandinsky builds an entire teaching system on this dogma' (Schlemmer [1958] 1977: 86). Uncomfortable in the Constructivist era of the Bauhaus after 1925, he wrote to Otto Meyer:

> Kandinsky's lecture is still running strongly through my head, so I am planning to reply, in a roundabout way, in a talk I shall be working on soon: 'Theatre at the Bauhaus'. I'll only give you a hint: but I shall be obliged to say critical things about the Bauhaus, and to discuss basic principles, in order to prepare the ground for what will emerge from the stage in the Bauhaus. For my theatre must do more than mirror chaos and shadow box with itself. It must—if only it would succeed—offer 'enchanting pedagogy' and be founded on Schillerian principles. Oh

for success with the setting, the proposition, the language, the speakers, and the audience! A stage thought out like this could become a powerful force for order at the Bauhaus (Schlemmer [1958] 1977: 86).

Schlemmer here sees theatre as a 'powerful force for order' but what he is really doing is countering intellectual arrogance, and I suggest his humility derived directly from his personal experiences of performing. He knew 'knowledge' was not always a thought.[14] Taking the individual and their perceptions into account prevents easy answers, promotes a healthy self doubt. Schlemmer's theatre placed the human (body) as central to discovering 'truth'. Realising the importance of the body in our construction of meanings, as Schlemmer did, anticipates another key development in phenomenology, long after the lights were dimmed on the Bauhaus stage. Not until two decades later with Maurice Merleau-Ponty did philosophers at last begin to take account of the body. Even Heidegger for all his emphasis on 'Being' in the world and his stress on the situatedness of the human, failed to explore the body.

As explained in Chapter 2, the Husserlian term for a 'primary level of experience' when it is revealed is the ancient Greek term *epoche*. The term *epoche* suggests a stripping away of experience to reveal a transcendent 'core' or 'heart' of the matter; but the idea of a 'core truth' has a far more subtle sense today (and removed from the transcendental imperative) of rediscovering the hidden, and the subsequent unfolding of the embodied experience that is continually lost to us through the accretions of thought, culture, habit, familiarity and so on. This process is continual and not a fixed state we reach: an ongoing spiral rather than a progressive line of development is a better paradigm model to describe not only the process of our lived and developing and changing embeddedness in the world but also this process of 'peeling away' to gradually (re-)discover our experience. This thinking developed particularly within Anthropology in the last half of the twentieth century (Farnell 1994: 929–74, Classen 1997: 401–412, Howes 1991, Stoller 1989, Blacking 1977: 1–28). It claims that all constructs, artifacts, attitudes, ideas and languages are culturally specific and that they emerge from the body's interaction with the material world, and that the interaction itself is shaped by cultural and historical contexts, in an unending reciprocal interplay. In other words, there are no unchanging 'general superpersonal laws' which the Bauhaus spent so many years trying to identify, *even within a single culture*. An embodied approach to form acknowledges that meaning comes into being for each of us in our continual engagement with and therefore embodiment of the world: we are imbued with the world and it is imbued with us. The emphasis on the body within Western philosophy finally emerged with Maurice Merleau-Ponty writing in the 1940s, though it was very much then a minority view. Merleau-Ponty has already been referred to in relation to the experience of light, and the 'lived spatiality' we inhabit.[15] Merleau-Ponty identified the body as the hidden source of our ability to construct all meanings within the world. On the body, he claimed, depends our capacity to make language and consequently our very ability to think, since he maintained no thought existed outside language. Like Heidegger, he rejected the Husserlian 'idealistic self' grasping the *epoche*. He rejected all forms of mind/body dualism, including both the idealists who believed in an abstract world of thought divorced from the body, and the old empiricists who, whilst they believed (like Merleau-Ponty) that all mental life derived from our senses, still posited the existence of some intellect above sensation, which ordered all the sense data and built up our picture of the world. Merleau-Ponty identifies the questionable sense of linear progression in all the old mind/body dualisms, and ruthlessly exposes our false sense that eventually some final form of intellectual perfection can be achieved above and beyond the rather messy business of being in the world. Merleau-Ponty rejects this essentialist approach considering it a dangerous doctrine, a 'sleep, or nightmare, from which there is no awakening' (Merleau-Ponty 1974a: 281). In this, he echoes Schlemmer's earlier fears for the Bauhaus and its grand project.

The preface to the English edition of Merleau-Ponty's *Sense and Nonsense* declares: 'existence is the very process whereby the hitherto meaningless takes on meaning', that is, the advent of sense from non-sense (Merleau-Ponty 1964: xvi). Of course the choice of the word '*sens*' (sense) to pun on in his title is deliberate. The senses and how they work together is crucial for understanding the 'relation' of body and mind (Merleau-Ponty would not split them in the way this phrase implies). As Don Ihde (1976) points out, even a separation of one sense from another can distort the very experience of perception we are trying to understand. If we believe in an embodied existence as fundamental, then the five senses of sight, hearing, smell, taste and touch cannot be neatly separated into categories (such a paradigm model is only an intellectual construction). Similarly, if there is no all-ruling intellect, separate from the body, then there is no mind receiving myriads of sensory information of which it *then* 'makes sense'. Rather, there is a system of senses working together *at the point of reception*, actively seeking out sensation selectively, filtering out some sensations and linking others to form patterns we recognise, and thus forming our consciousness of what is outside ourselves (Gibson 1966). In other words, we do not perceive every sensation there is to perceive at any one moment, only what we seek out. The pattern, moreover, can suddenly be noticed and possibly be changed, temporarily or more permanently, either suddenly or over time—for example, a shock, perhaps a near miss that alerts you to a hitherto unnoticed danger around you, or perhaps thinking you have seen a ghost; or viewing a challenging art object/theatre performance. This is a very different and perhaps startling way of considering the mind as extended into the body or equally, the body extended into the mind. Until this century, indeed until Merleau-Ponty, Western philosophy never articulated such a radical possibility; but certain artists, painters, sculptors, poets and especially dancers, have always 'known' it. It is radical because our strong feeling and idealistic illusion that we do have a separate inner life—separate, that is, from our bodies—may distort the true way meaning in the world is made for us; we may actually have a very different kind of mind to our 'inward' sense of it, our world of thought. Merleau-Ponty insists that we continually lose the actual origin of that thought and fail to see where our mind originates, each and every moment in the ever changing bodily engagement with space, objects and people. Without completely endorsing Merleau-Ponty at this stage, since he eliminates any metaphysical dimension, this essentially phenomenological and embodied model of being (i.e. how the world and our self within it takes on meaning) has particular resonance for and insights into the non-narrative, non-mimetic and essentially *sensory* theatre/performance that is Schlemmer's legacy.

Compagnie 111's production *Les Sept Planches de la Ruse* (*The Seven Boards of Skill*) (Barbican Centre, London BITE09) demonstrates that Michaud's comments on the time locked nature of Schlemmer's 'forms' not only deny the complex relationship that Schlemmer has to his materials but underestimate the continuing explosively expressive potential today of abstract geometric form in relation to space and the body, acting as permeable 'symbols' in which our relationship to material form

Figure 5.1   Les sept planches de la ruse de Aurélian Bory, Cie 111 and Scènes de la Terre, 2009. Photocredit: Aglaé Bory. © Aglaé Bory.

and culture are worked out.[16] Aurélien Bory writes: 'Geometry is what inspires my work because the stage is first and foremost a space in which any form of action is subject to the laws of general mechanics. It's a place of fiction where poetry is related to the dialogue between man and space. Between what's human and what's not. This led me to search geometry for a starting point to my work' (Bory 2009). Bory's piece sets 'geometry' in motion via the body: seven huge pieces of a 3-D Chinese tangram are continuously slid into multifold combinations, climbed, sat and sang on, fallen from, played with, resisted, slid between—in short, *lived* (see Figure 5.1). The combination of metaphysics and humour is pure Schlemmer. There are even direct echoes of Schlemmer's *Flats Dance* as figures hide from each other around a large block. Bory admires Schlemmer. But this work, so close to Schlemmer's method, is wholly original, a piece for our time:

> On stage the pieces become blocks. They slide against each other, rising to form mountains and towns and the opposing forces give rise to shapes in unlikely equilibrium. Rifts and breaches define man's position. *The Seven Boards of Skill* follows a changing future that human beings activate but are also subject to (Bory 2009: 3).

The abstraction in this piece lends the work a metaphysical dimension and avoids specificity of cultural reference, appropriate to its cross-cultural origins, working with the Chinese Beijing Opera. Bory's sensitive phrase here about the future 'that human beings activate but are also subject to' testifies there is form but endless change within that form. We are not helpless, but shapers of our culture and our destiny. It is the same ethical plea as that of Schlemmer.

Ethics are a vital aspect of Schlemmer's philosophy, and that of the Bauhaus itself. Gropius sees architecture as the symbol of the institution and its aims, since architecture has an ethical dimension over and above its practical functions: Rischbieter describes architecture as a 'social shaper' (Storch [1968] 1970: 14) and Susanne Langer characterises it as an 'ethnic domain' (S. Langer 1953: 95). Schlemmer often refers to the stage as a cheaper substitute for architecture; that is, study of space on the stage is similar to studying space of a constructed building. However, whereas the Bauhaus tended to stress the plastic form of the building, its mass and its spaces, Schlemmer places the body in those spaces. Architecture was at the heart of the ethos of the Bauhaus, enshrined in its name, and founded by an architect who continued to practice throughout his time there. Walter Gropius wrote at the foundation of the Bauhaus:

> The ultimate aim of all visual arts is the complete building! . . . Architects, painters and sculptors must recognise anew and learn to grasp the composite character of a building both as an entity and in its separate

parts. Only then will their work be imbued with the architectonic spirit which it has lost as 'salon art' (Gropius in Wingler 1969: 31).

Architecture, like the stage, is plastic form carving out, articulating, making visible the space, and Schlemmer would have us remember it is a space surrounding us as much as a space we look at and into. It has a purity of aesthetic that unlike the stage or visual arts is never involved in questions of either mimesis or meaning. In Gropius's Constructivist phase of thinking, architecture, always an important symbol to the Bauhaus, became the ultimate example of pure aesthetics and utility not conflicting. Schlemmer agreed with this idea, and was only too aware of this conflict within the Bauhaus, where 'pure' painting (tending towards 'salon art') came to be suspect under the reign of Maholy-Nagy. Schlemmer himself felt there need be no conflict if the building and art works were conceived as a whole. Unfortunately, architecture was expensive, and the Bauhaus had no architecture department until much later; but it had a stage at Dessau, and a stage moreover placed at the heart of Gropius's exemplary building.

The parallel the Bauhaus made between architectural space and stage space has contributed to misunderstanding the stage's role within the Bauhaus, since the twentieth century came to be dominated by the (Bauhaus) International Style in architecture: utopian, rational, functional. Ironically, the style failed ultimately through less talented practitioners not acknowledging that the bodily feeling is profoundly affected by surrounding space and ultimately can have a huge social impact. Originally they attempted to use 'pure' shapes to make satisfying wholes, where form followed function, and where there was no extraneous decoration; the impetus was of course also ethical and partly economic, designing cheap but well designed housing. The ideal went wrong because the body was not taken into account and a pure intellectual ideal began to dislodge the human element. This is recognised (perhaps in the midst of the worst 1970s excesses of tower blocks and grey urban sprawl) by Bloomer and Moore (1977) in their book *Body, Memory, and Architecture*. They attempt to define this elusive bodily 'feeling' in detail, and draw heavily on the earlier work of Paul Schilder (Schilder 1950)[17] and James Gibson (Gibson 1966). Schilder first expounded ideas of the body-image in 1923, and it can be related to Schlemmer's use of built-up and heavy costume, his use of geometric shapes as 'performing objects', and to puppets and objects on the contemporary visual stage.

It is worth pausing here, before drawing on Schilder's observations, to offer a definition of a 'performing object', which is a rather vague term found in contemporary critiques of visual and object theatre. There really is little consensus on this term and a definition is offered here for clarity's sake, at least in terms of discussing Schlemmer's work, as puppet and performing object can be usefully distinguished. 'Performing objects' share some of the important characteristics of puppets. However, not all performing objects are puppets. I define a puppet as a 3-D animated representation of a living person or creature.[18] Performing objects remain objects (and not representative) whose quiddity or material essence is harnessed to performant function.[19] They are objects whose material function is essential and central to the performance.[20] For example, La Ribot in her performance piece *Panoramix 1993–2000* (Live Culture, Tate Modern 2003) explores the physical nature of a folding chair exposing its flatness, its three-dimensionality, its strength, its sound, in such a way that its physical qualities are revealed through her body's engagement with it, overriding or at least challenging its semiotic significance (school rooms, picnics, village halls, etc.). La Ribot's performance makes an interesting contrast to one shown in the Brighton New Visions Festival in 2004, *Habitable* by Là Où Théâtre where a folding chair, again central to the realisation of the performance (so clearly more than a 'prop') is manipulated by the performer but becomes lover, friend, jailor, comforter—in other words, it is a puppet and the action is mimetic. This is not to be disparaging, merely to point out there is an essential difference between a performing object and a puppet, and both are more than 'props'. Despite close affinities, puppets are mimetic, performing objects are not, and differentiating them is useful for understanding the dramaturgy of puppetry and object theatre, as well as the dramaturgy of Schlemmer's stage. I suggest the puppet belongs firmly in the theatrical tradition whereas in performance art and dance the object resists the mimetic possibility. It also resists it on Schlemmer's stage. What will emerge is that both the performing object and the puppet derive their power from the same body/object relationship.

According to Schilder, our sense of ourselves does not stop at the surface of our skin, even though when touching something, we feel the object and the surface of our body as separate.

> The body-image can shrink or expand; it can give parts to the outside world and can take other parts into itself. When we take a stick in our hands and touch an object with the end of it, we feel a sensation at the end of the stick. The stick, has, in fact, become part of the body-image . . . It is new proof of the lability of the body-image that whatever comes into connection with the surface of our body is more or less incorporated in the body (Schilder 1950: 202).

This seems to connect with performers wearing built-up costumes, like those of *The Triadic Ballet*; but this also applies to the objects in performance at Dessau such as the sticks in *Stick Dance*, and especially the heavy suits that the performers wore at Dessau. Built-up costume gives any performer an enhanced sense of their own body, a deeper sensitivity to its position in the space of the stage, and the heavy weight of the padded costumes (made of 'batting' or cotton wadding (Moyniham and Odom 1984: 54)) had a deliberate and practical aim over and above their visual purpose of smoothing out of the body shapes into 'neutral' figures. Even the way the head is held and turned in order to see alters drastically when wearing a full head mask so that the head is held in a highly poised way, and each 'glance' is a deliberate look, a turning of the head in order for the performer to see out of the eyes of the mask. The importance of this basic enhanced sense of physicality is confirmed by Raman Schlemmer's interview with Albert Flocon in 1994 (Flocon 1994: 67) where Flocon says that the costumes were 'dreadfully heavy' and the performers sweated and made them heavier, but the 'heavier they were, the better we danced'. He says that the light costumes of today (presumably specifically referring to those used in reconstructions of Schlemmer's dances) mean 'light movements' and they 'lose part of the character' of Schlemmer's dances. In other words, the heavy body suits were absorbed into the body image of the performer: 'the material and the costume determined the movement' (Flocon 1994: 67). Hubert Hoffman in his reminiscences of the Bauhaus says something similar: 'He [Schlemmer] had always stressed that a uniform changes a man. In the moment that I get dressed, I am someone else. The dancer ought to feel the costume more strongly. That's how the thick padding worked' (Bogner 1997: 29).[21]

Similarly, in Stefan Brecht's two volume study *The Bread and Puppet Theatre*, the performers, observers and Schumann himself struggle to articulate the 'non-acting' Schumann requires from his performers, often described as a 'feel' [sic], enacted into being, not thought up in advance (Brecht: 1988: 254–269). One performer describes:

And they needed people underneath the giant puppets. And we were given rhythms to count: and two and three. I couldn't see where I was going. I simply had to step up over steps and over a dam with a great puppet over my head. And as I stood under there and counted, I began to change too, you know, this physical change was happening, and it became a wonderful experience (Brecht 1988: 267–8).

Despite suspicions by frustrated actors in Schumann's troupe (Brecht 1988: 292), the aim is not to become a mindless automaton but to become open to the physicality of the experience:

[A]nd my impression was that he anticipated the physical difficulty of it to get the effects . . . he would build the difficulty into the puppet . . . like Yama, King Hell was a huge, monstrous thing, and it took some holding so that you saw this monster like wobbling and having a little trouble holding himself up, you know, and you actually transmit it, feeling your whole body through the puppet. The way you'd have to make it move. It would have to move the way he wanted it to move. You couldn't move it any other way (Brecht 1988: 259).

The changes in the performer's body (image) described by Flocon strongly parallel this description of the acute awareness of a puppeteer of their own body performing through an object as an extension of themselves. This sense is precise and yet not under the control of thought. Although Ronnie Burkett gives voice to his puppets and his work is embedded in a narrative tradition of puppetry and marionettes that pushes his work towards an extreme of naturalism that to my mind at least feels awkward, no one can fail to be impressed by his consummate skill in operating his puppets—for example, in *Happy* 2001 (Barbican Centre, London BITE01). The grace and intensity of the operator moves the figures with precision and apparent (if not actual) ease. Burkett exhibits an absolute concentration that is not self-conscious about performing. There is a grace in his motion which would have been unattainable without the necessity to move through an object. The object in turn obtains its grace of movement from the body manipulating it. When watching Ronnie Burkett part of the pleasure comes from his performed actions that are not Burkett himself but puppeteer and puppet, a mental and physical oneness. This can often be observed on the contemporary stage where puppets are now frequently used as a dramaturgical tool within other modes of expression.

In Gibson's new model of the five senses, usefully, the 'haptic sense' replaces touch (see page 47, this volume). The haptic sense, we remember, is the *whole body* sense of touch: 'to sense haptically is to experience objects in the environment by actually touching them' (Bloomer and Moore 1977: 34) (e.g. to experience a mountain haptically is to climb it, not just to look at it). Moreover, 'you may sense body motion haptically by detecting movement of joint and muscles through your entire bodyscape' (Bloomer and Moore 1977: 35). The key observation is that the haptic sense can extend into an inanimate object, so that in using a stick, for example, to explore an object, the haptic sense extends to the tip of the stick, and when using a pair of scissors, the tool becomes an extension of the hand (Gibson 1966: 112). Schilder (1950) of course does not call this sense 'haptic' which is Gibson's later coinage, but it clearly is the same extended bodily sense. The inanimate object is absorbed into our body image and becomes part of our physical movements and part of our mental image of ourselves. The effect is similar in regard to costume, if it is recognised as plastic form placed against the body: a hat with a large feather extending upwards extends our body image (Schilder 1950: 204) and helps us to relate haptically to the intensified, focused stage space around us. Schlemmer makes the same observation, pointing out that actors (and women!) are especially sensitive to what they are wearing, and how the use of uniform can draw on these kind of sensitivities (Schlemmer [1929] 1965: 17). In addition, Schilder observes that objects and movement make us more aware of our bodies:

> We do not feel our body so much when it is at rest; but we get a clearer perception of it *when it moves* and when new sensations are obtained in contact with reality, that is to say with objects [my italics] (Schilder 1950: 87) .

Our normal unconscious relationship with the physical world around us, from which 'meaning' bodies forth, is intensified and exposed and, in Schlemmer's case exaggerated, on the stage: our perception of the world through the medium of space is scrutinised. Although this is communicated to the audience in varying degrees, the most intense experience, as Schlemmer knew, is that of the performer themselves.

The idea that performance is an intensification of perceptions, as in the happenings, compared to the 'semi-conscious behaviours' of ordinary life is explored in an essay by Etzel Cardeña and Jane Beard, 'Truthful Trickery: Shamanism, Acting and Reality'.

> Performance can be defined as a series of purposeful, intentional acts, rather than as a form of deception . . . One of the first paradoxes we encounter in a discussion of illusion and acting is that what we define as being 'authentic' or 'real' is, in many instances, a collection of automatic, semi-conscious behaviours, thoughts and experiences (Cardeña and Beard 1996: 33–4).

Analysing the Bauhaus stage as an intense physical experience is more fruitful than dwelling on the theoretical ideas and historical purpose behind the costumes (as Michaud does). In the light of Schilder, Merleau-Ponty, Gibson et alia, the earlier quotation from Schlemmer about applied objects (such as the red glove with a white costume) having psychic effect (Schlemmer [1929] 1965: 13) is demonstrably true, since perception is labile and not entirely 'physical' nor entirely mental ('the emphasis has been moved, not only visually, but also as something felt: the equilibrium of the body and mind is upset' (Schlemmer [1929] 1965: 17)).

As Nancy Troy observed, 'the actor, thus reduced to a type, could still be "altered, transformed, or 'entranced' by the addition of some applied object" or prop that would influence "his habitual behaviour and his physical and psychic structure"' (Troy 1986: 143). Schlemmer (quoted here) is talking in the Gestalt terms of his era but it has a much wider application as I have demonstrated. Sally Banes comments on an 'intensified concept of bodiliness' being communicated to her when she watched McCall's reconstructions of Schlemmer's work: 'the performers animate and humanise the abstract geometric landscape . . . they seem larger than life, an intensified concept of bodiliness' (Banes 1982: 80, 82). One way of describing this in Schlemmer's work and that of others who realise their performances with deliberate manipulation of material form is that the performer/puppeteer's body image and haptic sense flows into the object/costume/puppet which is/are being animated, and meaning is literally 'bodied forth' before our eyes in the moment of performance and forms new perceptual 'Gestalten' in the audience—all of which are moments that are fundamentally implicated in the shaping of our culture. They both reflect the culture and are proactive in its formation.

The juxtaposition of visible puppeteer and puppet, or performer and performing object, common in postdramatic theatre (Lehmann 2006: 72–4) and in performance art is a 'bodying forth' of meaning. Of course semiotic and cultural reference is also present and strongly communicating to the audience but the physical form of the action, the animate and inanimate together, are equally vital. Compagnie Mossoux-Bonté in *Twin Houses* (Purcell Rooms, South Bank Centre 2006) demonstrates this 'physical meaning' throughout: for example, in the opening scene a male puppet head is attached beside the head of the female performer, 'sharing' her body and taking over the act of writing. Performance art too draws its meaning from the 'bodying forth' as much as semiotic content. For example, even Franko B's controversial blood performances in the 1990s (such as *I'm Not Your Babe*, Chapter Arts Centre, Cardiff 1997) showed a performer working intimately with a material substance, blood, albeit a material charged with cultural associations and taboos, transforming thought into an action. The puppeteer or performer becomes the intermediary between mind and matter, equivalent to Kleist's bear (Kleist [1810] 1994), hitting precisely with unconscious accuracy because it hits without thought. There was a 'terrible beauty' in Franko B's gesture (Campbell and Spackman 1998). In contemporary theatre, the visible operator figure moves us beyond the logical, the linear and the thought through, into an active experience of embodiment.[22]

This bodying forth of meaning is so strong in certain performances using puppets and performing objects that the objects used are not merely animated but momentarily persuade us of the very animism of the material world. Here we move beyond Kant's limits to our perception, and beyond Merleau-Ponty's existential embodiment, and into the 'magical nimbus' of the stage space.[23] In Faulty Optic's *Horsehead* (ICA, London 2006) the puppet protagonist saws off the deformed leg of his lover. This was a scene of extraordinary horror when a puppet leg was torn apart muscle by muscle until it was a stump. Matter apparently taking on 'life' in performance is very common in puppetry and its power is being increasingly recognised by 'mainstream' theatre directors. It is hard to envisage, for example, any other way of staging Philip Pullman's *His Dark Materials* at the National Theatre (South Bank Centre 2003/4) without the puppet Daemons, and the scene of Lara being severed from her Daemon derived its power from the Daemon being perceived as so much more than a scrap of white fur. Audiences often put this down to empathy and emotional involvement but this only seems superficially to explain the theatrical illusion with puppets. 'Truths' like these (i.e. putting the response down to empathy) may seem self-evident, even trite, but paying attention to the apparently 'self-evident' reveals much more about the 'emotion' itself. Theatre has the capacity to evoke a power we cannot fully grasp, and I suggest with puppets and performing objects it has more to do with touching, evoking, and, at its strongest, realising this fusion of body, mind and object than it has to do with 'empathy'.

There are performing objects which provoke an intense emotional reaction. Objects on stage can gather a force around them beyond the facts of their material reality. Robert Wilson is a master at this. In *A Dream Play* (Barbican Centre, London BITE01) we see a 'Sitting Room' in scene 2 which is set up like a tailor's factory. The large black cloak (we feel it could have been made in this room) which the father holds is tossed in the air: the sudden short-lived thunder sound and then an immediate black out palpably charges this simple act/object with an energy beyond what the bald facts of this description might suggest. Similarly, Wilson's capacity to charge the ordinary is felt in Scene 13 of *The Burning Castle* where each character leaves a 'token of sacrifice' before Agnes enters the burning castle. These are raised up on invisible threads above the performers' heads—a book, a pair of glasses, a hat—and hang in the air, the trite objects of human lives somehow here fully charged with poignancy and long use: and Agnes at this point is about to quit this world and return to Heaven. Geometry permeates Wilson's stage world and can itself acquire a Wilsonian 'charge'. In *A Dream Play*, as in Schlemmer, especially in his paintings, chairs and tables are used as geometrical sculptural objects that simultaneously connect to human life so that form becomes resonant with meaning. The vastly long table, solid, rectangular, on a slight diagonal, so carefully placed, spans the stage in the Lawyer's Office, 'his home' (see Figure 5.2). Its uncompromising plain angular lines echo the diagonal line down which Agnes travelled from heaven to earth in the opening scene. This is not a table for convivial eating and drinking, but it is at the same time an intensely human object, emotionally if bleakly evocative, boding ill for Agnes's marriage. In an Arena video interview (Brookner 1985) a friend describes the way Wilson would arrange objects in their shared flat so that you seemed to see them for the first time; and Wilson himself says that placing a Baroque candelabra on a rock rather than a sideboard—'well, that's something different'. Wilson's performances give access to this sense of discovery, an enrichment of the ordinary. More broadly, applying these experiences outside the theatre, when we have recognised how not merely to look but to see, a rich visual world of pleasure opens up: even taking a walk down a street with 'new' eyes can be intense. The most famous walk of all perhaps is John Cage's walk with the painter John Tobey following a visit to his exhibition, where Cage seemed to see the world with entirely new eyes (Kostelanetz 1988: 175). Within a performance space this translates into theatrical power. As one reviewer said of *Monsters of Grace* (Barbican Centre, London BITE98) and its extraordinary 3D visuals, 'the computer animation allows Wilson to see through obstructive matter and make spirit visible. A white, frugal table top, set up for a minimal Japensese meal, suddenly becomes transparent, throbbing and pulsing, we see molecules circulating inside it like bleached blood—a truly Einsteinian triumph of X-ray vision' (Conrad 1998: 7).

Figure 5.2 A Dream Play directed by Robert Wilson, Stockholms Stadsteater, 1998. Photograph courtesy Lesley Leslie-Spinks.

These observations about the 'super-charging' of objects on stage can be pushed even further in an attempt to understand stage illusion. An example of prolonging illusion into almost hallucinogenic intensity appears in the work of Il Theatro della Socìetas Raffaello Sanzio (SRS). *Il Buchettino* for example is described by Stephen Di Benedetto (Benedetto 2003: 102–106) as a sustained experience of sensory elements, voice and story, in 'a constructed architectural environment' (104). One child, tucked under the coverlets of the bed where she listens to the story, is so terrified of the 'ogre' summoned by the reader's voice that she cannot even move to seek the comfort of her mother near-by in the next 'bed'.

Di Benedetto's article exposes the embodied reality of the performance experience in phenomenological terms. Interestingly, Di Benedetto summons Rudolf Arnheim, a Gestalt thinker on visual perception, to back his terms of analysis. SRS are conscious of the manipulative ability of the theatrical form upon the physiological body—of what Arnheim describes (oddly) as 'cognitive' [sic] thinking, where there is little distinction between real and unreal in perception. What we perceive is part of our experience and it 'incorporates itself in our thought processes' (Di Benedetto 2003: 102). The stress upon the material world as an intrinsic part of the 'Gestalt' of cognition, apprehended in one moment as a whole, was always fundamental to Gestalt thinking. Moreover, Arnheim's point that that the 'real and unreal' do not exist in perception echoes that of Merleau-Ponty cited earlier in relation to light (Chapter 3) that at the moment of perception (though the word 'moment' indicates a condition in time but it is actually continuous) we accept what we perceive and it is only subsequently (again falsely indicating a sequential process) in thought, far distanced from perception itself, that we stop, fragment it, and work it out. Theatre works against our tendency to break up experience, and to categorise, analyse and separate. But because of its power to make us 'think' through objects rather than rational thought, it can take us beyond the rational and can, as any art has the potential to do, touch the sublime, which I characterise as a fusion of mind, body and object.

Kleist's 1810 essay (Kleist [1810] 1994) on the marionette theatre is relevant here. One hundred years before phenomenology and later theories of embodiment are formulated, it describes a subtle linkage of body, mind and material world; and a hundred years before Henri Bergson, it identifies a state of being beyond rationality, logic and even time. Without the human, organic reality controlling it, Kleist's famous puppet would not have attained its unthinking, unselfconscious grace. There is reciprocity here. Kleist's puppet dances with grace because it is attached by artificial strings to a human body. The human body in turn attains a grace unattainable on its own by working an artificial extension of its own body, as if it were dancing through an object. If the strings were cut, the puppet would collapse. Equally trapped, humanity needs the artifice to discover its grace. Yet, artifice without humanity is cold and valueless.

Much of the power of Kleist's description springs from his choice of the puppet to demonstrate his idea, though he uses other examples, we remember, to exemplify 'non-cognitive' modes of being and action—the youth who lost his beauty when he became aware of it, and the bear who hit accurately because he hit *without thought*. All Kleist's examples illustrate the inadequacy of man's rational self to achieve wholeness and complete understanding, which links with the earlier ideas discussed regarding time and motion. In one way, his puppet can be taken as a symbol or metaphor for metaphysical ideas, and is often read this way. The West has a tendency to talk of 'symbols' so that what is presented is not the thing itself but a *representation* of the thing itself (symptomatic of the mind/body split of dualism). The strength of Kleist's essay however lies in his refusal to present the puppet as *only* a metaphor or a symbol: the story he tells of actually watching the puppet perform, and witnessing the living grace within the puppet has a power and a lived reality that still impacts upon us today. Schlemmer and Gropius both talk of finding new and better 'symbols' to express the inexpressible in art; in fact what Schlemmer was doing on the stage was discovering a much more direct experience rather than symbols, which was communicated to the audience in theatrical terms, as described by T. Lux Feininger, whose 'intuitions' seemed to 'acquire body and life' on the Bauhaus stage (Gropius and Wensinger [1961] 1996: 8).[24]

Peter Schumann has this to say about 'symbolism': he contrasts it with the direct power of communication which puppets have:

> In the Sicilian puppet show, when the Pope is sick, the sickness comes flying down from the ceiling in the form of blood and lands on him. When the sickness is taken away by the doctor, these spots are painted a different color and taken away in a bag. The translation of the language is so detailed, so real. We don't have that any more.We call it symbolism nowadays when someone does that, but that isn't symbolism . . . [W]e don't dare to use real language. Our language is only a destroyed small portion of language. We are inhibited by all the implications that we have learnt at school, by all the sciences. But we are looking for it, a real communicable language (Brecht 1988: 139).

This for Schumann is the 'radicality' of puppet theatre: 'Their creation has to be as far as possible removed from the purposeful definitions of dramatic characters or story. Only through this disconnected distance are they able to enter actively into the story as independent agents, not as providers of purposes' (Schumann [1990] 1991: 79). And again: 'Unlike most modern conceptual art, puppet theater realizes its conceptualizations in an atmosphere of what is possible or of what can be understood and taken from it [i.e. the material], and not as an exercise which demonstrates an extreme example of concept' (Schumann [1990] 1991: 81). Similarly, Schumann talks of the vital 'meaning' of the raw materials:

> The puppeteer whose performance starts somewhere else, namely with a passion for the correct or right raw materials, judged by their former uses, availability, cost, weight, beauty, can perform confidently with the help of those raw materials. None of these qualities is immediately obvious to an audience. The process of selection, their actual importance as participatory forces in the final product, are nothing more than a subtle presence, yet he owes his show to these invisible ingredients (Schumann [1990] 1991: 81–2).

Schumann's terms remind us of Schlemmer: 'Start with the materials, learn to feel the textural differences of such materials as glass, metal, wood and so on, and let them become deeply assimilated within you' (Schlemmer [1958] 1977: 112–3). In Susanne Langer's words, the artistic symbol 'negotiates insight not reference' and 'is deeper than any semantic of accepted signs' (S. Langer 1953: 22). Similarly, Svetlana Alpers, in her book *The Art of Describing: Dutch Art in the Seventeenth Century*, defines Dutch art of the period as not using symbols: the landscapes are what they are. Objects and scenes are not used as 'veils that conceal meaning' or as narratives. Merleau-Ponty is talking of the same direct presence of meaning in the paintings of Cezanne: 'Quality, light, color, depth, which are there before us, are there because they awaken an echo in our body and because the body welcomes them . . . there appears a "visible" of the second power, a carnal essence or icon of the first. It is not a faded copy' (Merleau-Ponty 1974a: 285). Henri Bergson talks of our urge to quantify and analyse and logically categorise the material world and make '*symbols*' of it, instead of 'entering into' the object to gain intuitive understanding of it and an 'absolute' knowledge of it (Bergson [1946] 1968: 190). In using Bergson again here, it must be remembered that Schlemmer, as far as we know, had no direct contact with his ideas; yet what Bergson has to say has curious resonances in relation not only to performance in general but to Schlemmer's own stage work, since Bergson draws us into questions of creative consciousness and the metaphysics of the eternal.[25]

According to Bergson, there are two ways of knowing something. 'The first implies going all around it, the second entering into it' (Bergson [1946] 1968: 187). The former involves a logical analytical approach, where we stand outside an object, using all our 'Kantian' constructs of time and space to grasp it, place it and relate to it. 'We shall say it stops at the relative'. The second position involves intuiting oneself into the object, so that the 'relative' positions of stability are left behind—'wherever possible, it attains the absolute' (187). Relative positions use symbols that 'mean' something, in a semiotic and therefore indirect way; absolute experience is direct and not translatable into (linguistic) symbols. It is this direct experience that lends power to any performer, but it is almost exclusively relied upon by Schlemmer in his non-mimetic stage, and is equally present when a puppeteer performs on stage; the simple power of presence is communicated to the audience. As before, it is important to draw attention to the difference between Bergson and later embodied thought, as well as the similarities: Bergson takes a mindful and not embodied approach to being 'in the object itself', calling it an 'effort of the imagination'. Bergson is talking about an irrational, non-cognitive relationship with materiality, even as Kleist does, but the body remains a vague presence:

> Take for example the movement of an object in space. I perceive it differently according to the point of view from which I look at it, whether from that of mobility or of immobility. I express it differently, furthermore, as I relate it to the system of axes or reference points, that is to say, according to the symbols by which I translate it. And I call it relative for this double reason: in either case, I place myself outside the object itself. When I speak of an absolute movement, it means that I attribute to the mobile an inner being, and as it were states of soul; it also means that I am in harmony with these states and *enter into them by an effort of the imagination*. Therefore according to whether the object is mobile or immobile, whether it adopts one movement or another, I shall not have the same feeling about it. And what I feel will depend neither on the point of view I adopt towards the object, since I

am in the object itself, not on the symbols by which I translate it, since I have renounced all translation in order to possess the original. In short, the movement will not be grasped from without, and as it were, from where I am, but from within, inside it, in what it is in itself. I shall have hold of an absolute' [my italics] (Bergson [1946] 1968: 187–8).

What Bergson says in this extract is equally applicable to the embodied art of performing with objects and puppets; however, clearly he has nothing like puppetry in mind at this point, even though he often uses art and the artist's practice and vision to illustrate his ideas. It also links with ideas of indivisible motion explored in Chapter 4. The balance is a delicate one between the liberating metaphysics of Bergson (which avoids the troublesome issue of the flesh), and the existential body of Merleau-Ponty where vision and transcendency vanish. But Merleau-Ponty's 'existential' bodies embedded in the material world in the 'halos of being' (Merleau-Ponty 1974a: 285) are the self same powerful performing bodies Feininger witnessed on the Bauhaus stage (Gropius and Wensinger [1961] 1996: 8–9); they are also the bodies of puppeteer and puppet which move in and through each other, where the motion of the puppeteer's body is indivisible with the motion of the puppet itself, and where this indivisibility is felt by both puppeteer and audience. When the theatrical experience is strong, the audience feels inexplicably enriched by it. Kleist dares to claim the object in performance can touch the sublime; and artists from Schlemmer onwards in the twentieth century rediscovered this alchemy of the ordinary.[26]

The yearning of an audience to be deceived, its illogical willingness not only to enter a space of spatial transformation but to accept all kinds of obvious and not so obvious tricks, devices and suggestions, seems to argue for a deep felt human need, a desire to glimpse the unknown, the irrational, a Bergsonian sensation of being 'wholly in flux' that can never be explained by our rational selves. Immanuel Kant in his *Critique of Pure Reason* knew he could never prove a transcendent reality, yet felt that the very human capacity to conceive its existence was significant in itself; it seems indisputable that the experience of watching theatre constantly offers us the same tantalising limitation and possibility. Whilst Kleist offers us the sublime object in theory, performance actively exposes it on stage. It makes its attempt to realise the sublime—momentarily, fragmentarily, sometimes unsuccessfully but always hopefully—through the embodied live experience of performer, object and audience.

6 Sound

Sound is ephemeral, fleeting, time specific. Sounds once permeated the Bauhaus and resounded in the Dessau corridors, sounds of a creative life lived with some real joy, the sounds of everyday living, learning and working, laughter, music, hammering, footsteps, voices. The Bauhaus Band practised in the basement, and as nearly everyone could play an instrument of some kind, live music was heard almost as a continual background to life at Dessau. Schlemmer and his student assistant knocked out rhythms on the piano in the theatre, underscored with percussion on drums and wooden claves, intercut occasionally with sirens. Public and private spaces rang with arguments about art, politics, personalities. The Bauhaus Band played until the early hours of the morning, and laughter animated the space as Schlemmer's Musical Clown scared himself by the noises he made when he moved. Hubert Hoffmann describes a Turkish student with a wonderful voice, singing early every Sunday from the Bauhaus roof as a 'Muhamaden' to provoke the good Christian folk of Dessau across the railway tracks (Bogner 1997: 18). These were the sounds of a life well lived and around them clustered an ideological and aesthetic debate that most commentators, at least in English, have missed. Sound—along with perhaps smell—is always the forgotten dimension of history. Ironically, it is also the forgotten dimension of our ever present perception: sound becomes so absorbed into the fabric of our everyday experience that most of the time we have to make a conscious effort to hear the dense fabric of sounds that continually surrounds us in perpetual motion: sound nevertheless profoundly shapes our experience on this earth.

Many commentators on sound have eloquently described its paradoxical and haunting nature. Sound is vibration and therefore a physical sensation which literally enters the body of the listener: it is promiscuous, spilling over into space after space, rebounding off and articulating surface after surface, reminiscent of the bouncing rays of ambient light described in Chapter 3, until its vibrations are too faint for the human ear to pick up. David Toop describes the passive but absolute penetration of body by sound: 'sound comes from everywhere, unbidden. My brain seeks it out, sorts it, makes me feel the immensity of a universe even when I have no wish to look or absorb' (Toop 1995: 1–2). Shirley MacWilliam communicates a material presence of sound that is linked to its penetrative flowing qualities, its 'physiological aspect': 'the physical sensation of hearing is not so discretely localised to the ear as is the experience of sight to the eye. We hear through the volume of the body, through the bones and flesh as well as the ear . . . Sound . . . vibrates through the producing and listening body. It reincorporates itself into the body of the listener' (MacWilliam 1998: 31). Victor Zuckerkandl, on the other hand, stresses the lack of material presence and alerts us to the mysterious power of organised sound, or as he put it, 'Gestalten', in music: 'the observation that we hear something in the tones of music which does not fit into the general context of the physical world is irreconcilably opposed to the assertions that our sense organs are organs for perceiving the physical world and that the world perceived through the senses is physical throughout' (Zuckerkandl 1956: 24). Daniel Barenboim comments: 'although sound is a very physical phenomenon, it has some inexplicable metaphysical hidden power' (Barenboim 2006: 2). This phenomenon, sound, is variously described for both its materiality and its non-materiality, its liquidity and its viscosity, its ethereality and its density, its vagueness and its precision. It is these paradoxical qualities of sound, the combined intangibility and physicality (vibration), the ethereality and the materiality, that makes sound perhaps the most elusive of the stage elements so far discussed.

We attempt to access the sound of the past despite its silence. But of course it is the silence itself we must access, a void in an imagined space: there is Schlemmer's silence, which gently invites engagement and eschews 'radical interpretations' (Schwartz 1999: 8–11).

One summer's Sunday evening in 2008 I approached the Dessau Bauhaus from the direction of the station, walking up Gropius Allee: the Bauhaus rising ahead of me was white, huge, enigmatic, its impact seemingly unaffected by the houses that have crept closer to its walls since the 1920s. I recalled Hoffmann's description of his walk towards the stark and isolated newly built Bauhaus building so long ago in 1925, walking from the station, no doubt following my same route (Bogner 1997: 14–5).

> I found it sensational: how could anyone put such a raw structure in a field! . . . as we climbed the stairs there came the sound of music from below, from the cellar . . . music that I had never heard before . . . fantastic rhythm . . . 'That's our Bauhauskapelle Band' (Bogner 1997: 15).

Almost deserted and with grass growing from between the pavement slabs, the courtyards on the evening I arrived seemed utterly devoid of people, and above all (*pace* Cage[1]), eerily yet eloquently silent.

> Harpocratic silence is the empty silence of reflection and meditation. Larundic silence is the full active silence of communciation. Harpocratic

silence depicts the notion of emptiness, which is how silence is most commonly perceived. Anything can be done in this emptiness; it is pure freedom for creativity and imagination without constraint. On the other hand the myth of Larunda and Hermes accounts for our intuitive perceptions that silence sometimes contains and transmits meanings (Schwartz 1999: 8).

The horizon of silence that rimmed the Bauhaus that evening was Larundic in Schwartz's sense, communicating how much we have lost of the Bauhaus more strongly than the weekday noises of work and visitors and study and performances which currently fill its corridors and spaces.

It could be argued that there is another Bauhaus silence, this time operating on the original Dessau Bauhaus stage, in Schlemmer's refusal to fill up the aural spaces of his dances with ambient background music. In performance at least (less so in rehearsals) he left gaps which, in Regine Elzenheimer's words, 'set hurdles on the track of speed' and wrung a 'place for listening out of noise, opening new sensitivities to minimal changes' (Elzenheimer 1999: 33). Elzenheimer traces and identifies silence as an aesthetic notion originating in nineteenth-century philosophy[2] and which developed throughout the twentieth century into a powerful and consciously used postmodern stage device, a 'transformation from a lack' into 'a qualitatively different comprehension of silence' (Elzenheimer 1999: 27) i.e. as standing in for the unheard, the unsaid, what is missing, the soundings we do not hear. Such are the blank spaces left between the lines on the page of an Expressionist poem (Kern [1983] 2003: 172–4). Elzenheimer sees this silence as essentially European and distinct from John Cage's American avant-garde, Zen-inspired silence. Yet, Cagean silence, a silence that negates the ego of self expression and lays us open to experience is also present in Schlemmer's pared down minimalist stage.[3] Arguably, these two interpretations of silence identify a similar goal, unspeakable, unutterable, unnamable—but not 'unexperienceable'. In the words of Schlemmer's friend the composer Stefan Wolpe: 'Good is not to know how much one is knowing' (Clarkson 2002: 108).

Sounds surrounding and penetrating the body engaged and frustrated Schlemmer's genius, as he sought to connect the medium of sound with the 'Gestalten' of the dance which he felt was the origin of all arts. In eventually restricting the sound on the Bauhaus stage to, largely speaking, basic percussion, he sought to understand something very simple that he also sensed was very complex: the relationship of the (moving) body to the making of sound. In the Bauhaus parties where the music of the Bauhaus Band infused and permeated the total social and aesthetic space he created, until dawn broke next day, he was recognising a dimension to music—and sound—that offers some of the strongest proof of his deeply human and ethical attitude. Music—a new music—would contribute to the shaping of the new society he hoped would emerge from Germany's chaos, perhaps from the Bauhaus itself, embedding the aesthetic in the heart of lived experience.

Schlemmer's ideas on sound appear on the surface to have resulted either in limited practical solutions on stage or even in unfinished projects, such as *House of Pi*, but in his practical research he was, as ever, far in advance of Expressionist thinking. In contrast to most of his colleagues at the Bauhaus, such as Itten, Klee and Kandinsky who preferred to concentrate on the intangible and mystical dimension of sound, producing elaborate unprovable theories of colour correspondences and imagined new 'Gestalten', Schlemmer followed his usual path of caution and restraint, handling the materials and and letting them speak. He concentrated on the physical and material qualities of sound in relation to the body in an attempt to discover its metaphysical, aesthetic and ethical role in the particular kind of non-representational theatre he wished to make. I argue that his desire to harness sound to spatial articulation could not be realised with the technology available in the 1920s, but its potential has since been recognised and to some extent realised over the past thirty years or so, most obviously in the development of sound art, but primarily with the development and sophisticated use of soundscapes on the postmodern stage that connect intimately with the live performing body upon it.

The history of Bauhaus sound is the familiar early Modernist eclectic mix of the traditional and the new, Expressionist and Constructivist, mystical and scientific: man, machine and (largely but by no means exclusively) music. The blend of mysticism and science, a prominent feature of Modernism in the first thirty years of the twentieth century, was manifested in the widespread interest in the supposed connection between sound and colour, music and painting taken by many German painters, of whom Paul Klee at the Bauhaus was one of the most persistent and vigorous exponents (Maur 1999: 12–17, Gage 1993: 227–246, Vergo 1994: 131–7). These links had first been explored in the nineteenth century. By the time of the publication of Kandinsky's writings in 1912, the ideas had developed to parallel closely those on 'Gestalt' and colour, explored in Chapter 2. The intention was either to produce paintings structured like music, or, less commonly, to produce performances of music/sound with corresponding staged visuals. Those painters who were most active in tracing the supposed correlations between the structures of colour (as represented in the colour wheel[4]) and the structures of sound (as demonstrated in music) were also musicians, or at least played an instrument with confidence, though this of course was not unusual at the time, even up to professional level in the case of Klee (on the violin) and Feininger (a composer). Many of these 'musical' painters had strong connections with the Bauhaus or taught there. They included the Stuttgart based teacher and painter Adolf Hölzel, who played the violin (and who was the painting teacher of key Bauhäusler Schlemmer, Itten and Hirschfield-Mack); Kandinsky, who played the cello and was moreover a synaesthetic who actually did 'see' colours when he heard sound; and Johannes Itten, who had a detailed knowledge of music theory. At the Bauhaus, ideas on the equivalence of sound and colour remained active: strongly so in the Weimar years, less so at Dessau. Whereas Paul Klee was vehemently opposed to modern music and considered that the music of the eighteenth century had touched the heights of development possible (a rather Spenglerian view of Western culture[5]), Johannes Itten worked closely with Josef Matthias Hauer on developing a colour wheel that corresponded to Hauer's version of the twelve tone system of atonal music. Kandinsky was particularly interested in developments in early Modernist music that included the use of dissonance and he saw parallels in the dissonant music of Schönberg with the development of his own abstract art and its use of colour described earlier. He had of course included Schönberg in his seminal Expressionist text, *The Blue Rider Almanac* (Lindsay and Vergo 1982: 229–283). The key point here is that these 'musical' painters were all thinking in the 'Gestalt' terms laid out earlier; in other words, what was sought was not some simple system of equivalence between colour and sound but a colour system (like musical structure) that had both constant form and an in-built dynamism or change, and which also (like music supposedly did) referred to the deeper reality, higher law, 'universal formula' or Goethe's 'Urplantze'. '[C]olour and music were capable, as Goethe had insisted , of being "referred back to a universal formula . . . both are derivable, though each from itself, from this higher law"' (Vergo 1994: 135).[6]

Within the Bauhaus there was disagreement as to whether the new twelve tone system of music, developed by Schönberg in the early 1920s, was sufficiently radical an approach to musical structure within atonality to yield the correspondences and new 'Gestalten' that were sought. Many students thought not, and this is reflected in the interest in avant-garde composers and modern music that developed in the Bauhaus, eventually resulting in the founding of the Bauhaus Band in 1924 by Andreas Weininger, influenced at least in Weimar by anarchic and youthful Dada ideas of throwing out the old and traditional. Before that, there was interest in, for example, the music of Erik Satie, Arnold Schönberg, George Gershwin, Henry Cowell and Kurt Schwitters (Eisenhardt 2006: 1–2). Interest in the experimental music of George Antheil, whose ideas were so far in advance of his age that one of his works was only fully realised in 1999,[7] was so strong that a Bauhaus book was planned on his work, though it came to nothing.

As to the Bauhaus Band, it would be hard to underestimate its impact upon the Dessau Bauhaus's daily life since its sounds, as Hoffmann testifies, filled the corridors and flowed out of windows, and its impact on Bauhaus celebrations and parties is incalculable. It was not primarily a jazz band but took much of its inspiration from the fiery rhythms and tunes of East European folk music, overlaid with improvisation and inspiration. It was not alcohol that fuelled the wild dancing through the night, only the band. Unfortunately, no musical scores have survived but everyone pays tribute in their memories to the urge to dance that the band induced, the rhythmic force of the music, the sheer joy of hearing them. The band incorporated sirens, bells, whistles and other 'real sounds' in their exuberant 'modern' compositions, echoing thereby Dada and Futurist ideas on sound, and perhaps debunking the preciousness that surrounded music theory at the Bauhaus.

The one CD published that purports to be *Music at the Bauhaus* (Schleiermacher 1999) in fact gathers together composers who had some association with the Bauhaus (Antheil, Hauer, Stuckenschmidt, Vogel, Wolpe) but gives no idea of the true Bauhaus music, which was that of the 'Bauhauskapelle', or Bauhaus Band, heard moreover in its proper environment, the unified social and aesthetic space of a Bauhaus Party, organised at Dessau by Oskar Schlemmer (the Dessau band line-up only really formed in the latter months at Weimar). The band did not play for Schlemmer's performances though key members of the band were also involved with the Bauhaus stage, such as Xanti Schawinsky and Andreas Weininger. Musicians were utilized on occasion for *The Triadic Ballet* (Bogner 1997: 26–7).

A loose grouping thus emerged whose attitudes were more mixed, more experimental and less rigid. It was open to new possibilities and provided the kernel of later developments in sound in the twentieth century. Amongst them I would count Schlemmer, Maholy-Nagy, and the members of the Bauhaus Band. Most of them had an interest in the possibilities of technology for developing music and, more broadly, sound itself: live, recorded, broadcast and amplified. Linked to this group is the composer Stefan Wolpe, not a student at the Bauhaus but a frequent visitor up to 1925 and a friend of Schlemmer's.

Maholy-Nagy's 'scratch' treatment of records at the Bauhaus (the 'Schallplatten', old-fashioned 78 speed phonograph disks, an early version in shellac of what is now called 'vinyl') to produce new sounds prefigures much later work by scratch DJs in the 1980s. It parallels Maholy-Nagy's work in photography, in that here he was again seeking new 'Gestalten' by pushing a recording medium from 'mimesis' into a creative tool (see Chapter 2, this volume). It also indicates his desire to 'make physical' the sound visually, seen again in his later practice of drawing shapes and 'translating' them into sounds (Manning 2003: 9–10, Kahn and Whitehead 1992: 11). This was made possible through the invention of the sound track on films at the end of the 1920s. Maholy-Nagy was never 'mystical' in his approach to sound and music but neither was he a prosaic engineer. He was excited by the technological possibilities to make new art: he was, like Schlemmer, a visionary who also demonstrated, in his own way, a 'terrestrial anchoring of objects and bodies' (Kahn and Whitehead 1992: 15).[8] Interest in the concrete nature of sound, its physicality, and how this might be worked on, grasped and changed, reached towards its establishment as a medium in its own right, and were notions that anticipated developments much later in the century in 1950s Europe and America.[9]

The music scene and mixed attitudes within the Bauhaus are only partially reflected in the public face that was offered in the Bauhaus Week of performances in Weimar from 16–19 August 1923, which opened the Bauhaus Exhibition. When this week was planned, prepared and finally took place, the Bauhaus was in a state of transition from the excesses of Johannes Itten and Gertrud Grunow, both of whom had keenly promoted the etherial and mystical approaches to music/colour correspondences outlined above, into the more Constructivist phase of the Bauhaus, driven by Maholy-Nagy. Hans Heinz Stuckenschmidt captures the atmosphere well in his account of being invited to take part in the Bauhaus Week and of his arrival there (Stuckenschmidt 1976). Stuckenschmidt, who was a well-known figure amongst the avant-garde at least, and familiar with the work of George Antheil for example, entered and helped to shape the music milieu of Weimar Bauhaus for a brief period in July/August 1923. Maholy-Nagy had cornered him at a dinner party in Berlin and invited him down to the Bauhaus to work with Kurt Schmidt on his piece *The Mechanical Ballet*. That summer Itten and Grunow had just left and Maholy-Nagy was newly in post. The Exhibition of material works from the Preliminary Course and the workshops, running from August through September, was a vast public relations exercise to demonstrate the Bauhaus ideals and achievements to the local government who provided the funding, but it was also, more importantly, a nationwide, if not international, publicity event to boost the fortunes of the institution. Masters and students alike threw themselves into it and preparations dominated the year leading up to it, which included Schlemmer producing reliefs for, and painting, the vestibules and staircase of the Workshop Building with various student apprentices as his working team. The performance week to kick off the Exhibition opening in August included a triumphant performance of *The Triadic Ballet* (which was perhaps the start of the Bauhaus taking much of the credit for this piece which was created independently and financed always by Schlemmer himself); an evening of 'Mechanical Cabaret' including Schlemmer's *The Figural Cabinet* and Kurt Schmidt's *The Mechanical Ballet*; and several concerts of contemporary music, including that of Hindemith, Busoni and Stravinsky. Contemporary music was thus featured prominently. Gropius enjoyed music and was married to Alma Mahler (widow to the composer) who herself played at concert pianist level. He clearly wanted to place the Bauhaus at the leading edge of all the avant-garde in Germany, if not Europe, and music gave him the opportunity to make an unmistakable and strong statement. The inclusion of music was also a gesture towards the overall cultural Gestalt that the Bauhaus was aiming for. He finally managed to persuade the composer Hermann Scherchen, well known in Germany at that time, to take on the role of conductor, and a programme was arranged that declared the Bauhaus position at the cutting edge of the arts.

By the time Schlemmer had joined the Bauhaus in the late 1910s, no longer did he share the Expressionist hopes of reaching the 'Gestaltungen' through the equivalence of colour and sound. However it is true that around 1912 Schlemmer had appeared to share some of the hopes of his contemporaries regarding the deep correspondence of colour and sound, and these hopes are apparent in the plans for his Expressionistic dance work of that same year, *The Courtship* (see also Chapter 4, this volume).

Schlemmer's original plan was to approach Schönberg to write for this ballet. Schönberg was a pioneer of the new 'atonal' music creating dissonance and entirely new sounds, but still within recognisably musical paradigms. Although it was nothing like the extraordinary attempts at simulated real world sounds in the 'noise music' of the Futurists (which Schlemmer had probably not encountered at this point) it was a radical and exciting recasting of musical form that had not been systematically attempted before. Schlemmer heard the 'Sprechstimme' atonal piece *Pierrot Lunaire* in 1912, a spoken voice text solo, half sung against music. The female lead, playing Pierrot, sings three groups of seven poems, twenty-one in all (this number is significant within the structure of the work: Schönberg, like Schlemmer, was interested in numerology). The poems have titles such as 'Moon-drunk' 'Night' and 'Journey Home'. There are echoes of popular cabaret in it, and it is played by five instruments (flute, clarinet, violin, cello and piano) which are stretched into producing a larger range of sounds. The work is around thirty to forty minutes long at most. This half sung, half said poetry set to music has a non-realist, slightly 'otherworld' atmosphere. What would have appealed to Schlemmer, apart from the 'low' or popular entertainment feel to it, is the novel atonality of this piece which obviously does not depend on traditional musical harmony for its effect. As Schönberg pointed out to Schlemmer the music also lacked traditional dance rhythms. Schlemmer felt it might be suitable for his dance because he was trying to forge a new kind of dance which directly expressed his metaphysical ideas rather than narrative story lines or lyrical expression with which dance rhythms had traditionally been associated. In fact, within a few months Schlemmer had started to develop a different way into the 'new' dance he sought, through costume, and he left ideas of heightened expressivity behind.

In Chapter 4, this shift away from symbolic expression to using material form and the body as his starting point for finding motion was explored. Such a change fundamentally affected Schlemmer's attitude to the accompanying music. A solution to the auditory dimension of his new approach proved a lifetime's problem. It is hard to understate the radical nature of his shift from Expressionism, driven by ideas, into a phenomenological and embodied approach driven by material form. The implications in relation to sound are profound. Many of the problems Schlemmer encountered are issues explored and mined in sound art and the postmodern stage much later on: sound's physical qualities, the problems of highlighting sound's 'quiddity' as against its evocative properties, sound as an articulator of space, sound as an equal element alongside the domination of vision. Above all, Schlemmer sensed the problem lay in his hunch that the 'new' music he wanted would spring primarily from rhythm and movement rather than harmony, and he believed strongly that it would emerge from the new dance he was creating.

Whilst Schlemmer was convinced that the solution to the new music lay in dance itself, its motion and its rhythms, he was equally sure that it lay in his own disciplined dance of form, not that of Jaques Dalcroze's Eurythmics or Wigman's Expressionist 'hand wavings' (Schlemmer [1929] 1965: 13). He considered dance as a purer art form that provided the chance of a new beginning to revive the German stage, in his case using 'brightly coloured masquerades', reviving the old form of 'theatrical costume dance', in contast to Eurythmics (Schlemmer [1958] 1977:88). His 'silent' dance, with its cool and objective Muse[10], who says nothing yet means everything, contained the starting point for a 'theatrical renaissance' (88). Schlemmer's embodied vision of dance and music was not the untrammelled release of bodily motion, and as long as he worked within the somewhat restricted bodily engagement of *The Triadic Ballet*, he encountered problems in realising the connections he sought. In a 1927 essay on abstraction in dance and costume, he talks about how Bach's music follows contrapunctual and mathematical laws, constrained by the physical nature of the instrument being used and compares this to a body dancing in space, equally constrained by the geometry of 'laws' of the space or room surrounding the dancer: 'The music of the future approaches this strictness of law, and the abstract dance will do the same, following or leading it' (Schlemmer [1927e] 1961: 28).

However, the rigid form of *The Triadic Ballet* not only restricted the body but appeared, for the time being, to silence its music. This interest in the formal structures of music obviously connects to his emphasis on form in his ballet. In June 1920, he wrote to Otto Meyer:

> Yet there remains a geometry that belongs to the surface of the dance floor, even though it is only as part of and a projection of the stereometry of space. I am working out a similar surface geometry of the fingers and the keys on the piano, endeavoring to identify that geometry (or the unity of movement and bodily form) with music (Schlemmer [1958] 1977: 41).

He talks of the 'Musikalität der Formgestaltung' or 'musical form' of *The Triadic Ballet* costumes which 'arose from the joy in playing with form, colour and material' (Schlemmer 1927b: 523). In other words he continually identifies the costumes with the aspects of music he considered 'material': primarily structure. Until he encountered Hindemith however he was frustrated in his attempts to find music that 'identified' with the worn costumes in motion, and in choosing Hindemith's music, ironically, he removes himself from all bodily 'contact' with the music since Hindemith's music was produced not by a played instrument but a piano roll (used for the abridged 1926 performance in Donaueschingen). The 'exactitude and precision of the music, determined by the mechanisation, was in extraordinarily harmonious rapport with the formal precision of the figures' (Schlemmer 1927b: 523). Elsewhere, in a diary entry of 5 July 1926, written immediately after the Donaueschingen performance, he asks 'Why Hindemith?' Besides citing Hindemith's ability to span the range of mood in the piece 'from merry grotesque to full emotion' (July 1926) (Schlemmer [1958] 1977:88)[11] and also mentioning the spiritual depth he brings to the music, Schlemmer directly links the sound Hindemith makes with the form of the dance. There is also the visual aspect of a mechanical piano as the strings are mechanically hit, so that the audience sees something 'visual' corresponding to a sound, but not a human movement: instead they see something closely tied to production of the sound itself:

> And why a player-piano? Because on the one hand the mechanical device suits the template of the dance style (a style which is partly conditioned by, or even aspired to, through the costumes), in contrast to the usual spiritual and dramatic exuberance of today; on the other hand, it forms a parallel to the mathematical costumes, which follow the mechanics of the body. Furthermore, the puppet-like quality of the dances will conform to the musicality, which has a 'music box' quality about it. In all probability it will create 'Unity', which corresponds to the notion of 'Style' (July 1926) (Schlemmer [1958] 1977: 88–9).

Nevertheless, more was needed:

> Unfortunately, the full potential, already limited by the mechanical organ, had to stay more often than not unrealised. For example shiny metal spheres call for the sound of a trumpet; one shape demands a large drum, another the sound of fine glass. This ideal harmony still awaits its realisation (Schlemmer 1927b: 523).

It is significant here that he mentions 'the sound of fine glass', an actual material and its 'sounding', alongside the trumpet and drum. Schlemmer was aware of possibilities of recording and amplification of sound. It might have offered him the solution he needed for *The Triadic Ballet*, providing amplified sounds of the (worn) materials: However, the technical knowledge was simply not widely available at that time, tending to be in the hands of engineers not artists (Kahn 2001: 134). If anything, all his comments on Hindemith's music connect it closely with the material forms on stage, an impersonal unemotive sound/music which can then be detached from source, moved around and distorted.

> Mechanical reproduction through technical devices makes it possible to separate the human voice and the sound of the musical instrument

from the human body in order to enhance them, beyond their dependence on real time and physical limitations (Schlemmer 1925: 10).

This is very close to the work of certain contemporary directors such as Romeo Castelluci or Robert Lepage where the soundscape has 'direct action' on the space of the stage and is often formed out of 'sounding' objects on that stage.

In fact, new 'Gestalten' of sound on stage have only been realised in recent years on stage, where technology has enabled directors and sound designers to exploit the phenomenology of sound—the 'sounding' rather than, or in addition to, the sound itself—and harness its spatial properties to communicate in new, highly effective and possibly largely unnoticed ways. An audience's ability to hear sound varies as much as the senses of smell, sight and taste, and although many will naturally recall every detail of the soundscape (and natural abilities in the senses can of course change or be improved by training) on the whole it is probably true that audiences find sound the hardest element to recall from a theatre performance. This does not mean that the sound has not been working directly upon them, phenomenologically, in the moment of their reception of it. It can be said that the receiving of the sound alongside the visuals fuses into a new stage Gestalt.

For example, Robert Lepage's *The Dragon's Trilogy* (Barbican Centre, London, 2005) covers the best part of a century from 1910 to 1986 when Haley's Comet reappeared in the sky, and luminous light is used throughout the piece—the comet, the shining ball of light that Stella plays with, the lit up floor. Analysis of this visual aspect of the piece, light, belongs more properly in Chapter 3, except it is impossible to separate off our sensory experiences and the receipt of ideas in a categorical fashion like this. Sound and light together articulate the space alongside motion and plasticity. *The Dragon's Trilogy* not only spans a huge period of time but covers interlinking stories and characters. The use of space is perfectly suited to the content: whilst retaining specificity of each place, space is fluid and permeates every boundary almost as soon as it is established, as do the many stories themselves. The story is in one sense a single one and linear, easy to follow, but it is also circular, 'reflecting', sinuous, non-linear. Lepage gets larger perspectives into his story by weaving in Hiroshima and the Chinese Revolution, and other spaces continually intrude and overlay each other, so that a bigger world or perspective presses in continually, but the particular and personal is not lost. One world that continually presses in is an unspoken metaphysical presence that resonates around the human action without detracting from the absolute humanity of what we see.

Sound is an important device that enables Lepage to realise this 'metaphysical presence', this sense of the 'significant human', whose actions seem to resonate beyond the moment of their doing. He mixes live and recorded sound to articulate the extraordinary envelope of space in which the characters live their lives. He plays with recorded off stage sound as if it emerges from a 'larger' dimension and plays with live sound on stage as if it were tied to the human dimension. Often a live sound on stage seems to draw down an off stage sound, welding the 'beyond' to the human here and now: for example Françoise appears live on stage in the front of the screen where we have seen and heard the recorded concert, and sings. Her human presence is doubly felt: both vulnerable and vivid. Conversely recorded 'off' stage sound picks up live sound on the stage and can seemingly spin it into orbit and even cross swathes of time. In part 1, the live click of the two (gambling) sticks by the Englishman as he watches the barber wager his daughter away, picks up and seems to complete the loud rhythm of the same recorded sound off stage. The effect is as if a larger metaphysical world was brought down to a human time and place, but equally a human moment (the idiocy of gambling and losing so much) cannot be contained in that specific time and place and will resonate, true enough, through the years to come. Such moments take a great many words to describe but an instant to receive and interpret: except that we do not 'interpret' these moments intellectually. They are simply 'present' to us: the way we receive the 'soundings' shapes the meaning in a phenomenologically direct way that often escapes our consciousness. Lepage is a master at building up such effects through a performance, using variation in sameness, sameness in difference. The clicks were first heard in part 1 and associated with poker; similar sounds punctuate the stage in other places, such as the paintbrushes of the old woman tinkling against the glasses on the table in part 2, the clacking of typewriter keys in part 3.

It was said earlier that the receiving of the sound alongside the visuals results in a new stage Gestalt. Another example is Romeo Castellucci's *Inferno* (Barbican Centre, London BITE09) where a young boy enters and bounces a ball: when it hits the ground it causes a vast sound utterly charged with energy, amplified beyond reason, the break, crash, smash, a momentous something—not necessarily destructive, just magnificently powerful (see Figure 6.1). The palpable power of its 'sounding' actually derives from the immediately preceding scene where we first hear (and 'see') the crashing sound. At the rear of the stage in this scene is a large black screen. It rises on a tilt to reveal a smallish triangle of lit space. The atmosphere is now very still (when we have just had a great deal of loud noise). Then we hear crashes, very amplified, which seem to body forth the unknown and unseen space behind the curtain, a space that we only ever hear but do not see. Then, startlingly, china smashes, apparently thrown upon the stage below the curtain, objects that are very human, very sharp; an action very violent, very noisy. At one point, innumerable feet appear along the gap of the lifted curtain, lined up, a whole population, a town, a holocaust, who can tell (see Figure 6.2)? Somehow the ball's crashes as the boy bounces it gather up and embody all of this mysterious unseen space behind the visible envelope of the stage.

Figure 6.1 *Inferno*, directed by Romeo Castellucci, Socìetas Raffaello Sanzio, 2009. Photocredit: Luca del Pia.

Figure 6.2 *Inferno*, directed by Romeo Castellucci, Socìetas Raffaello Sanzio, 2009. Photocredit: Luca del Pia.

These uses of sound are exactly parallel to Peter Schumann's eulogy of the puppet, quoted in Chapter 5, as not a symbol but the thing itself: like the theatre of Achim Freyer, puppets are not an idea but an experience. So is the noise of the ball, hitting us with a palpable force. And this of course is exactly the heart of early twentieth-century Gestalt thinking where the virtual space of a painting was treated as another *lived* experience of (a different kind of) space. This theory was articulated by Adolf von Hildebrand and read by Schlemmer, Itten and others (Hildebrand 1907).[12]

As Schlemmer's attention focused away from his ballet to the research space of the Dessau stage, concerning sound as with other stage elements he was forced to work with very pared down means, beginning with his exploitation of a simple fact: sound is vibration, the heard motion of the physical element, penetrating the body.

In the early non-narrative pieces, he was inclined to cut out tonal harmony all together and concentrated on duration or rhythm, either using simple percussion on drums to accompany the movements (*Space Dance* and *Form Dance* seem never to have had music with them) with various live sounds overlaid (he even used voiced grunts and so on in *Gesture Dance*). There were at Dessau, with one significant exception (*House of Pi*), no words, and this decision may well have been influenced by his predecessor Lothar Schreyer's excessive emphasis on words and the decisive rejection of him by the Bauhaus. Scheper, who at the time of his research had access to the archive, says the music Schlemmer wrote for rehearsals has no merit (Scheper 1988: 186). On the contrary, Scheper is wrong: the scores that gradually emerged from rehearsals were fit for purpose and deliberately concentrated on and developed out of the pounding rhythms that Albert Flocon describes:

> We were not supposed to collide—and the music which Schlemmer played himself was percussive, and it gave the rhythms, he sat at the piano often. For the performance we had a student who did the music and had studied what we did, and he did it beautifully, also using wooden and metal claves. It was more a 'Bruitage', sheer noise to maintain the rhythm (Flocon 1994: 65).

The rhythms did not stay as 'sheer noise'. Schlemmer was an accomplished musician and a particularly fine pianist. He eventually wrote the piano music to accompany the 'Bauhaustänze' for the tour (whose scores still survive[13]). For the non-narrative more 'metaphysical' pieces he linked sound closely to the action and materials of the piece, and used either swift, urgent and insistent rhythm (*Metal Dance* (piano and percussion) and *Hoop Dance* (piano, claves and drum)), or delicately repeated high piano chords, some dissonant, in *Glass Dance* (piano, triangle, glass) which also had running 'ripples' of notes as it moved to its end; in *Stick Dance* (piano, cymbals, triangle, claves) he used punctuating single notes as the sticks fixed to the body were held and moved, held and moved. For this dance, the piano softly built under the single percussive notes which seems to give the impression of the dance unfolding smoothly and rhythmically in its motion even as it maintained its 'freeze frames' of form between the percussion sounds. His scores for the most theatrical and comic dances such as *Gesture Dance*, *Three Women* and *Box Play*, resembled the highly rhythmic and illustrative piano music supporting silent movies of the day. Here we see, or rather hear, Schlemmer once again connecting action with 'material' form (here, sound) and his unfailing reverence for the comic as supplying the most simple Gestalt forms on stage, the comic being the closest to both humanity and to metaphysical 'truth'. It is significant that he developed a friendship in the Weimar years with Stefan Wolpe, who in later years wrote an article on film music that developed Busoni's idea that music was the art of movement: 'Rhythm is the primary technical basis for the music' and percussion 'expresses essential relationships and reconciles the effects of the action'. Finally, 'aesthetic harmony is achieved by transforming a "depsychologised music" into sublime energies' (Clarkson and Shin 2006: 262) and 'Motion—motion of intervals, rhythms and formal contrasts—belongs to the absolute nature of music. The first characteristic of motion is variation. I believe it is a spiritual principle' (Clarkson and Shin 2006: 263). His words uncannily described the 'music' of pounding rhythms and percussion on the Dessau experimental stage of motion. 'Dance represents the highest degree of perfection, a blend of mind and mathematics; it provides intelligent gracefulness, joy, utmost liveliness and the energy of abstract designs. It is space alone that is always danced' (Clarkson and Shin 2006: 265).[14] It seems Wolpe also wrote some music for *The Triadic Ballet* but it has not apparently survived (Clarkson and Shin 2006: note 8).

In 'bühne' (Schlemmer 1927c) Schlemmer talks first of all about why his theatre work does not use *'laut, wort, sprache'* [sic] or sound, word and speech:

> Sound, word and speech: we confess until now we have carefully not used them, not in order to cut them out but conscious of their significance, to grasp them slowly. For the time being we are satisfied with the silent play of gesture and motion, with pantomime—and we believe firmly that the word will one day inevitably develop from this. This area is a particular problem for us because we want to grasp it with a special emphasis on the non-literary aspects, that is to say the physical elements: sounds as a phenomenal event, as if apprehended for the first time (Schlemmer 1927c: 2).

The widely published English text of this lecture in the Gropius and Wensinger edition of 1961 (Gropius and Wensinger [1961] 1996) is problematic. After the insertion (by Schlemmer) at this point into the original German published version (Schlemmer 1927c) about the brief lived project *House of Pi* (which used words and was discussed in Chapter 3, this volume), Schlemmer describes his attempt to use word and language as a 'phenomenal event' or in Wensinger's translation, in its 'primary state', 'als ereignis' [sic]. 'Ereignis'[15] confusingly, inaccurately and but perhaps understandably (in an over enthusiastic attempt to link Schlemmer with the then current experimental American theatre 'happenings') was translated as 'a happening' in 1961, a very time specific performance term and subsequently very particular in its meaning, rather than 'event'. This experience of language, says Schlemmer, 'as if apprehended for the first time' applies equally to the musical sound and 'note'. The 1961 edition again confuses by translating 'Ton' as harmony thus:

> What has been said about word and language applies to SOUND and HARMONY. Here too we try in our own way to create out of necessity and need an appropriate aural expression for each experimental production (*Gestaltung*). For the time being, such simple 'stimulators' as the gong and kettledrum are enough (Schlemmer in Gropius and Wensinger [1961] 1996: 91).

'Note' and not 'harmony' is a better translation as Schlemmer deliberately avoids any harmony in an Expressionistic sense on his Dessau stage. The 1961 translation also fails to make clear the Gestalt thinking underlying Schlemmer's aims. We arrive in preference at:

What has been said about word and speech also applies to the musical sound and note. Here too we have necessarily had to to seek our own method to create the expression of the respective Gestalt forms, and we use for the time being the simple sounding drum and gong (Schlemmer 1927c: 2–3).

This description of the attempt to approach the 'word' and the 'musical sound and note' as if it were 'apprehended for the first time' parallels Maholy-Nagy's comments on the 'apperceptive' reception of sounds (and colour) being preferable to 'associative' reception: he talks of 'the sensory, technical effect of interconnected sounds' (Maholy-Nagy 1925: 48) being no longer the monopoly of poetry[16] as if these aspects were separate from the intellectual meaning or thought communicated by them.[17] Maholy-Nagy's note on 'apperceptive' reads:

> 'Apperceptive' (the opposite of 'associative') ought here to mean an elementary step in perception and the formation of concepts (psychophysical assimilation). For example, to take in a color = apperceptive process: the human eye reacts without previous experience to red with green, blue with yellow. Whereas an object= the assimilation of color + matter + form = connection with previous experience = associative process (Maholy-Nagy 1925: 48).

'Apperceptive' is clearly a phenomenological reception of stimuli or 'Gestalten' in the Husserlian idealistic sense, and reaches towards the 'type' or basic form that was consistently sought. Schlemmer, in his desire to hear sound as an 'event' or 'as if apprehended for the first time', is also talking about a similar 'apperceptive' reception of sound—in other words, a phenomenological and at the same time essentialist perception of sound, though he would never of course use such words. It is hard to envisage what such pure forms of sound might be. Schlemmer's purpose in 'stripping back' sound to its essential elements is part of his Modernist agenda to reveal the 'laws' of sound, which is an essential part of his wider intention, that of laying bare the stage 'Gestalten'. This is clear in a 1927 article, where Schlemmer says: 'We want to master language and musical notes according to the laws which we have extracted from forms and colours, so as to understand the complex totality of the stage' (Schlemmer 1927a: 71). But in Schlemmer's case the body always plays a crucial role. Because of this there are wider implications to Schlemmer's essentialist phenomenological approach to sound that again prefigure work on the postmodern stage.

Schlemmer's practice anticipates ideas articulated much later in the century, particularly by the late John Blacking (Blacking 1973, 1977: 1–28), whose writings on music, and particularly the music of the Venda tribe, provide an insight into the reciprocal co-existence of music and society that an embodied understanding reveals. Daniel Barenboim in the Reith lectures (2006) demonstrated the 'connection between the inexpressible content of music and the inexpressible content of life . . . music has another weapon that it delivers to us, if we want to take it, and that is one through which we can learn a lot about ourselves, about our society, about the human being, about politics, about society, about anything that you choose to do' (Barenboim 2006). Blacking and Barenboim share the awareness of the social and cultural embeddedness of sound, and its dynamic capacity to effect and reflect change in the social body—literally in the body itself, because as the original music maker, music is founded there: and metaphorically in the 'body' of culture and society where the literal body 'sounds' as receiver and transmitter. In Schlemmer's case, this awareness is reflected in the 'stage' of his Bauhaus parties and the Bauhaus Band that poured life into them, as well as his determination on stage not to succumb to the blandishments of harmony and ambient music.

Blacking's embodied thinking about music is immensely useful in relation to the cultural shift that took place at the start of the twentieth century and which was reflected in changing attitudes to music—that is, the inclusion as Maholy-Nagy says of 'sounds of all kinds' (Maholy-Nagy 1925: 48) and the development of atonal music. Blacking prefers to call music 'ordered sound', which makes more sense when trying to understand this period of change that seems to redefine 'music':

> Music is a product of the behaviour of human groups, whether formal or informal: it is humanly organised sound. And, although different societies tend to have different ideas about what they regard as music, all definitions are based on some consensus of opinion about the principles on which sounds of music should be organised. No such consensus can exist until there is some common ground of experience, and unless different people are able to hear and recognise patterns in the sounds that reach their ears (Blacking 1973: 10).

The shift in the early twentieth century away from the structures of the well tempered keyboard also indicates a new stress on listening and the listener, since their compliance could no longer be guaranteed. This propels them into prominence. Blacking's point is that to ask the difference between noise and music, or sound and music, is to fail to see the origin of music in people's embodied engagement with the world: redefinitions of music indicate a shift in cultural norms.

> We can no longer study music as a thing in itself when research in ethnomusicology makes it clear that musical things are not always strictly musical, and that the expression of tonal relationships in patterns of sound may be secondary to extramusical relationships which the tones represent (Blacking 1973: 25).

Blacking sees music as originating in the body and bodily engagement with material form.

> Both Stravinsky and the Venda insist that music involves man. The regular beats of an engine or a pump may sound like the beats of a drum, but no Venda would regard them as music or expect to be moved by them, because their order is not directly produced by human beings. The sound of electronic instuments or of a Moog synthesiser would not be excluded from their realm of musical experience as long as it was only the timbre and not the method of ordering that was outside human control. Venda music is founded not on melody, but on a rhythmical stirring of the whole body of which singing is but one extension. Therefore when we seem to hear a rest between two drumbeats, we must realise that for the player it is not a rest: each drumbeat is the part of a total body movement in which the hand or a stick strikes the drum skin (Blacking 1979: 27).

New stage 'Gestalten' consist of fusing the visual and the heard into new forms. The phenomenology of sound, recast since Husserl into embodied thinking, helps us to understand how directors harness the 'apperceptive' quality of sound to immediate communicated meaning. Don Ihde offers a visualisation or model of how each sense, seeing and hearing, works. The visual field can be described as a circle of vision which is 'constantly full' but has a very central focus, like a bull's eye at the centre with the field. This was touched on earlier in regard to light. Around the bull's eye objects gradually fade in clarity to the 'horizon of invisibility'—the edge of the field. The auditory field in contrast is much more like a sphere with a far less well defined 'horizon of silence'. In the visual field are mute, still objects, and moving sounding objects. To create a sound, movement must take place. Within the field of hearing, there are (obviously) no mute objects but there are objects that are seen to move and make a sound. There are also objects that you hear, but cannot be seen. Thus it is the *overlap* of visual and auditory fields (moving objects that are seen and heard) and the ability to wrench these apart, where I suggest that new stage 'Gestalten' emerge. This is exactly the overlap where skilled directors like Lepage work. His visible clicking of moving sticks on stage suddenly connects to an area outside the 'overlap', an invisible area which cannot be seen but is heard loudly via recorded sound—co-present space, all permeating, timeless. Use of sound in this way makes the absent and the unsounding suddenly present.

This is well illustrated by John Collins's descriptions of his formative encounters with sound when he first recognised it as a 'performance' as opposed to a 'design' element.[18] His first realisation came from witnessing Kate Valk of the Wooster Group raise her arm to make the gesture of throwing a shot glass to the floor. She paused, and the sound effect, which went ahead anyway, made her look up to the sound box in surprise: Collins described his realisation at that moment that there was another 'performer' there besides Kate Valk; and as if in confirmation of this, Valk began to play with the sound, throwing her arm up again and again to hear the sound of glass shattering. Subsequently, he began to look for actions to assign sounds to—for example, sampling the creaking of the set as performers moved on it. The sounds he created for *To You The Birdie* (Riverside Studios, London, 2002) rely on the overlap of visual and auditory fields described above, since he created a sound for everything the 'birdie' hit in the game of badminton—for example each different racquet, the floor, or the softer sound of it hitting the trough behind the stage. He had no cues, just a set of rules and live action: as he described it, 'sixty one keys and two eyes'. The result was a highly active and highly unpredictable soundscape, a vital performative element of the piece. He also talked about playing with the sounds of things you cannot see, which is in effect playing with the visual and auditory overlaps: in production of *Hamletmachine* by Marcus Stern (Yale 1990) which Collins referred to, a performer walked off stage and the audience heard sounds of him destroying the lobby, but as he walked back on stage the sounds continued.

One of Schlemmer's own methods of 'terrestrially anchoring' the sound of the spheres is discovered in the overlap of visual and auditory: getting the materials themselves to generate the noises on stage.[19] This is true of *Glass Dance* and *Stick Dance*, for example, where the noise of the material itself was used (glass and wood claves). Less easily recognised but equally metaphysically suggestive is the sound of his famous musical clown character, sound that was earthed into the material of his costume. We remember Schlemmer's reverence for the holiness of clowning and popular theatre forms. Albert Flocon recalled in conversation with Raman Schlemmer in 1994:

> Sometimes the Musical Clown used a cello . . . a sort of case whose strings were electrified, I think, so that they sounded different, or the sounding knobs were left open, I don't know, but he pulled out the most wonderful things from it. Later I saw the clown Grock and I found that there was a great similarity between them, for example the instrument would make a sound and he would go round and round as if it were a bomb, and you wondered what on earth it was, it was like a haunted object. Then he came back again and another sound came out, and he was absolutely shocked, and ran around again . . . All these features, the movements, the curiosity, the fright and finally the triumph were wonderfully expressed (Flocon 1994: 68).

Here sounding material drives the action.[20] In contrast, he once cast overt metaphysical material into a 'Gestalt' of sound/words and action in *House of Pi*. The difficulties of this piece demonstrated the complexity of words and confirmed to him the need to retain the more direct link to materials. With the spoken words of *House of Pi* (consisting of the strings of phrases by the Astrologer on the roof) he felt unable to be sonically as precise as he needed to be. Precision was always essential in his stage action (Flocon 1994: 63). The piece was abandoned. Sound was complicated enough to mould into stage 'Gestalten' without the richness of semiotic import.

Schlemmer always wanted to articulate the stage space using the elements in their simplest form. In the case of sound, this meant recognising and harnessing its phenomenolial essence, i.e. the fact that sound is either directional or surrounding within the auditory field.

Schlemmer himself simply (at least at Dessau) tended to avoid the surroundability of sound: instead of music he accentuated the directionality of sound by using percussion, and sharply sounding humanly generated noises (grunts and howls and whistles and so on) and thereby attempted to make it a more precise dramaturgical instrument. Both apects of sound however, its surroundability and its directionality, are the key to successful employment of sound theatrically:

> This double dimensionality of auditory field characteristics is at once the source of much ambiguity and of a specific richness which subtly pervades the auditory dimension of existence (Ihde 1976: 76).

The twin aspects also reveal why sound presents particular problems and opportunities when moved around. The auditory field or sphere is itself omnidirectional, that is sound can come from any direction, and 'while the field of sound surrounds me it does not do so with anything like a constant homogeneity' (Ihde 1976: 75). In other words, sound can be quite dense from one direction and slight from another, and this can change constantly. The sounds are either directional or surrounding—that is, they either draw attention to where they have come from (sharper directional sounds, for example clicking type noises) or they tend to envelop the hearer (surrounding tones). Despite this, some extravagant claims are made for sound revealing space:

> The thing about sound is that it doesn't travel through out the universe, it's kind of locally produced. It's incredibly site specific in that sense, so that you and I talking in this room are sounding differently than we would in any other room . . . Through acoustics you actually sense volume, texture and configuration . . . I'm acutely aware, when I go into a space, of listening to the space (Helyer 1999: 2).

and:

> The spatial properties of sound, usually relatively ignored, are for Audio Arts[21] at least as interesting as its temporal ones. In fact the two are interwoven. A sound is not instantaneous but exists for a period of time: how it modifies over that time, how it decays, will depend on

the acoustic qualities of the space, and it is therefore possible to 'map' a space using sound, producing an audible imprint or image of it (Furlong 1994: 121).

Despite such optimistic claims for the power of spatial articulation through sound, on the whole the clues it gives through its echoes are not at all precise, though they may give a rough indication of the size of the space for example, since sound is good at revealing distances; and possibly in the case of very acute listeners, it may reveal the nature of some of the materials contained within the space, through echo. Failures in 'moving' sound around a space are to do with not taking account of the 'surroundability' of sound and the way we tend not to notice the specific origin of the sound if it is not sharp. To move sound around the space effectively requires exploiting the directionality of sound and selecting sharper noises.[22] When a more suitable sharp directional sound in a space is used to 'move' around the space this can be harnessed to theatrical ends. Any attempt to articulate space through sound needs to understand and use the sharpness of directionality. Schlemmer's percussion was chosen, instinctively, for exactly this reason, whilst remaining on a fairly basic level of space articulation. As technology became more available to exploit the 'sounding' of space, sound quickly moved away from the mechanical into the meaningful. What sound does do well, and which Schlemmer recognised in his Musical Clown, is display simultaneous concreteness and fluidity, and it is this that contemporary art exploits to the full: its phenomenological qualities. This is particularly apparent in the growth of sound art over the past fifty years. Fluxus artists were perhaps the first to harness the phenomenology of sound to their art (Kahn 1993: 101–120) including Joseph Beuys who also used the 'sounding' as much as the sound in his work (Tisdal 1979: 86, 95). But with the growth of technology, artists have fully realised the 'new music' Schlemmer dreamed of: spatial articulation via sound, intimately harnessed to communicated meaning.

Bruce Naumann's installation in the Turbine Hall of the Tate Modern in 2004, *Raw Materials*, consisted of bands of sound crossing the space from twenty pairs of speakers. Although Laura Cumming as reviewer (Cumming 2004b) does mention the semiotic content of the voices, impact really arose from the low level of noise from the speakers ('A big party of children would have to be silenced to hear it'), from the discrete beams of sound in 'that grand canyon of emptiness', and from 'the experience itself, which is of pausing, wandering, listening, drawing close to a speaker, ascending staircases, returning to the start'. Certainly, from personal experience, the physical experience of moving amidst the sounds is the strongest memory of it. 'Coming in feels almost like going out—an audible breeze threatening to swell into a blizzard, waves breaking and withdrawing, the open air tuned to so many sounds that your own are absorbed in the rise and fall of murmurs, shouts, susurrations, plosives, stutters and echoes' (Cumming

2004b: 13). And the sound itself is abstracted, semiotic content reduced: 'words decoupled from meanings, signs from signifiers, voices from decontextualised, disparate works opposed'.

Similarly, in Susan Hillier's work *Witness* the mysterious words ("'It had wings like a bat', 'It flew faster than any jet', 'There was a sudden silver light', 'I know I didn't dream it'") seem to owe their impact as much or more to the way the phrases hit your ears as they do to their semiotic content: 'You are in your own dark cloud of unknowing. The wires tremble, the light flickers, the chorus fluctuates, now here, now there. And somehow, the voice you are listening to so closely becomes the only audible voice, echoing from somewhere else as the room falls silent. The piece feels like a phenomenal visitation in itself' (Cumming 2004a). Janet Cardiff too uses the phenomenology of sound, the way it hits your ears, to create her sculptures. At its simplest her sublime *Forty Part Motet* (National Gallery of Canada, Ontario) simply sets up forty speakers in eight groups to enable the audience to wander round and sample the individual voices of the polyphonic music. As an 'audience' you can play with the streams of music by moving around the sound sculpture, letting it hit your ears differently minute by minute, second by second, or simply sitting and absorbing the directional sounds. This splitting up of separate parts of the orchestra was used similarly in Anna Best's *PHIL* (2002), except that the different instrumental parts were separated in time and place before being brought together in a final performance. The listening was delicate, intimate, personal, a solitary player and a single instrument, placed centre stage in people's living rooms, the audience honoured, elevated in status: oddly moving and strangely emotional, the piece derived its impact from the phenomenology of its presentation, the embodied experience of its initial and solitary reception by the chosen few.

Ross Brown postulates, rightly I believe, that whereas in the Enlightenment visuality moved to the fore, being more akin with rationality and logic, now the 'Postmodern processes belong more to the ear' (Brown 2005: 105): that is, processes involve motion, together with shifting and permeable boundaries. Anthropologists and art critics have demonstrated how visualism continues to dominate consciousness, at least in the Western world, to the devaluing—even exclusion—of the other senses (Bloomer and Moore 1977, Classen 1997, Jay 1988, Kahn 2001 and Synnott 1991). Paul Stoller worked as an anthropologist amongst the Songhay of the Niger, who told him continually that he would have to learn to hear; his Western ears simply could not perceive as theirs did (Stoller 1984). David Howes examines this dominant visualism in Western art, symbolised by Dürer's alienating drawing grid, objectifying the world in a framed perspectival picture, a space created by logic, that nowhere actually exists (Howes 1991: 5). In this way, the use of perspective in visual art reinforced Western ideas of a mind/body dualism, feeding the sense of abstract, mindful perfection just out of reach. Compared to the clarity of vision, with its ability to define and clarify instantaneously, the sense of hearing seems clumsy, vague, elusive, the sounds it grasps forever vanishing; most of the time we hardly hear all there is to hear, as Cage reminded us in *4'33"*. Yet the very fact the postmodern stage has grasped the endless capacities, capabilities and possibilities of this stage element is testimony to the loosening hold of the dualist mind cast of the Enlightenment. Perhaps it is only now that Modernity on the stage is truly beginning.

If Schlemmer felt safest harnessing and simplifying the quiddity or essence of sound rather than its liquidity, through the 'sounding' of physical form, and pushing it therefore towards the articulation of space and not Expressionist 'vibration', he was nevertheless fatally limited by the technology of his day. But he anticipated the future by identifying and working with the phenomenology of sound, recognising its intimate links with motion, plasticity and the body. He moved beyond the Bauhaus essentialist 'apperceptive' reception. There are two aspects to this: firstly, the development of experimental sound and sound art since the 1920s, and secondly, the use the postmodern stage has made of sound. Both these developments owe a huge debt to technology. Those practitioners, some of them at the Bauhaus, who were moving away from the Expressionist ethereality of sound into manipulating its physical properties, moving into a phenomenological, physical and 'terrestrial anchoring' of it were stopped in their tracks by the upheavals in Europe but in doing so they liberated sound from much of the baggage it carried from the eighteenth and nineteenth centuries in relation to sound/colour correspondences, theories that were equally poised between science and, frankly, mumbo-jumbo; at the same time sound was established as a spatial articulator that could synthesise idea and action, both off stage (as sound art) and on stage. The Bauhaus stood at the cusp of this final abandonment of Romanticism and the beginning of the phonograph revolution in attitudes to sound, as described by Douglas Kahn (Kahn 1992: 5–14).There is increasing recognition in Germany that music and sound provide a far clearer linking thread between the Bauhaus and the later avant-garde in America, than performance *per se*, particularly via Black Mountain College (Schoon 2006). The following chapter pursues 'phonographic' sound further in relation to our perception of time: it moves into areas that are necessarily speculative as far as Schlemmer himself is concerned, but areas that are central to the postmodern stage.

7 Time

It is May 2007. I am at the MACBA (Museu d'Art Contemporani de Barcelona) exhibition *Un Teatro Sin Teatro* (*A Theatre Without Theatre*). I watch films of events that took place when I was a child: Allan Kaprow's *Fluids* (1967), where heavy blocks of ice continually threaten to dissolve as a wall is agonisingly built by the participants, pressing their foreheads to the unyielding surfaces, and a blow torch melts and joins the seams, after which the wall is lovingly hand scrubbed and textured into existence; Robert Whitman's long vanished *American Moon* (1960) in the Reuben Gallery New York with its 'very rough' set of card and polythene, daubed paint, cloth and canvas making 'layers of space' continually revealed through the polythene, the figure on a swing sweeping suddenly and startlingly above the audience in the circular central enclosed space. Claes Oldenburg explains how Whitman has a 'feel for slow time' and can put you in a space and make it feel different, creating a claustrophic, intimate experience, opening up the space or closing it down 'one way or another'. Judith Malina of the Living Theatre describes how her mininalist sets are brought about through lack of money not aesthetic principle and yet how the sparseness suits the work; how when we are on stage we are in a heightened state, responsive and alert—'then I am responsible, aware'. Finally I stare at a video by Peter Friedl, *Liberty City* (2007). I am drawn to this sequence of a policeman being beaten up over and over again. I feel voyeuristic but am compelled to watch it to the end. Eventually I realise it is on an endless loop, the beating will never end, time has been stretched and I have been fooled. My mind is ever in the Schlemmer room on the second floor, where next to the photographs of Schlemmer as Musical Clown, and opposite the mounted production photographs including Feininger's photograph of the white figure standing on stage amidst the taut white rope lines,[1] and behind the glass cases of documents and published works, the space is dominated by the huge reconstruction of *Hoop Dance* (see Figure 4.1) on a stage at the end of the room. Periodically set in motion mechanically, its intriguing space, both centreless and multicentred, connects in my mind with the fluidity and materiality of Kaprow's ice wall, with the expanding and contracting space of Whitman's *American Moon* and its 'slow time';

with the performer's heightened sensibility on stage at the Living Theatre that Judith Malina identified and the minimalism of means she used; and finally with the sense of linear time slipping away from me in Friedl's video. In all these there are pluralities of meaning and the uncertain contours of experience; yet they also appear to engage with form in a particularly rich and enigmatic way. This tension is exhilerating. Moreover the aesthetics are intimately connected to the material world from which and for which these artists forged their works, not a mystical 'beyond' which as Molina pointed out avoids the here and now reality.

This theme of structure and form will be played out in this chapter at least initially in terms of time, analysed through sound, before returning to the question of formalism within postmodern performance. Of all stage elements, time is most closely associated with space and motion, Schlemmer's chosen material. Time is at the very heart of the stage at the Bauhaus in that (as I have shown) it directly confronted, examined and asked questions of dynamism, change and motion: in short, time itself.[2] His treatment of it was very different from that of his painter contemporaries. As explored in the previous chapter, it was partly because they were aware of the 'limitation' of painting (i.e. it was not a time-based art) that by translating musical structures into painterly terms they attempted to supply the missing element of time. Schlemmer, however, plunged into time itself via performance. He was acutely aware of the ability of performance to embed the spectator in an experience unfolding in time, though he did not necessarily value painting any the less for lacking it:

> In Kierkegaard I recently came across an idea, roughly this: the most abstract idea conceivable is sensory, erotic genius, and music is its one and only form of expression. Surely dance must also be counted as part of this realm, because it, like music, is a portrayal of the immediately-present erotic as a 'succession of moments,' in contrast to painting and sculpture, which realize it in a single moment (February 1918) (Schlemmer [1958] 1977: 28).

Painting in the early twentieth century had always had a status which most stage work then lacked, and he often referred to the stage as a temptation, an ephemeral art with no artifact to survive the ages, which he should perhaps resist. Yet it is the very capacity of stage work to realise itself in time that he values.

> I readily acknowledge that I came to the dance from painting and sculpture, and as a result I am bound to appreciate dance's essential element, movement, more keenly, because the expressive range of painting and sculpture by their nature is restricted to the static and rigid, to 'movement captured in a fixed moment' (September 1931) (Schlemmer [1958] 1977: 131).

Questions about time and the audience's experience of time are insistently present within contemporary stage performance and performance art. This is not a new phenomenon. Our apprehension of time in the course of witnessing a performance, even a straighforward fictional tale, is complex, and always has been. Aristotle was aware of the slippery boundaries between fictional time/space and 'real' time and space. Hence he carefully set up his rules of unity, in order that form and control were not lost, and one of these was unity of time, where the performance of fictional action was supposed to cover the same time as it approximately would in real life. In fictional drama as it later developed in Europe, from the medieval Mystery Plays onwards, the ability of drama to span times and places was used to create rich fables, and only rarely was a playwright's conscience troubled by the tricky demands of the classical models of Greece and Rome; attempts were made to conform but, in the main, not strictly. More recently in the twentieth century certain playwrights have played with and distorted the *idea* of consecutive time when unfolding plot;[3] but far more exciting and radical experimental approaches to time took place in the live art of the late 1950s and early 1960s. John Cage radicalised music into a different performed art, more closely allied to performance art than to music as traditionally defined, by concentrating on duration rather than frequency (harmony) in sound: '[T]he important perameter of sound, is not frequency but rather duration, because duration is open to noise, as well as to what has been called musical' (Cage in Kostelanetz 1988: 51). Joseph Beuys played with our sense of time in his performance events. In *24 hours . . . and in us . . . under us . . . land under* the use of sound is described as 'disrupting the physical perception of time' (Tisdall 1979: 97).[4] Whilst Robert Wilson's use of slow motion action and repetition beginning with his earliest staged works has long been acknowledged as disrupting our sense of time, in the forty or so years since he began his extraordinary articulations of space many other groups on stage have consciously focused on the experience of time. Contemporary performance often provokes us into losing the sense of time passing when watching the non-narrative, fragmentary, and repetitious action of groups such as Goat Island and Forced Entertainment (especially their durational pieces). Bock and Vincenzi clearly play with time as part of their physical and visceral interrogation of philosophical enigmas.[5] *The Infinite Pleasures of the Great Unknown* (Toynbee Studios 2008) pointed up time as one of its subjects by the presence of a huge digital clock face at the front of the stage which seemed to bear no relation to the repetitious and nightmarish action taking place in the performance space behind, a sense heightened by the beat of the relentless music. I would like to suggest, however, that ideas of form and structure, in Kaprow's sense, can be applied to the stage in relation to time and our perception of it less randomly than these examples suggest. Sound, which has been (rightly I believe) described as challenging the hitherto dominant visuality in our Western culture (Brown 2005), is a major stage tool that enables us to work with time, since sound space is not Euclidean space (whose measurable delineations 'match' clock time): it surrounds and it invades us. Why we should want to enter such a space, and do so frequently and willingly on contemporary stages, will emerge in this chapter. Meaning and directorial intent is intimately tied up with the physical deployment of the stage elements, and the ability to manipulate the fluid and interpenetrating structures of the postmodern stage distinguishes the best of latter-day directors, who are surely and truly the 'poets' that Schlemmer envisioned (Schlemmer 1925: 19, Gropius and Wensinger [1961] 1996: 29).

Time cannot be apprehended by any of our senses; we cannot see, hear, smell, taste or touch time, yet we are all aware of it. And our personal sense of time, the way time presents itself to us as we engage with the world, seems to run alongside, but rarely matches, the evenly measured divisions of the clock. We have to keep checking, to see how much time has passed. In Chapter 4, the shortcomings of 'clock-time' were revealed through the paradox of Zeno. The primary purpose there was to demonstrate that motion was not a simple phenomenon, since space cannot be divided up into so many discrete units and neither can time. Logic of course demands that we do both in order to think and make sense of the world and our dealings with it. Such logical systems have their limits, as the nonsense of Zeno's paradox demonstrates; logic cannot cope with time and change, such as takes place in motion. Our personal experience of time is nothing like the seconds, hours and minutes of measured time; it seems to run fast or slow depending on what activity we are engaged in. The logic of present, past and future is of course also a nonsense, since what is the present? How small a unit of time constitutes 'now'?

Allan Kaprow, with echoes of Bergsonian time 'durée', records that time moves at different speeds for different people as if it is a well-known truth:

> Time, which follows closely on space considerations, should be variable and discontinuous . . . this is 'real' or 'experienced' time, as distinct from conceptual time . . . Real time is always connected with doing something, with an event of some kind, and so is bound up, with things and spaces (Kaprow 1966: 191–2).

Kaprow takes as self-evident that time is bound up with 'doing something' and with 'things and spaces'.[6] Similarly, Yvonne Rainer says:

> Thirty seconds began to seem like the right interval length. I did not realise until much later that a given duration can seem long or short depending on what is put into it (Sandford 1995: 163).

This notion of 'experienced' time is that of Henri Bergson, whose ideas have already been discussed in relation to objects. Bergson's perception of the indivisibility of space and objects extends into the indivisibility of time, to what he calls 'duration' (Bergson [1946] 1968: 176, 212–3). Kaprow and Rainer are both arguing for a Bergsonian view of time, time as 'duration' or *durée*, not measured by the clock, not subject to cognitive division and measurement, time experienced without reference to past and present and future. Laermans describes the use of 'affective silence' by some directors as a pause between two aesthetic communications that is 'elongated, stretched and thus stressed. Time becomes *durée*, 'felt' or experienced Time'(Laermans 1999: 4). But Bergson, clear as he is in his metaphysics, in all puts little emphasis on practical measures as to how we can deliberately place ourselves in durational time, seeming to assume that once its existence is recognised, we can always move from 'clock time' to 'time durée'. On the contrary, this challenge exercises the minds and the imagination of performance artists like little else. Kaprow and Rainer insist, like Bergson, that it is reached via experience of the material world, but unlike Bergson give plenty of exercises (at least in Kaprow's case) for reaching it. This is another 'alchemy' of the ordinary, to use Kaprow's words (Kaprow [1958] 1993: 9), in this instance in terms of time.

Writing on contemporary performance often refers to this different experience of time as 'durée' or felt time while watching productions, in Robert Wilson particularly (Quadri 1984: 76–82). Holmberg comments that Wilson 'moves the theatre towards interior time: the infinity of meditation . . . a process of distension' (Holmberg 1996: 162). His elongation of a single action—famously, the mother murdering her child in *Deafman Glance* (Holmberg 1996: 4–5) and taking forty-five minutes to do so—is a visual device but enveloped in the power of silence, punctuated by two screams. The fusion of the concrete and experiential (itself ephemeral) is theatre's enigma: and also that of sound. There is no way of knowing if it is the sound or the hypnotic visuals, or a combination of the two that most contributes to the variable sense of time that we experience watching Wilson. However, the connection between sound and time persistently intrudes in any analysis of the postmodern stage.

The notion of time has proved to be one of the greatest problems for philosophers, but continues to be the richest of mysteries for artists and directors, and often sound, and our reception of sound, seems intimately bound up with it:

> 'From the beginning of recorded time', says la Monte [Young] 'people have always wanted to understand their relationship to a universal structure and time. Even in as simple a way as where do we come from, why are we here and where are we going? I point out that our entire concept of time is dependent on an understanding of periodicity. Time is depending on night and day, the periodic rotations of the planets, the stars, the periodic functions of our bodies, and the seasons, all these various periodic events, and without them we really have no universal structure. What I have learnt is that it goes very slowly' (Kahn 1993: 104).

Leaving aside Young's enigmatic comment here that 'it goes very slowly', he is right that periodicity structures our perception of time. This is important in the context of the Bauhaus stage, because, as I have argued in the previous chapter, Schlemmer came to concentrate in the Dessau work on a new function for sound in performance, one that in effect concentrated more on the periodicity and materiality of sound than its harmony. Later in the twentieth century, a whole branch of avant-garde music, led by John Cage, and which (to avoid confusion) perhaps is more properly designated performance art than music *per se*, rejected harmony in music and experimented instead with its periodicity and functioning or material action in space.

Since clock time (that is, the time that most of us think of as time, i.e. seconds, minutes, hours etc.) is closely bound up with space and spatial divisions in the attempt logically to quantify and measure it (for example, object A or planet B takes so many seconds/minutes/hours to pass point Z etc.) these new approaches to sound via periodicity implicate time. When artists address the problem of more fluid, personal and phenomenologically perceived time, it is periodicity to which they turn. Goat Island commonly use this technique, in for example in *The Lastmaker* (BAC, London 2008). Goat Island's website (Goat Island 2009) describes the 'architectural dance' in this piece which is performed in lengthy 'detailed triadic rounds' with a temporal dulling effect and which are followed by faster (and often noisy and disparate) action. Repeated action is, however, rather a blunt instrument for the manipulation of time in the audience and, from personal experience, can pall. A better and more accurate tool is sound, and frequently and consistently it is the periodicity of sound—and silence—that artists turn to. Applying Schlemmer's analytical methods of space to sound (i.e. concentrating on how it presents itself in space, what it *is*, rather than what it means) may enable us to understand how space affects or even structures the perception of time for the audience in some highly visual and often non-narrative contemporary work.

As Shirley MacWilliam points out, sound is more obviously connected with time than other phenomena: 'Sound is qualitatively governed by time and the ear is subject to a linearity of perception, the attack and decay of sound' (MacWilliam 1998: 32). If sound and time are so intimately connected, the clue may lie in the phenomenon of sound and how it presents itself. Such an analysis takes the phenomenon of 'perceived time' beyond assigning its effects to 'subjectivity'. In pursuit of this recognising the attack and decay of sound is extremely useful, as here:

> When I listen to auditory events there seems to be no way in which I can escape the sense of 'coming into being' and a 'passing from being' in the modulated motions of sound. Here temporality is not a matter of 'subjectivity' but a matter of the way the phenomenon presents itself. I cannot 'fix' the note nor make it 'come to stand before me', and there is an objectivelike recalcitrance to its motion (Ihde 1976: 94).

Ihde goes on to explain in fairly complex philosophical terms how the phenomenon of sound presents itself. For our purposes, however, to understand how a sound might function in the theatre, it is enough to recognise that every sound presents itself as a temporal unit, which has three parts. The first is a welling up, or coming into being which has a 'leading edge' or a 'source point'. The second phase is a 'running off' of the phenomenon in retentions such as reverberations and echoes. These 'sink into the just-past' so that the horizon or edge of the auditory field then appears (i.e. the sound is no longer heard) and the sound becomes memory (the third phase) for the first time. Don Ihde's three ways of listening are, firstly, that we focus on the leading edge of a sound, or, secondly, the trailing off period, or, finally, we can have a much more general experience of the sound 'washing over' us, and these three modes of listening roughly correspond to the three parts of the temporal unit of sound. Theatre can deliberately oscillate our focus between these three listening modes so that meaning emerges not only from the semiotic content of what we hear (which is not dealt with here) but its mode of reception in the space—which is the same as its articulation of the space.

The first mode of listening is when we focus on the leading edge of a sound, for example being told to listen for a sound as a signal, such as a buzz or a click to prompt us to press a button. An example of the second mode, when we focus on the trailing off period of a sound rather than the leading edge, might be listening to a tone of a musical instrument to determine what note it is. In these two modes of listening there is normally the 'ratio of focal-to-fringe inversions' as there is with a visual focus. This means that the part focused on tends to have the effect of pushing the other part that is not in focus into the fringe of the field; as we shall discover, directors can use this for their own purposes. The third type of listening, the broad or open focus, can be compared to the sudden visual opening up of a vista before our eyes.[7] In the parallel auditory experience, the field is opened up, letting the experience surround and enrich us; Ihde uses the example of listening to an orchestra. Ihde's descriptions are a plausible paradigm model, useful in understanding how sound hits our ears in a space thereby contributing to the articulation of space, perception of time and engendering of meaning. The models are especially useful to understand the rather focused act of listening that a performance involves. The types of listening or different modes of focus can occur separately as Ihde describes but they also work together in theatre, and can be deliberately structured to do so.

In the Lepage example given in the last chapter, the clicking of gambling sticks in *The Dragon's Trilogy* (Barbican Centre, London, 2005) are 'leading edge' sounds but because they are subsequently amplified off stage and through the space (into a 'charged' space, we remember, where clock time retreats) the 'running off' phase is more noticed. Each sound ceases and sinks into a 'remembered thing' but within a whole fabric of remembrances.

What are created within the (ultimately) resulting 'broad and open focus' listening mode (i.e. all the clicks taken together rather than each 'temporal unit') are Bergsonian 'memory images' or Deleuzian 'Time-images' (Sayre 2004: 42–3), themselves closely related to the Derridian interpretation of Freud's 'Mystic Writing Pad', where the present is constantly perceived but overlays an ever-changing-by-being-added-to and ever-diminished-by-forgetting past.[8] Lepage is thus deliberately using the three parts of each temporal unit of sound to build meaning in the piece, a satisfying structured whole. Romeo Castellucci, who always carefully controls and structures the sound within his pieces sometimes in collaboration with the composer Stuart Gibbons, often varies the mode of listening focus so that sound becomes a crucial element in his created 'worlds' (Ridout 2009: 9), and, I would argue, creates the predominant sense of being 'outside time' (12). The intrusion of the leading edge of a sound will often shock the listener and in Castellucci's work frequently is used to return us somehow to the 'present' moment, and that present has all the power of the 'time' or 'memory' image. In *Purgatorio*, the father is lying on the floor of the living room writhing with (quite literally) uncontrolled movements[9] and the music that is playing in contrast to the movements has a compelling rhythm, a pulsating sound as if from a synthesiser, a rhythm faintly picked up in the subtle pulse of lights in the window stage left; the rhythmic sense is compounded by a deep bass heart beat also underlying the music. Our mode of listening here is 'broad and open focus'. Cut into this is the irregular loud sound of something breaking, perhaps bricks or rubble, one cannot tell precisely, but because of its irregularity one is forced to listen out for the leading edge of the sound that continually disrupts the rhythmic sounds. In each 'temporal unit' of this sound (because they repeat often close together), our focus is split since the trailing off period seems equally to demand attention since it is irregular in length and therefore not temporally helpful (i.e. not helpful in placing us in clock time). Later this irregular sound changes (when the grown up son, rather than, as earlier, the father, is writhing on the floor) to something sharper, perhaps more like breaking crockery but the mode of listening is the same. As always, this takes many words to dissect and analyse but is experienced all in one moment rather than cognitively grasped. Oscillating patterns of listening also seem to operate in the unbearably long sound tape, 'The Music' which accompanies the abuse of the young boy by his father, acts unseen upstairs, but heard. I have no idea how long this scene lasted except that we seemed to move outside time in the endless unrecognisable random sounds of supposed and unbearable violation that are intercut with the clearly heard and recognisable sounds of the boy's words as he speaks. Again I here omit what is actually said to concentrate on what meanings are communicated by the phenomenological perception of the sounds. It is hard to describe the tortuous effect of this oscillation between the two modes of listening, leading edge and focused, except to say that it somehow returned the listener to the continuous and unending present of oneself sitting in an audience seat, forced to witness a 'present' and presence, reinforced by the naturalistic unchanging broad image of the domestic living room set, somehow impersonal, unyielding, filmic, black and white, muted behind a screen, that situated itself before our gaze. The 'focus to fringe' ratio mentioned earlier may also contribute to the unbearable intensification of sound here as each sound 'unit' seems to demand equal focus on its leading edge and its trailing off period, both screaming as it were for our attention. And the third phase, when the sound becomes remembered for the first time, is never allowed to become 'past' because of the inexorable repetition of the units. This was time harnessed for dramaturgical effect and immersive experience, largely achieved by sound articulating the space.

The distortion of time is the focus of many sound artists whose work and techniques have largely developed over the past forty or so years. David Toop quotes Pauline Oliveros who describes recording in a large reverberating cistern that exaggerates and makes physically obvious the temporal aspects of sound units. She describes what happens when the units breakdown as they collide and overlap:

> In 1988, that's when we went into that big cistern and recorded . . . When I was trying to write the linear notes, I was trying to come to some conclusion about what it was we were actually doing in there. The two words came together—deep listening—because it's a very challenging space to create music in, where you have a forty-five second reverberation coming back at you. The sound is so well mirrored, so to speak, that it's hard to tell direct sound from the reflective sound. It puts you in the deep listening space. You're hearing the past, of sound that you've made; you're continuing it possibly, so that you are right in the present, and you're anticipating the future, which is coming at you from the past . . . So it puts you into the simultaneity of time, which is quite wonderful, but it's a challenge to maintain it and stay concentrated (Toop 1995: 248–9).

Oliveros claims here to have experienced a 'simultaneity of time' through the breakdown of sound's temporal units. This would seem to refer to the letting-go of notions of past, present and future on which clock time relies. When La Monte Young wrote his piece *Composition 1960#7*, which consisted of the notes B and F sharp being held for a long time, he too appeared to be getting away from the periodicity of measuring time (which he describes in the quotation earlier), a periodicity which was telescoped, though in a different way, in Oliveros's work in the resounding chamber. In both cases, though Kahn is here only referring to La Monte Young's piece, it could be said that 'Time could no longer be measured as units of sound passed by, nor could any sequential organisation of sound'—and, one might add, time—'exist' (Kahn 1993: 108). An extreme example of this is the use of 'white noise' to distort the audience's perception of space; and equally, the use of silence.

White noise is 'acoustically colourless—equally anonymous, feature-less and unpredictable at all frequencies, and hence at whatever speed it is played'(Barrow 1995: 20). The effect of white noise filling the space is very disorienting. The word 'disorientating' indicates a spatial orientation (or that at least is the first assumption) but it is possible the disorientation extends into time, given the links between sound and time:

> Conversely when one is purposefully placed in the presence of a single sounding tone which does not vary and in which the depth of fore-ground to background features is eliminated, this presence can not only be deeply disturbing, but it begins to approximate the solid 'now-ness' of the stable visual object and time sensing 'returns' to its location 'in oneself' (Ihde 1976: 94).

In hearing white noise, this field becomes a solid surrounding sphere with no variation of directional sound, and no sense of a border to the audi-tory field, no horizon of silence. It is important to understand how sound fixes time as direction, that is, the minute *time difference* between a sound hitting first one ear and then the other is crucial for orientating ourselves in space. The Gestalt thinker David Katz makes explicit the crucial con-nection of the directionality of sound and space with time: 'It is as if time "stiffens" when direction is localized in space'(Katz 1950: 36). White noise denies us this fixing of time as direction through sound.

Similarly, silence denies us this fixing of time as direction through sound, and all that was said of white noise applies to silence. Again, Castellucci is acutely aware of the power of silence, or at least the oddly quiet, to distort our sense of time in this way and uses silence to devastating effect in *Purga-torio*.[10] In the first half of the piece, sound and its absence builds to distort our apprehension of the 'naturalistic' action in front of us so that the action (to use the words of Nicholas Ridout) 'seems to take place out of time' (Rid-out 2009: 12). Silence dominates the action until 'The Music' (the sound sequence of abuse described previously). This is in stark contrast to *Inferno* where sound is a dominant force from the start. The silence that leads us into *Purgatorio* is not complete, however, but mixed with subtle features that further distort our sense of place and therefore time. There is the muted sound of the television which the little boy watches but whose screen we cannot see; in this piece, screens are used throughout to implicate us in the act of viewing. Occasional words are spoken but they are further 'silenced' and removed from their utterance in time by their subsequent repetition in written form on the 'invisible' transparent projecting screen that covers the stage opening in front, even as the actions themselves in the living room are distanced into a filmic space by their being always anticipated by the pro-jected words. The projection screen clouds and faintly blurs our grasp of the space/time. In contrary fashion to silencing the words, the ordinary sounds of washing up and slicing fruit are magnified and so, conversely, point up their silent envelope (see Figure 7.1). Nothing seems quite to match up: the sound hitting our ears does not square naturalistically with the visuals we see. We start to lose our temporal bearings as the space and action begins to recede into filmic distance, somehow utterly ordinary yet utterly obscure and impenetrable. Finally of course the silence is broken; that it is done so by 'The Music' further intensifies our loss of temporal markers.[11]

The work described above is a deliberate manipulation of the space/ time continuum via visuals and sound and is a carefully structured and unfolding series of overlaying structures; we remember definition by Arne Naess of Gestalt structures: 'wholes that are perceived to have an organic identifiable unity in themselves, as a network of relations that can move as one' (Naess 1989: 6), and that 'identity is inherent only in the *relationships* which make up the entity'. Unpacking the relationships is a wordy business, but in the moment of reception they are received without thought.

Music is a particular instance of organised sound[12] and intimately connected to time. Putting aside its capacity for strong emotional effect, music like theatre creates a 'virtual time', that is, a time that is experienced by the listener who simultaneously lets go of 'clock time'. Susanne Langer's *Feeling and Form* (S. Langer 1953: 104–119) and Victor Zuckerkandl's *Sound and Symbol, Music and the External World* (Zuckerkandl 1956: 201–247)

Figure 7.1 *Purgatorio*, directed by Romeo Castellucci, Socìetas Raffaello Sanzio, 2009. Photocredit: Luca del Pia.

fully explore this notion. I want to use insights into time in music to further illuminate the experience of listening, and beyond that, the experience of witnessing a dynamically structured theatre piece, both in terms of its organised soundscape and also in terms of every stage element working together. John Blacking, anthropologist and expert on the music of the Venda tribe, whose ideas were used in the previous chapter, believes that the organising principle of sound is ultimately the body, but the body as it is lived within a culture. There is in other words a symbiotic relationship between organised sound and the culture it both embodies and is born from. Blacking describes hearing music:

> The sound may be the object, but man is the subject; and the key to understanding music is in the relationships existing between subject and object, the activating principle of organisation. Stravinsky expressed this with characteristic insight when he said of his own ethnic music: 'Music is given to us with the sole purpose of establishing an order in things, including, and particularly, the co-ordination between man and time' (Chronicle of My Life [London, Gollancz, 1936], p.83). Every culture has its own rhythm, in the sense that conscious experience is ordered into cycles of seasonal change, physical growth, economic enterprise, genealogical depth or width, life and afterlife, political succession, or any other recurring features that are given significance. We may say that ordinary daily experience takes place in a world of actual time. The essential quality of music is its power to create another world of virtual time[13] (Blacking 1973: 26–7).

Within Western genre terms there is a difficulty differentiating sound and music.[14] Zuckerkandl and Langer, writing in the early 1950s, assume a distinction between sound and music is self-evident. It is worth thinking oneself back into such a pre-Cagean mode of thought, since Zuckerkandl in particular has interesting and illuminating things to say in regard to the properties of music that are more widely applicable to sound and the 'sound space' itself. Despite Zuckerkandl's own awareness of the hermeneutic circle of interpretation, it has to be born in mind that his comments are couched almost solely in terms of Western Classical music, a fact he never mentions (Zuckerkandl 1956: 11–12). His ideas are, however, still valuable, and deserve to be better known. Despite music being the ostensible subject, it is rather Ihde's 'broad and open focus' or MacWilliam's 'reduced mode' of listening (MacWilliam 1998: 33) which is the real subject under discussion in the following pages. Increasingly on the postmodern stage the sound scape is deliberately structured, comparable to a musical piece, and the same is true for many pieces of sound art.[15]

Gustav Mahler says that music may lead to 'the "other world"—the world in which things are no longer subject to time and space' (Blacking 1973: 51). Taking his cue from Schelling, whom he quotes at the start, Zuckerkandl asks, 'What must the world be like,what must I be like, if between me and the world the phenomenon of music can occur? How must I consider the world, how must I consider myself, if I am to understand the reality of music?' (Zuckerkandl 1956: 7) Zuckerkandl is arguing for a transcendence that surpasses our logical constructs of time and space, that is revealed in the actuality of music.[16] He argues for a force, or living dynamism, in music, discernible in terms of musical motion, musical time and musical 'space'. Whereas we normally know a force from the material traces of its action, he points out there are no material phenomena in sound (Zuckerkandl 1956: 56). The dynamic qualities of music will not show up on an oscilloscope. By dynamism he is referring to the way that tones, as 'Gestalten', contain within themselves more than the physical reality itself—for example, he analyses how two notes in a Beethoven piece are in isolation indistinguishable regarding their proper place in the melody, but when combined with the other notes *demand* their appropriate position. This force or dynamism is not part of the make-up of the bare physical vibration of the note itself (which is all the oscilloscope would show). This dynamic sense and power in a piece of music derives from the innate sensitivity to structure, which the audience always has. This sense of structure does not depend on cognitive thought.

In his analysis of musical motion, he concludes, along with Bergson, that the Zenonian analysis of physical space is a nonsense; actually it is the curious 'space' and 'motion' found in music, rather than Zeno's analysis of the 'space of places', that helps us to understand the real nature of the 'normal' physical space around us, the space that was analysed in Chapter 3. This physical space around us is *apparently* a 'space of places' but, Zuckerkandl maintains, music demonstrates that 'Motion must be something else than things changing places' (Zuckerkandl 1956: 128).'Real motion', Bergson asserts, 'is rather the transfer of a state than a thing' (Zuckerkandl 1956: 115); in other words it is a palpable force and the space it takes place in is indivisible. Certainly there are curiosities in sound. Zuckerkandl describes how two voices singing in harmony would, according to physics and analyses on an oscilloscope, be technically 'out' but are 'correct' to the ear (Zuckerkandl 1956: 79–81). Jonathan Rée talks about the 'oil and water mix' of voices, the capacity of sound to be in two 'places' at once, as in a sung or played chord (Rée 1999: 297). 'Formulations that in the world of space are a paradox, indeed nonsense—where ever we go, we return, start and goal are one and the same; all paths travel back to their own beginnings—are in the world of tone simple statements of fact'—all of which Zuckerkandl demonstrates in terms of musical motion and space. He argues convincingly for the indivisibility of space and motion in music, and claims that the space and motion of music are truer descriptions of physical motion and space, were we able to recognise it. Thereby of course time is in reality indivisable. [17]

Zuckerkandl maintains that each tone in music is a 'temporal *Gestalt*'. 'The present of musical metre . . . contains within it a past that is not remembered and a future that is not foreknown—and not as something to be supplied by thought but as a thing directly given in experience itself' (Zuckerkandl 1956: 227). This means that the past and future, that are in fact present in a tone, are not there because of any cognitive act on the part of a listener. 'If we tried by remembering, to make "one" present simultaneously with "two", all perception of metre would instantly cease'; and the same goes for consciously anticipating the metre that we expect to follow.

> Let anyone who is capable of it call to mind the immediately preceding tone of the melody that he is hearing. The instant he does so, he will have lost the thread of the melody . . . It is even a condition of hearing melody that the tone present at the moment should fill consciousness entirely, that nothing should be remembered, nothing except it or beside it be present in consciousness[18] (Zuckerkandl 1956: 231).

The future is part of the temporal Gestalt not through cognitive anticipation; but it is nevertheless sensed and felt, an integral part of the form. This state of being is the exact parallel of Kleist's knowledge without thought, the puppet dancing, the youth who lost his beauty when he thought about it, the bear who punches with accuracy because he does not think, discussed extensively in Chapter 5. The reception of the musical Gestalt takes place outside our normal structures of time: and the musical Gestalt moreover is a temporal Gestalt of past, present and future.

> The totalities that are called *Gestalten* are distinguished by the characteristic that in them the individual part does not acquire meaning from itself (or not exclusively from itself) but receives it from the whole (Zuckerkandl 1956: 225).

The 'whole' in this context is time itself; each tone in a melody contains within it past, present and future. 'The simplest temporal *Gestalt*, the melody, shows the erroneousness of the view that the past can only be given as memory, the future only as foreknowledge' (225). Zuckerkandl's argument for the existence of a non-cognitive perception of time is densely structured on the idea of music and melody, i.e. music as a discrete and special art form. As was said earlier, such a distinction between music and sound is difficult to maintain; a more useful distinction broadly depends on the mode of listening which each kind of sound draws upon. In the 'broad and open' mode of listening, or 'reduced listening'[19] this non-cognitive 'holding' in perception of past and future is exactly as Zuckerkandl describes. This non-cognitive awareness of the 'simultaneity' of time is present in the audience throughout the experience of a theatre piece, and it is this that the structures of theatre depend upon.

Jaqueline Martin and William Sauter address the problem of structure taking into account the perception of the audience, and this is closely tied up with time. The process of the audience making sense of information they describe in terms of the 'hermeneutic circle', which is itself a Gestalt, and closely connected to phenomenological perception. They change the closed circle idea into a 'spiral' of understanding in the audience—'[t]he hermeneutic circle is in reality a spiral, where both beginning and end are open':

> This process proceeds from part to whole and back again to part. It is not necessarily a once-only operation, but in fact takes place as many times as required until a final interpretation is reached. The effect is a snow-ball one; it relies upon a feedback function, or interaction between established knowledge, informed guesswork, or what Hirsch calls 'leaps of the imagination'[20], as well as newly- accumulated knowledge. This means that as soon as one had gained more information about separate parts, and attempts to understand their relationship with the whole, one goes back to the parts and adjusts them (Martin and Sauter 1995: 66–7).

A circle, or spiral, seems the only metaphor that can escape the concept of linear rational growth of understanding, and get anywhere near identifying the process of audience perception, especially on the contemporary stage, which oscillates between cognitive and non-cognitive understanding. Beckerman is identifying such a spiraling of 'understanding' when he talks of the audience's intermittent attention, probing and scanning over the material 'with our alerted sense systems', and '[f]rom time to time we temporarily and provisionally surrender ourselves to the impact of the object' (Beckerman 1979: 168). Much of the continual scanning of 'information' received takes place at the non-cognitive level in the way that Zuckerkandl describes the formulation and reception of musical 'Gestalten' and it involves the building of our expectation and its fulfillment or not. The structuring is subtle, intelligent and immensely flexible, but structure there is, even within the apparent loose and fragmentary action of the postmodern stage.

The danger is seeing this perception of time in a theatre piece as undirected and unstructured; for example, at the end of her analysis of *King Lear*, Fischer-Lichte writes: 'The awareness of space changes according to the interweaving web of light and sound . . . Time, seen subjectively, becomes a thoroughly subjective quality' (Fischer-Lichte 1995: 209). The comment is not helpful. 'Subjective' indicates an uncontrollable element, but theatrical time is not like this. In controlling the theatrical structures on stage, the director and performers are also able to some extent to control the sense of time in the audience. This sense of time is a shared one, and not entirely 'subjective'. Judging the 'correct' timing within the structure(s) set up and developed relates to a 'truth' that depends on manipulating the twin qualities of fluidity and form. When we hit such moments in rehearsal, we know that something has 'worked' and it is a sense that practitioners cannot always rationally articulate. It can be planned for and worked at

(Schiller's and Schlemmer's serious 'play') but in the end is a synthesis that lies beyond thinking. It is a skill that may fail director or performer, and the result is a violation of the unity of the stage elements or 'Gestalten' so carefully built up. Such a violation may be temporary and forgiven by an audience, but too many of them shatters the delicate balance of concentration and engagement.

Careful structuring of the stage elements belies Fried's argument that 'theatricality' is the endless freedom to interpret, throwing meaning back upon ourselves in an endless circularity of barren interchange (Fried 1967). The plea is for a re-evaluation of form in terms of Gestalt modelling, a paradigm which I see as permeating, largely unrecognized, the structures of the best postmodern stages.[21] Recognition of structure and form is a healthy antidote, especially when teaching contemporary theatre, to the constant celebration of lack of closure, the freedom to interpret and the constant shifting of frames of reference where none have precedence. Gestalt ideas offer us a way out of this dilemma of absolute freedom which constantly threatens chaos, recognizing the structuring of material with innate fluidity and infinite freedom, deeply satisfying and endlessly creative. These structures Schlemmer reached towards at the Bauhaus, and we can see them present in the work of the best directors on stage today, who have managed to escape the formalizing structures of linear narrative and character driven theatre yet nevertheless create a stage that we know is structured, formal and reflective of an age where boundaries permeate, binaries collapse and the time/space continuum seems imploded in multimedia and Internet complexities. From chaos, artistic form inexorably emerges. And the best artistic form of our times retains the Bergsonian motion within motion, the escape from linear thinking and cognitive straitjackets, and allows the leaps of imagination that both form and are formed by our present day culture.

Form is the key in communicating a sense of human purpose in art. Since Schlemmer worked his formal structuring of plasticity, motion and sound on the Bauhaus stage, form on stage and in performance has undergone some radical treatments and revisioning but is never eliminated. By using performance, Schlemmer sidestepped the dilemma of traditional form v. (Dadaesque) 'anti-form' that Kaprow later identified.

Jeff Kelley, in his introduction to Kaprow's essays in *The Blurring of Art and Life*, says that it is the expanding nature of our world that caused the unified centre no longer to hold (as it seemed to do in high Modernism). The unified centre is located everywhere and nowhere. Kaprow identified the new aesthetics of postmodernism when he declared that 'when it turns out that the whole can't be located precisely, or, if approximately located, cannot be limited with an outline or kept still, either all hell has let loose or we're in another ball game' (Kaprow [1974] 1993: 161). In this new ball game, 'Anti-formalism is not the answer'. In other words, Kaprow considered that the Dadaesque 'antiformalism' prevalent in the early years of the twentieth century with its anarchic response to form was clearly not the aesthetic answer to the dilemmas posed by the increasing confusion and inclusion of modern life. 'Antiform' is the 'structure of hell as the nether image of heaven' (Kaprow [1974] 1993: 157) [22] (i.e. one implies the other): 'When the enemy zigs you zag' (Kaprow [1974] 1993: 158). In other words, binary thinking had to be sidestepped and ideas about 'formalism' had to be transformed. Similarly, Schlemmer rejected the anti-formalism of Dada, and began to explore the new 'formalism' of performance. In doing so, he began to unravel—or perhaps complete—the Modernist project.

Early American performance artists and 'Happeners' in the late 1950s and early 1960s can be seen rejecting or revolutionizing the traditional idea of 'form' and developing a new aesthetics of performance (and dance) that shifts the emphasis away from shared cultural norms into individual experience. Schlemmer's embodied approach to form in fact moves him closer to this work; and this work moves closer to Schlemmer *via* its formalism. Kaprow himself openly acknowledged his formalist approach, even if he radically recast it, and indeed it was his formalism that alienated John Cage. Yet even Cage is implicated in formal questions since he never ceased to place a frame around his art works. Duchamp tried to tear the frame away by playing chess, but even this was an aesthetic act. The challenge that Schlemmer faced (and by the 1960s this problem had become acute) was a fast changing world of increasing complexity that art seemed, and perhaps still seems, unable to deal with. As Kaprow said, the unitary centre or whole ('universally acknowledged truths') simply cannot be located and the 'different ball game' (Kaprow 1993: 161) requires new rules.

Goldberg first claimed a connection between the Bauhaus stage and the development of performance art (Goldberg 1977), but failed to lay bare the formal and aesthetic problem in Modernism from which performance offered an escape. Schlemmer used 'abstract' material (even though it had a day-to-day significance and lived familiarity to Bauhaus students and teachers which we do not share) that is qualitatively different to a semiotically charged naturalistic *mise en scene* or expressionistic dance movements. Similarly, when making a 'happening' as a 'new' formalist fifty years later, Kaprow suggested trying to choose objects that lacked too much semiotic significance to get away from the usual (usually narrative) meanings which audiences will strive to put upon the images presented (he suggests Kleenex in the context of a happening will draw unwarranted attention to its intimate uses, for example) (Kaprow 1966: 201). He suggested a formalist painter (like Schlemmer) can use an impersonal statement such as 'The sky is blue' far easier than 'horrifying records of Nazi torture chambers'. In the happenings, Kaprow manipulates the events of life as a formalist painter shifts colour and shape around the (abstract) canvas but 'it is better to approach composition without borrowed form theories *and instead let the form emerge from what the materials can do*' [my italics] (Kaprow 1966: 202) . The example he gives is a performance script where disparate objects are chosen and their circular form emerges from engagement with them—Cheerios cereal, lifesaver belts and so on, and from this evolves the unpredictable themes of nurturing and regeneration (milk, eating, lifesaving). These meanings emerge from the context, time and cultural milieu of the art work itself, and this is actually exactly what was happening on the Bauhaus stage in the manipulation of hoops, sticks and sets of treads. Certain mid-twentieth-century artists (and dancers) at the cutting edge of performance shared with Schlemmer a rejection of mimetic art coupled with a strong desire to root themselves in lived experience. They do not identify personal insight and transformative experiences as *transcendent* (i.e. cut off from the material world) and 'beyond ourselves'. A different sort of transformative experience is sought, rooted in the here and now, within the grasp of each and every participant and audience member. The possibility of magic is never banished. Schlemmer was aware that narrative can develop and deliberately courts it at times (as in *Gesture Dance*), because he wants to know the relationship between his phenomenal, embodied and non-mimetic stage and the stuff of life which fell short of his visions: the result was often humour. Although Kaprow's whole method precludes narrative, it is utterly rooted in the stuff of life. *Calling* for example offers a transformative (but not transcendent) experience to participants (the audience) through actual physical experiences of restriction, wrappings, isolation and freedom (Kaprow [1965] 1995: 195–201). It attempts to move art and life closer together by imposing a formal structure upon lived actions. Antony Gormley, talking here particularly in relation to *Event Horizon* (Hayward Gallery, South Bank, 2007) similarly wants to create a shared social space of a 'new kind' (Gormley 2007: 5) 'creating objects that would transform the context of everyday life into a crucible for remaking the human project' (51). 'What I am interested in is how that immersed existence with its shorthand mental references can be renewed by looking at the world as a picture, a living picture that we are in, but having been given this instrument of distance, we are also removed from' (47). Compagnie 111's work demonstrates that pitting the body with and against geometric forms like those of Schlemmer can still today yield rich sequences of action, transmuted beyond narrative into expressions of current human experience. As Barry Schwabsky points out, 'the revolt against formalism in American art . . . has never been more than its radicalization . . . When the artist becomes his own creation, he finds the most rigorous impersonality of all' (Schwabsky 1998: 42). This aesthetic rigour is today deeply satisfying. It is a rigour, moreover, that was rediscovered with the happenings and a radical recasting of 'form' to accommodate flux, flow and change.

Kantor recognized this in his own journey from painting to theatre, then via happenings to theatre again. In 'The Theatre of Death' (Kobialka 1993: 109), he describes how theatre eventually discovered it was not an either/ or choice on stage between naturalism and a disembodied 'autonomous art/intellectual structure'; and this led to the happenings. If we accept that performance is an intensification of everyday experience, as argued here in relation to Schlemmer and so many artists whom I have paralleled with his work, then performance takes formalism to its radical conclusion and embeds it in life itself. Only Gestalt structures can cope with such fluidity of form.[23]

Schlemmer faced the artist being reduced to an engineer; Kaprow, on the contrary, saw art being elevated by the Greenbergs of his world to a rarified plane disconnected with life. But the objects and events of performance art, and this is especially apparent in 1960s work, are essentially no different to the hoops, sticks and boxes that Schlemmer used or the translucent box of Anthony Gormley, which Rugoff describes as a 'Bauhaus structure with the cloud of unknowing within it' (Gormley 2007: 55). All are attempts to escape from 'art for art's sake' and simultaneously to move art and life closer, without either losing the art or losing the human.

8   Afterword

The leap from Schlemmer to Kaprow and to the postmodern stage outlined in the last chapter may seem a huge one, but one that is no longer, I
hope, implausible, impossible or unthinkable. The exhibition *Un Teatro Sin
Teatro* laid out the history of 'the relationships and interchanges between
theatre and the visual arts during the twentieth century' (MACBA 2007). It
made glaringly clear an identifiable cusp between Modernism and postmodernism that occurred around the mid-1950s. Before that the battle between
Modernist form and Dadaesque anti-form had largely been played out in
precisely these terms in performance: form *versus* anti-form or as Kaprow
put it 'you zig, I zag' (Kaprow [1974] 1993: 157). As Schlemmer observed
of the students at Weimar, in their Dada-inspired efforts to make fun of
anything approaching solemnity or ethical precepts (Schlemmer 1927c: 1),
they considered all that was 'outré' and unconventional worth doing: zig,
zag. Schlemmer sidestepped this reactive process by refusing to dispose of
form, but insisting on recasting form in terms of space and time. It was
Kaprow who articulated the boundless, centreless and motile spaces of the
'new ball game' in the second half of the twentieth century and it is a les-
son we are still absorbing and playing out today on the postmodern stage.
Kaprow proposed a new formalism that took account of the multiplicity of
daily life in the twentieth century. As Jeff Kelley explains in the introduction to *Essays on the Blurring of Art and Life* (Kelley 1993: xvii), a work of
art has limits: but what are they? To Kaprow, according to Kelley, all forms
are provisional '[t]emplates for modern experience, they are situational,
operational, structural, subject to feedback, and open to learning' (Kelley
1993: xvii). Merleau-Ponty was talking of exactly this when he defined
great works of art as capable of being continually 're-written' or remade:

> As for the history of art works, if they are great, the sense we give
> to them later on has issued from them. It is the work itself that has
> opened up the field from which it appears in another light. It changes
> *itself* and *becomes* what follows; the interminable reinterpretations to
> which it is *legitimately* susceptible change it only in itself (Merleau-
> Ponty 1974a: 300).

Academic formalism, far from both Schlemmer and Kaprow, is 'finally a secular essentialism driven by a closed fundamentalist belief system intent on self purification through rituals of rational renunciation' (Kelley 1993: xvii). Schlemmer, devoted to form, would have nevertheless agreed with this damning judgement on form divorced from feeling. He asked much more complex questions of form than those of his colleagues, even those of Klee, concerning shape and colour, harmony and colour correspondences. He suspected the answers are much more than any formula can contain, and that the modern world needed radical new thinking concerning the synthesis of life and art; he thought the solution lay somewhere within the boundaries of the Bauhaus stage. He felt his methods would lead 'to the keyhole to the riddle' which the Bauhaus Theatre posed (May 1929) (Schlemmer [1958] 1977: 113); he was never arrogant enough to claim he would lay hands on the key itself. He subjected the essentialist phenomenology and 'Gestaltungen' of the Bauhaus to embodied experience, lived engagement, human handling. He transformed the excessive mysticism of Itten and Grunow into present action, grasped objects, breathing bodies, experienced motion; in other words, he demonstrated Kelley's 'process of transformation, and the hope of transcendence' (Kelley 1993: xv), and above all he engaged with life. The work on the Dessau stage was not an isolated aesthetic act but infused the whole functioning of the Bauhaus, even as the Bauhaus itself was meant to shape and influence the whole of German society. In this sense, Schlemmer's parties at Dessau, driven by the same values that underlay his stage work, epitomise not only his desire to infuse life with aesthetic values but represent his total Gestalt vision of society that included art; and the parties at Dessau anticipate the participatory and joyful art that Kaprow—and indeed John Cage—later in the century identified and to which they devoted their lives. The parties are truly the social spaces that the participants themselves forged: a powerful unity of shared cultural, aesthetic and social will. The bond between Schlemmer and later artists, a shared aesthetic of human contact and the emergence of form in what is 'wholly flux' (Zuckerkandl 1956: 241) has never been sufficiently recognised.

In some senses Schlemmer took the opposite journey to Kaprow and Cage in that he found flux and change in what he thought was wholly form. The early chapters of this book laid out the Gestalt principles of form as they were adopted and adapted in the Bauhaus as a whole, and the in-built dynamism of structural form was recognised in Gestalt thinking. The odd mixture of science and mysticism, the holistic and the analytical, deriving from Goethe, was carried through to some extent into the Dessau Bauhaus. The new sense of 'realism', so often attributed to the Dessau years of the Bauhaus and the influence of Maholy-Nagy, was not only practised in the curriculum changes but actually more present on the Bauhaus stage than anywhere else. Instead of Schreyer's mystical and expressionist performances, the physical components of space were being moulded and shaped into a living and 'lived' architecture, plastic articulations of the 'void' (space) that imposed no etherial agenda or mystical imperative or narrative mimesis, but simply took their form from actions, objects, the body and motion: as Kaprow suggested years later, let the form emerge from what the objects can do (Kaprow 1966: 202). When 'expression' is superseded by reception, as it was on Schlemmer's stage, action then becomes a cultural form that is itself subject to change, a reciprocal flow where meaning is continually made and remade in terms of the ever-just-past, the present 'moment' and the future that is anticipated. The social order can be questioned, re-ordered; we are empowered, and the order happens not to us but because of us. Schlemmer discovered that what is apparently fixed begins to move, as in the shifting boundaries of light and objects, the changing dynamics of scenery and the human body, the varied actions of stage action and stage business. As he immersed himself in the possibilities of changing space(s), the real and 'illusory' inevitably became one: instability and endless play opened and opens up the possibility of the sublime, the unrecognised Bergsonian flux, which is always banished by logic and linear structures.

Gradually, Schlemmer came to accept the indivisibility of the material world and 'Geist', and embraced the absolute physicality of his stage and the emergence of meaning through the physical: more than this, he realised the absolute necessity of the physical for any ethical system of aesthetics to emerge, any cultural change to take root, any moral values to emerge. He reached towards a Bergsonian indivisibility of mind and matter that is momentarily realised upon the stage for actor and spectator alike. For him, no other art form could achieve exactly this because live performance included motion and time. Schlemmer's absolute respect for the physicality of the stage elements is realised nowhere more strongly than his respect for sound, his minimalist approach refusing to succumb to the false blandishments of a sublime, harmonious experience that was separate from the heavy, fleshly, dancing body on stage. How often has a piece of music been misused to carry the inadequacy of a piece of stage action? His precision and exactitude simply would not allow re-ploughing old furrows, an approximation, a fudge. All Schlemmer did was utterly new, utterly original. In his isolation of sound in percussive modes refusing musical harmony he opened it up to periodicity and phenomenological power, which took another thirty years and more to be re-discovered and many more than that to be truly applied and exploited in performance.

And what of the Bauhaus as a whole, the project which Hoffmann claims will take another three hundred years to play out, the modern which has not yet arrived but is always about to come (Bogner 1997: 15)? Are we right confidently to assume that Modernism is past, 'post' modernism or even 'post'postmodernism has arrived, and we have thrown off the shackles of form follows function, rejected Gropius's 'superpersonal' laws, and the straight white lines, glass walls and chrome door knobs of the Dessau Bauhaus? But these are of course not 'shackles' at all: the deeply held ethical and holistic values nurtured at the Bauhaus alongside functional grace and human comfort infused the Modernism of the Bauhaus and speaks loudly to us today in an age that badly needs to face up to the urgent changes demanded of us. Findeli rightly argues for a re-evaluation and reapplication of the holistic Bauhaus ethos, within design, design teaching and architecture. But this ethos can be taken further.

Sally Jane Norman applies Schlemmer's spatial wisdom, the pitting of object and body, into the realms of the virtual stage (Norman 2001). She argues for the absolute necessity of the visceral body being accounted for, as the ultimate space shaper, and for the need never to forget its organic realities: 'The modernity of Schlemmer's researches bears witness to his clear vision of the contemporary world' (Norman 2001: 162). She recognises a new (virtual) world has emerged and is emerging, that demands we come to terms with and explore new embodiments; and Schlemmer's theatre, founded on 'Schillerian' principles and acting as a 'force for order' (January 1926) (Schlemmer [1958] 1977: 86) can still act as our model and our guide. More widely, there have been calls to apply Bauhaus thinking to the world of digital design and digital education (Findeli 1991/1992; Ehn 1998; Beardon 2002; Malmborg 2004; Prager 2006). Ehn calls for 'a comprehensive sensuality in the design of meaningful interactive and virtual stories and environments' (Ehn 1998: 210). A holistic and embodied approach to computer technology has been sadly lacking (though there are signs that this is changing as haptically sensitive systems emerge) in an industry that once could envisage a 'thinking' robot without investigating or even being aware of how the mind and 'meaning' comes into being through, and indeed is indistinguishable from, a long embodied engagement with the world. The baby which first moves and feels pressure on its back 'knows' the difference between front and back long before it 'thinks' it: knowledge becomes a lifetime's continuous reciprocal flow between object and subject, perhaps impossible to replicate in a machine, but a necessary challenge and a call for much more enlightened research. There is surely a role here in the new millennium for performance research, and moreover research of a type formulated long ago in the tiny space of the Dessau Bauhaus stage, a space shaped by a singular, quixotic and engaging mind—a materialist metaphysician, an idealist Constructivist, a practical visionary and master magician: Oskar Schlemmer.

Notes

NOTES TO CHAPTER 1

1. Schlemmer in fact said that studying the precepts or rules he set himself for working, involving simplicity and lack of presuppositions, would lead 'to the keyhole to the riddle which the Bauhaus *Theatre* apparently poses' [my italics] (May 1929) (Schlemmer [1958] 1977: 113).
2. Paul Overy describes the fatal beginning of the process of creating a fixed 'Bauhaus style' that never really existed, at the Werkbund Exhibition in Paris, 1930 (Overy 2004).
3. The evocative description of Schlemmer is that of Walter Gropius, finally paying tribute to him in his introduction to the 1961 English version of *The Theater of the Bauhaus* book (Gropius and Wensinger [1961] 1996: 8).
4. For example, Michael Billington, 'The Troll in the Drawing Room', *The Guardian*, 15 February 2003: 17.
5. The noun 'Gestalt' or 'form' is capitalised in German, but English-language texts use both the capitalised form and its anglicised version, 'gestalt'. The same word is used for both noun (usually translated as 'form') and adjectival use. Normally in this book the capitalized version 'Gestalt' or plural 'Gestalten' is used, or sometimes 'Gestaltung'. 'Gestaltung' implies process or as Paul Klee says 'the paths to form' (Klee [1956] 1961: 17) rather than the form itself and is often preferred within Bauhaus. Klee says, '*Gestaltung* in its broader sense clearly contains the idea of an underlying mobility and is therefore preferable' (Klee [1956] 1961: 17).
6. Robert Wilson, for example, directly quotes Schlemmer in *Einstein on the Beach* (Schober 1997). Tadeusz Kantor admired Schlemmer, especially his sense of humour (Kobialka 1993: 220) and his exercises on abstraction on the stage are clearly influenced by Schlemmer (213–215).
7. The reference to the cathedrals in medieval times was to evoke a period before the fundamental 'split' between mind and body (which can be equated to aesthetic artwork and handcraft work) came about in Western philosophy and culture around the time of Galileo and Descartes. See Findeli 1989/1990: 59.
8. See note 2.
9. Strangely enough the split between theory and practice had already manifested itself in philosophy, a split which will be dealt with in Chapter 2, when theoretical philosophers had to come to terms with psychologists in the same departments who were advocating practical experimentation on the mind.
10. Schlemmer was stage and costume designer for Paul Hindemith's version of Kokoschka's *Murderer the Hope of Women* (*Mörder Hoffnung der Frauen*) and Hindemith's own short work *The Thinga-ma-jig* (*Das Nusch-Nuschi*), Stuttgart, 4 June 1921.

11. For details of Schlemmer's background and childhood, see Maur 1979a: 17–20 and Kunz 1991: 19–25.
12. *oskar schlemmer: tanz theatre bühne*, Kunstsammlung Nordrhein-Westfalen Düsseldorf, 30 July–16 October 1994, Kunsthalle Vienna, 11 November 1994–29 January 1995, and Sprengel Museum Hannover 19 February–21 May 1995.
13. See for example Maciuika 2006.
14. Tut Schlemmer, aware of the ephemeral nature of performance, made huge efforts so that Schlemmer's stage work should not be forgotten.
15. Arnd Wesemann links the aesthetic of these Bauhaus open air parades to street parades today using as they did built-up costumes and masks, and he talks of the 'decentering' of man in such parades, and the merger of audience and performer: 'In spectacle, man and architecture constitute and celebrate a grotesque social re-experiencing of urban space. Schlemmer's own inspiration, the street carnival, erupts nowadays in street parades' (Fiedler and Feierabend 2000: 550)
16. The correct spelling is Jaïna Schlemmer.
17. Compare Schlemmer's own dance plan in 1912 described in his diary (December 1912) (Schlemmer [1958] 1977: 10). See Chapter 4, this volume.
18. This use of language had appealed to Schlemmer in his early encounters with avant-garde dance, when he had seen Schönberg's *Pierrot Lunaire* (January 1913) (Schlemmer [1958] 1977: 12).
19. See Schlemmer's plan for the stage workshop at Weimar which included 'decoration for shop windows' (Schlemmer in Wingler 1969: 59).
20. There was a desire in the Bauhaus to create immersive performative environments, evident in for example Molnár's U Theatre design or Gropius's Total Theatre (Gropius and Wensinger [1961] 1996: 11–4, 73–80; Prager 2006: 200–1).
21. 'Die Bühne' is more accurately translated as 'the stage' of the Bauhaus, as it is in fact translated in Schlemmer's grid 'Schema' ('scheme' or 'lay out') showing the range of performance types possible in any era (Gropius and Wensinger [1961] 1996: 19). In this grid scheme, 'Stage' broadly covered all types of performance whereas 'theatre' (placed in the centre of the scheme) was reserved for a particular kind of stage work.
22. In outlining this vision for a new theatre there are few more useful documents than a 1929 manuscript plan for a lecture 'Tanz und Pantomime' by Schlemmer, which is unpublished and only accessible at the moment through Dirk Scheper's commentary on it (Scheper 1988: 249ff). Schlemmer divides theatre into five divisions of Place, Actor, Speech, Music and Dance, not in order to understand their history, but to 'discover anew the pure basic forms of each type of stage event' ('die ursprünglichen reinen Formen jeden Bühnengeschehens neu zu entdecken' (Scheper 1988: 250).
23. See Schober 1994: 334–5 and Schober 1997: 26–7.
24. See Gropius on 'The Work of the Bauhaus Stage' in Wingler 1969: 58 and Scheper 1988: 250–3.
25. Spengler's book was published in two volumes, the first in 1918 (*Untergang des Abenlandes, Gestalt and Wirklichkeit* [*The Decline of the West, Form and Actuality*] München: C.H. Beck) and the second volume in 1922 (*Der Untergang des Abenlandes, Welthistorische Perspektiven* [*The Decline of the West, Perspectives of World History*]). Obviously Schlemmer is referring to volume 1.
26. Schlemmer continued stage design work in 1925 with Hans José Rehfisch's *Who Weeps for Juckenack?* (*Wer weint um Juckenack?*) (Volksbühne Berlin), Christian Dietrich Grabbe's *Don Juan and Faust* (*Don Juan und Faust*)

(Nationaltheater Weimar) and Shakespeare's *Hamlet* (*Hamlet*) (Volksbühne Berlin). These were not happy experiences for him involving much compromise 'in the service of writers' (October 1924) (Schlemmer 1972: 155). The designs are on the whole spare, abstract and dramatic divisions of space.

27. See Schlemmer's letter to Otto Meyer (May 1924) (Schlemmer 1972: 154).

28. The series of photos that end the 1925 book (mainly those of student 'mechanical' productions as Schlemmer described them) are used in 1961 to illustrate Maholy-Nagy's essay.

29. Constructivism had its origins in the 1910s in Russia alongside visionary Russian Futurism and Suprematism, and it was embraced by both Malevich and Tatlin, who managed to turn its ideology to their own ends. See Lodder 1983.

30. See Anker 2005 for a portrait of Maholy-Nagy that puts him more in line with contemporary vitalists and late twentieth-century deep ecologists than Constructivism.

31. In 1922, van Doesburg held a joint Dada and Constructivist conference in Weimar. The united front shown by these two movements at this point should warn us against easy paradigm models in the history of the avant-garde. At that time the division between sceptical Dadaism (which, conversely, had so recently been under the tutelage of the mystic and dreamer, Hugo Ball) and exciting new Constructivist ideas originating in Russia from before and especially after the 1917 Revolution, was much harder to distinguish. They were united in their opposition to the high flown Expressionist idealism which the painters of the Bauhaus seemed to represent, rejecting this as so much claptrap, unlikely to fashion a new Germany.

32. Itten undertook analysis of form, often via studying paintings, but overlaid it with his own particular brand of mysticism and 'empathy'. See Schlemmer's letter to Otto Meyer amusingly describing Itten's 'Analysis' class (May 1921) (Schlemmer [1958] 1977: 49).

33. After Itten resigned, Kandinsky taught classes on 'The Basic Elements of Form' and on colour, and Klee contributed later.

34. See Maciuika 2006.

35. At least, Schlemmer's affectionate letters to his wife, and her devotion to his memory after his death, would seem to attest to this.

36. '[D]ie Typenbühne' is very hard to translate because it refers to the basic ('Ur-') form of the stage which Schlemmer was trying to recreate/discover. See Chapter 2, this volume, on Gestalt thinking and the 'Ur-form'.

37. This lecture-demonstration was first given to the Friends of the Bauhaus in 1927 at Dessau; the text also appeared in the Bauhaus publication *bauhaus 3* (Schlemmer 1927c)

38. *Box Play* was also a commentary on human cooperation in the task of building, and Schawinsky indicates that at least one version of *Flats Dance* played with a German pun—'what is going on "behind the flats" [i.e. backstage] (political tricks, clever manipulation, fraud)' (Schawinsky 1971: 43).

39. Schlemmer drew up extensive plans for developing *The Triadic Ballet* in the 1930s, but sadly the resources were never forthcoming.

40. In fact, the home of Tut Schlemmer in Stuttgart from 1949 developed into a meeting place (and occasioned many parties) for Bauhäusler for years and throughout Raman Schlemmer's childhood in the 1950s and 1960s: a testimony to the love and affection both Oskar Schlemmer and his wife generated in those around them.

41. John Cage for example was taught by Maholy-Nagy in the New Bauhaus and Stefan Wolpe (not a Bauhaus student but someone who had close contacts

there including Schlemmer) opened up his own school of music on Bauhaus principles.

NOTES TO CHAPTER 2

1. See Burwick and Douglas 1992.
2. See, for example, the séance in Thomas Mann's *The Magic Mountain* (*Der Zauberberg*) (Mann [1924] 1960: 653–81) or the scandal over Zöllner described by Treitel 2004: 1–28.
3. For an explanation of the opposition between the terms 'Seele' and 'Geist' in German metaphysics, see http://www.revilo-oliver.com/Writers/Klages/Ludwig-Klages.html (accessed 27 September 2007), 'Understanding Klagesian Terms'. Some of the material on Ludwig Klages—one of Schlemmer's recommended writers in his course 'Man' (Schlemmer [1969] 1971: 144)—has to be treated with caution, since strongly vitalist modes of thinking have been too easily harnessed to quasi and actual racist views in the twentieth and twenty-first century.
4. This phrase is picked up by Lucy Embick Kunz (Kunz 1991: 91–4, note 66) who explains it appears in an unpublished diary entry (December 1920) (papers which are no longer available to view) and another diary entry quoted by Karin von Maur, 30 November 1919 (von Maur 1979a: 354, note 335).
5. Galison demonstrates that the Nazis castigated both the Bauhaus and the Vienna circle for their lack of holistic tendencies; the political situation really forced an alliance between the two, and it is not surprising that Meyer, true to his anti-fascist principles, made no concessions and played down the former vitalist and more metaphysical sympathies within the Bauhaus.
6. This is true of Michaud throughout his commentaries, and in Scheper (Scheper 1988: 242).
7. Both Carus and Klages appear on Schlemmer's booklist for the Psychology lectures in his course 'Man', making up no less than six of the thirteen recommended books. See Schlemmer [1969] 1971: 144. On Klages's theory of physiognomies and personality types, see Frank 1994: 147.
8. Paul Klee had read Wertheimer's essay on 'Laws of Perceptual Organisation' dated 1923 (Ellis 1938). For cumulative evidence of Klee's knowledge of Wertheimer and Ernst Mach, see Cretien von Campen 1997 and Teuber 1979.
9. Heinrich von Kleist committed suicide allegedly following his so-called 'Kant crisis' where he grasped the bleak implications of the unattainable nature of the noumenon.
10. Philosophers distinguish between 'transcendent' and 'transcendental' following Kant, who defined 'transcendent' as referring to an existing reality which transcends our own in perception (the noumena), and 'transcendental' as referring to the *concept* of that transcendent reality, a concept which we can neither prove nor dispense with. Husserl does not use these terms in this way. See Koestenbaum 1985: LII.
11. Translated in Haus 1978: 46–77.
12. On Ernst Mach and early embodied thinking, see Kern [1983] 2003: 133–5.
13. In Schlemmer's course on Man he was still using Wundt as a source whereas recent developments in Gestalt Psychology were in fact much more in keeping with Bauhaus thought. This was not realised until Durkheim's lecture in 1928: see Wingler 1969: 159–60.
14. See Debra McCall's comments in Moyniham and Odom on Schlemmer doctoring photographs (1984: 46–66:56).

15. Dada's simultaneous poetry was in effect a similar search for 'new previously unknown relationships' (see Melzer [1976] 1980: 36) and Maholy-Nagy's experiments with sound and the gramophone are noted in Chapter 6: see Haus 1978: 46–7.

NOTES TO CHAPTER 3

1. Schlemmer himself saw Russian theatre in Berlin in 1912 (Maur 1979a: 39)
2. *Ruheraum* refers to the resting room in a spa. *Quiet Room* might be a better translation, avoiding suggestions of 1950s English sitting rooms.
3. See Schlemmer [1958] 1977: 71 and R. Schlemmer 2001: 25.
4. See Herzogenrath 1973: 50–4.
5. The Bauhaus printing style was to simplify German by not using capitals for nouns.
6. The detailed plans for the Dessau Bauhaus following its recent reconstruction list the basic likely lights but state it is impossible, even studying the original plans, to tell if the stage even had a primitive dimmer facility (Meier 2006: 20, 24–6). It seems unlikely.
7. The origins of *Reflected Light Play* were in the Lantern Festival at the Weimar Bauhaus in 1922 (Scheper 1988: 108 ff). Kurt Schwerdtfeger developed a 'Art Laterna Magica' with a hand held lantern and paper figures making a shadow show on a screen. However, Ludwig Hirschfeld-Mack swopped the light for a powerful acetylene lamp to get a livelier colour light play. The result was a doubling up of the shadows; and further play, including doubling the number of lamps themselves, revealed interesting effects of repeated reflected shapes, one behind another but overlapping, and warm and cold shadows with colours drawing nearer to what Hirschfeld-Mack described as a 'new artistic genre' (Hirschfeld-Mack in Scheper 1988: 109). This connects to the exploration of photography described in the introduction where photography at the Bauhaus was primarily considered a play of light and a new means of artistic expression of *Lichtgestaltungen*. In performance, bright images were produced by moving lamps, with coloured glass filters, projecting on the back of a transparent screen. This in turn was viewed from the front as a continual light play of coloured shapes. There is no doubt here that what was presented were considered new 'Gestalten', linked to the discovery of absolute forms, not unlike Kandisnky's endless pulverization and rejoinings of colour and shape.
8. Baugh says of Stanley McCandless, an American who did much to advance lighting theory (Baugh 2005: 130), that for him 'the theatre space is not one that is illuminated in an overall general way, but fundamentally a place of darkness that is energised and brought to life by the performance of light' (135). This would be an excellent description of the Bauhaus stage experiments under Schlemmer at Dessau.
9. Indeed photos do exist where the body recedes. See those by Charlotte Rudolf and T.Lux Feininger in Fiedler 1990: 242
10. One doubts the sophistication of the lighting in the Bauhaus Dances from the evidence of the 'prompt copies' for the dances: reproduced in *oskar schlemmer tanz theater bühne*, exhibition catalogue Kunstsammlung Nordrhein-Westfalen, Düsseldorf, Kunsthalle Wien and Sprengel Museum Hannover, 1994: 218–225.
11. For example, on the cover of Rousier 2001.
12. See also Chapter 2, this volume, where it was explained that Schlemmer's preference in photography was to create new 'Gestalten', not to provide a record of the performance.

13. See Trimingham 2004a.

14. Low level light is a well-known device in puppet theatre known as the 'Curtain of Light' whereby a puppet figure can be made to dance in a beam of light by an unseen puppeteer standing behind the light rays; and it is a trick soon discovered by anyone experimenting with light and dark and shadows, as they did on the Bauhaus stage at Dessau.

15. From the personal notes of the author, taken as far as possible verbatim at the time.

16. See MacRitchie 1996.

17. One delightful example of the continuing fascination of magic and sleight of hand is Jean-Baptiste Thierree's and Victoria Chaplin's *Le Cirque Invisible* (Queen Elizabeth Hall, South Bank Centre 2009) which continues to entrance children and adults after many years of touring.

18. This is seen in the alluring, fantastic and sometimes faintly unsettling scenes from early films (mainly those of George Méliés), which relied on the transformative new medium of trick photography. The images were often taken from popular theatre, fairgrounds and sideshows, and were sometimes beautiful illusions (a butterfly woman emerging from a chrysallis) that hinted at an underlying magic and alchemy in the ordinary, or sometimes disturbing (a man's head being blown up by a pump). Horse and Bamboo Theatre's *Needles in a Candleflame* (1983) explored these ideas; they made a film as part of that performance, recreating scenes from Méliés's films. Today fantastic illusions are created on stage, and off, by digital technology, and the effect upon the body in the terms attributed here to live illusion, that is, both haptic displacement and intimations of magic, have yet to be properly researched.

19. The word 'Mobiliar', used in Schlemmer's essay 'Stage Elements' ([1929] 1965: 13) is a tricky one. He avoids the term 'Bühnendekoration' with its overtones of scenic design; and 'Kulissen' are the actual stage flats, which he isolates and plays with in *Flats Dance (Kulissentanz)*. 'Mobiliar' is therefore 'stage furnishings', translated here as 'scenery' and the word refers to moveable pieces of stage equipment such as flats, treads and rostra.

20. This was clearly demonstrated in numerous stage designs displayed in *Music and the Third Reich, from Bayreuth to Terezin*, Exhibition 27 February–27 May 2007, Fundació Caixa Catalunya, Barcelona.

21. The costumes of *The Triadic Ballet* are a 3-D realisation of this dilemma, and represent his first solution, that is, freezing into 3-D shapes the abstract 'lines', or rather curves, of motion. For example, the circular wrist movement with pointing finger is realised as a 'cuff' enclosing the enlongated point. The device is most obvious in the Spiral Wire Costume in section three, where the spinning of the dancer focuses absolute attention upon the motion pattern, accentuated to a high degree by the multifold curves of the costume. Instead of the bodies moving freely outside plastic structure they are encased within them.

22. In doing so he also begins to research motion in earnest. See Chapter 4, this volume.

23. Catherine Diverres's production *San* (Queen Elizabeth Hall South Bank Centre, 2005), a homage to Oskar Schlemmer, seems exactly to demonstrate this, in that she used two parallel large screens in conjunction with light, including an arc welding light, changing them from transparent to opaque by turn, and thus changing the space of the stage dramatically. Behind the back screen the space hung as a mysterious 'beyond' ('san') and between her screens figures could appear to float in the air.

24. This shift to articulating the response of both the performer and viewer is a crucial development in Schlemmer's sensibility, whose wider implications are explored in Chapter 5, this volume.

25. Didier Plassard (Rousier 2001: 65) sees Gesture Dance 11 and Schlemmer's unfinished remake of *The Triadic Ballet* in 1936 as both moving towards dramatic content.

26. This was picked up and directly quoted in Aurélian Bory's *Les Sept Planches de la Ruse* (*The Seven Boards of Skill*) (Barbican Centre, London BITE09).

27. This was clear from a concert of Schlemmer's music for *The Bauhaus Dances* (Tinguely Museum, Basel, 20 August 2009) where photos had to serve for the dance itself, and these alongside the Chaplinesque musical accompaniment still produced laughter in the audience.

28. The phrase is that of Torsten Blume, a current director of the Dessau Bauhaus stage.

29. By early June 1927 Schlemmer insisted on giving it up (Schlemmer [1958] 1977: 93). He cited two main reasons, the amount of rehearsal it would need, stretching into the autumn, and the impossibility of either keeping the cumbersome set in place or continually dismantling it and rebuilding it, to release the space for other activities. He also mentioned in letters to his wife the money worries of the stage workshop and had an eye on what work could be turned to some profit from touring and *House of Pi* clearly could not be toured.

30. The idea is that of Gemma Rowan from her MA thesis, *In Search of Other Spaces: The Panic of Lais- Between Arrabal and Kantor*, who contributed much to my understanding of Kantor.

31. Kantor references Schlemmer in *The Milano Lessons* (1986) specifically in relation to abstract theatre (Kobialka 1993: 209).

32. This sketch of Russian Constructivism takes no account of the strong mystical stream within Russian art from about 1913, characterised by Malevich's sublime paintings and the fascinating activities and interests of the Russian Futurists; but it is used here as a shorthand that utilises the commonly held notions about the 'Constructivist' Bauhaus after 1925.

33. See Peter Brook's comment after seeing Lepage's *Seven Streams of the River Ota*: 'They seek to create a theatre where the terrifying and incomprehensible reality of our time is inseperably linked to the insignificant details of our everyday lives' (Fisher 1999). Similarly, Robert Wilson 'supercharges' ordinary objects. See Chapter 5, this volume.

NOTES TO CHAPTER 4

1. Geometry tries to analyse space and its dimensions, to find ways to describe that space logically and realise it on paper. Euclidean geometry is both deductive and logical—an all embracing system that derives from first principles or axioms. It was developed by the Greek mathematician Euclid of Alexandria c. 300 BC. It was not until the nineteenth and early twentieth century that new geometries were developed, incorporating relativity and new ways of 'casting' reality and the space we dwell in—for example, the mathematical theories of Poincaré. It is impossible to understand fully some of Duchamp's work such as *The Large Glass* (*Le grand verre*) unless one is aware of his interest in flux, change and impermanence, and specifically the theories of Poincaré. See Henderson (1971), however, to counter blithe assumptions that artists were generally familiar with this material.

2. The best summary of their ideas is found in Lupton and Abbott Miller (1993: 22–33), especially the reproduction and explication of Kandinsky's diagram of the line as a moving point (25–6).

3. Kinetic sculptures relied in the early twentieth century on a visual experience. Arguably, the Robert Morris sculptures *bodymotionspacethings* at

the Tate Modern in May 2009 (originally shown in 1971) were kinetic in a fundamentally new way, offering an embodied and haptic experience as they invited 'viewers' to climb, slide, scramble and physically engage with them. The publicity described this as an installation. Like Anthony Gormley's *Blind Light* (Hayward Gallery, South Bank, 2007) it is closer to performance than to traditional sculpture.

4. See 'Man and Art Figure' (Schlemmer 1925: 7–20, especially page 15). Schlemmer's course 'Man' shows an endless dissection and analysis of the body in geometric and mathematical terms.

5. These definitions are entirely Nikolais's own.

6. For example, Lehmann describes the use of extreme repeated action on the postdramatic stage as a 'surge of signifiers that have been drained of their communicative character' as a device towards 'a constructing and constructive co-producing of the total audio-visual complex of the theatre' (Lehmann 2006: 157) and he identifies 'concrete theatre' (98–9). More recently Elizabeth Streb said in response to a question ('How useful do you find the term "dance" to describe your work?'): 'I think my subject should more accurately be called "action" ' (Streb 1999).

7. Schlemmer's term refers to a performer, neither a puppet nor an actor, simply someone on stage as a plastic but sensible element in the staging. The phrase 'art figure' originates with Clemens Brentano in 'Das Märchen von Gockel, Hinkel und Gackleia': 'neither man nor puppet but Beautiful art figure' (Brentano [1838] 1965: 543). Surely Robert Wilson's actors come closest to realising Schlemmer's ideal.

8. Schlemmer was keenly aware of the innate rivalry between French and German traditions, valuing always the sensibility of German painters over the (as he saw it) more superficial French inclination towards style. He always worried about the lack of emotion or empathy in the best of French painting, relying as it did (as Schlemmer thought) on formal innovations. He was clear headed enough however to want a combination of the best from both traditions. See especially his debates in his letters and diaries around 1917 (Schlemmer [1958] 1977: 26).

9. See Kern [1983] 2003 on William James and the unity of the perceptual field in Gestalt psychological terms: 'what we hear when the thunder crashes is not thunder pure, but thunder-breaking-upon-silence-and-contrasting-with-it' (Kern [1983] 2003: 176).

10. The Dessau Bauhaus reveals many examples: for example, the different bands of grey around the door openings in the office block have been faithfully reproduced and provide an extraordinary richness of texture and visual pleasure.

11. See Herzogenrath 1973: 33 for examples of Schlemmer's wall decorations in private houses.

12. This has especially been true in Anthropology where in the nineteenth and for a good part of the twentieth century anthropologists underestimated the efficacious nature of, for example, performance and artifacts, and their deep embeddedness within the lived and daily experience of the culture being studied, often explaining them as 'symbolic' of some larger, spiritual idea. In this way, anthropologists failed to engage with the lived experience of the culture, intellectualising it and distancing it into analysable pieces of 'knowledge'. See Howes 1991.

13. He also comments on the Essen mural work that he is using a dynamic element in it—'asymmetry as value in itself to offset the symmetry of the architecture' (Schlemmer [1958] 1977: 118).

14. This banding of similar colours was a common device at the Bauhaus: we see it in Gropius's Dessau study in an attempt to 'elevate' his desk area and also see note 10, this chapter.

15. Craig called them 'Übermarionettes' causing much confusion since this does seem mistakenly to indicate a preference for actual puppets over live performers.

16. A few years earlier the Gestalt Psychologists under Wertheimer claimed to have done exactly this in experiments with rotating discs.

17. Laurie Anderson describes the occasion of Debra McCall's reconstructions of the Bauhaus dances, and Andreas Weininger aged 'about ninety-five years old' telling them 'what went on in the Bauhaus and it seemed like it happened last week and then the performance began and it also looked like it had been choreographed a few days ago ... And it was a shock to suddenly feel this kind of continuity and to realise that artists have ideas and then they're used by other artists and it's not progress, but a long, long conversation stetching backwards and also forwards into time' (Anderson 1994: 218).

18. The ballet operates on the same principles as top fashion designers today who often display their garments as moving structures or sculptures: only today, the fabric is more often seen in motion and flow as it moulds and is moulded by the moving human body.

19. The phrase is apparently that of Schlemmer quoted in Scheper 1988: 255.

20. We are reminded of Duchamp's fascination with the game of chess, which similarly demonstrates flux and order.

21. The initial drawing that imposes cubes upon the body was never translated into a costume *per se*, but is crucial for understanding how Schlemmer saw the body echoing the cubical laws of the space in which it moved. On top of this unworkable rigidity the organic body adds flow and dynamism as demonstrated in the other three drawings. 'The functional laws of the human body in their relationship to space' rounds solids into curves, and their linear juxtapositions taper into circles, the joints that allow the body to move, subject always to 'der bewegungsmathematik, der gelenmechanik' [sic] the mathematics of movement and the mechanics of joints (Schlemmer 1927c: 3). 'The laws of motion of the human body in space' explain many of the odd shapes in *The Triadic Ballet* costumes. To put it simply, the 'functioning' body in the drawing just described ('functional laws' i.e. it now can move) is set into deliberate or *significant* motion. Schlemmer once said that the space around a dancer should be imagined as soft and pliable and solidifying into shapes as the dancer moves through it (Schlemmer [1929] 1965: 18), and this is exactly the explanation for the 'motion' shapes in this drawing: the solidified shapes are used in the built-up costumes of *The Triadic Ballet*. One 'hand', for example, is a circular bell like shape defining the circular sweep of a wrist while the forefinger points. The final bodily Gestalt 'The metaphysical forms of human expression' draws on more esoteric and ancient symbols for the infinite and holy, the double circle or 'leminscate' (the mathematical symbol for eternity), the cross with Christian ramifications, 'the double head, multiple limbs, division and suppression of forms' which derive from Schlemmer's wider reading in arcane texts of numerology and mysticism. These shapes too found their way into the costume designs for the ballet.

22. See note 12 this chapter.

23. *First Night* (Contact Theatre, Manchester 2002) deconstructed our expectations of what popular 'variety' theatre should be—entertaining, fun and full of theatrical tricks and illusions.

24. It has been dealt with in the past either by absorbing it into the semiotic coding of the performance, as naturalistic theatre might do for example, or foregrounding it (for example, casting Hamlet as a woman).

25. Three paragraphs of the following section are reprinted courtesy of Cambridge University Press. They first appeared as part of an article, 'Oskar

Schlemmer's Research Practice at the Dessau Bauhaus' (Trimingham 2004a: 128–142).

26. See his diary entry July 1914 (Schlemmer [1958] 1977: 14) and Kunz 1991: 76–8. The sculptor Adolf von Hildebrand, the art critic and patron Konrad Fiedler and the painter Hans von Marées all formed a sympathetic group around the end of the nineteenth century.

27. The thesis of Langer's book is that art is a direct, lived experience and not symbolic or representational of some other experience. In other words, this 'virtual' space is directly experienced by the viewer of the painting, and is not symbolic of some ideal 'Platonic' space that does not physically exist—it exists *in* the painting.

28. The German here is: 'wir werden das erscheinen der menschlichen gestalt als ereignis wahrnehmen und erkennen, daß sie, im moment, da sie teil der bühne geworden, ein sozusagen, 'raumbehextes' wesen ist. jede geste und bewegung wird mit automatischer sicherheit in die sphäre des bedeutsamen gerückt. (selbst 'der herr aus dem zuschauerraum' seiner sphäre entrückt und in die der bühne gestellt, wird vom nimbus des magischen umkleidet [sic] (Schlemmer 1927c: 3). The word 'Ereignis' here is not quite strongly enough translated as 'event'. Schlemmer is indicating that when the human figure appears, it is a significant event, creating a new 'Gestalt', a new element which changes everything including the space into which it enters and which it charges with energy, even as the space, in turn, charges the performer with energy.

29. As Ash explains, Bergson like the Gestalt Psychologists rejected associationist psychology that divided experience up into so many discrete 'units' and subjected it to logical analysis. Both took an approach to psychology based on experience and a holistic approach to consciousness but as Ash points out, both Köhler and Koffka taught Bergson not only because of his rejection of associationist psychology but also as an a example of what they wished to avoid! (Ash 1995: 69).

30. Marcel Proust, however, of course supplied exactly this illustration of Bergson's theories.

31. This was re-created in 1994/1995 for the exhibition *Oskar Schlemmer tanz theater bühne,* Düsseldorf, Vienna and Hannover, and exhibited in Madrid and Barcelona in 1996, and Barcelona in 2007. When shown, it is periodically set in motion mechanically which gives some idea of the shimmering motile space of this dance.

32. As, for example, *His Dark Materials* at the National 2004/2005: this was a scenographic dynamic researched by Schlemmer in *Flats Dance* on a very small scale.

33. By chance I viewed a rehearsal of the re-enactment of this piece for the Tate Modern in 2006. Stepping outside the building I glanced up and was shocked, disorientated and exhilarated to see a horizontal figure above walking apparently towards me.

34. See Norman 2001 for Schlemmer's ideas on embodiment in relation to new digital spaces.

35. See also Coppetiers 1981: 36.

NOTES TO CHAPTER 5

1. 'Requisiten' could be translated as 'props' in a theatre context but is here avoided because of the traditional overtones of naturalistic scenarios. See note 18.

2. There is no such struggle in Eastern philosophies, and the affinity between Schlemmer and Japanese sensibility has been noted by commentators (Niimi 1999). There have been several exhibitions on Schlemmer and on the Bauhaus in Japan, for example 'BAUHAUS experience, dessau', The University of Art Museum, Tokyo University of the Arts, 26 April–21 July 2008, Hamamatsu Municipal Museum of Art 29 July–7 September 2008, Niitsu Museum of Art 13 September–19 October 2008, Utsunomiya Museum of Art, 25 January–29 March 2009, co-organised by the Bauhaus Dessau Foundation.

3. Sally Jane Norman describes Schlemmer's work as supremely relevant to current experiments in virtual reality, in terms of his absolute insistence on the infusion of the inanimate with the animate presence of the human. See Norman 2001: 162.

4. See Michaud 1978a : 92–3. Others continue to tease out the meanings posed by the puppet on and off stage in early Modernism. See, for example, Franko 1989; Louppe 1999: 187–9; Koss 2003.

5. See notes 7 and 15 in Chapter 4, this volume.

6. Compare Franko 1989: 62ff.

7. See note 7 in Chapter 4, this volume, for the origin of this phrase. The significance of the elevation from humble 'puppet' into 'art figure' will emerge in the course of the chapter, especially in terms of Kleist's puppet.

8. Phenomenology was itself a reaction to excessively 'mindful' approaches to philosophy in the nineteenth century, though not idealistic ones (see Chapter 2, this volume). See Farnell 1994: 934 for a succinct summary of the problem of idealism and embodiment: 'bodies do not move and minds do not think—people do'.

9. Interestingly, George Steiner explains how Heidegger in *Letter on Humanism* gives up the struggle to express his notion of 'Being' in the language which Cartesian Western philosophy uses. Steiner says that the *Letter on Humanism* 'breaks explicitly with the logic of argument which has structured Western philosophical and scientific thought from Aristotle to modern positivism' (Steiner 1978: 129).

10. *The Triadic Ballet* was a project thought up on paper, the designs being theoretically driven, and Schlemmer encountered enormous problems when the costumes were first tried out in 1922 in performance. See Schlemmer's letter to Otto Meyer (October 1922) (Schlemmer [1958] 1977: 61).

11. See Schlemmer 1927c: 1.

12. Kantor's essay on 'The Theatre of Death' is devoted to this problem of the live body being part of the work of art (Kobialka 1993: 106–116).

13. See also Krukowski 1992: 203.

14. See Schlemmer's letter to Otto Meyer (September 1918) (Schlemmer 1972: 60): 'Everything would be different if I could paint, or at least think, in materials'.

15. See Chapter 3, this volume.

16. See Copeland 1998 on the abstract dance of Merce Cunningham and its continued relevance to our times.

17. This is usefully discussed in Wilshire 1982: 25 and Chapter XIII.

18. Neither are performing objects 'props', which in dramatic theatre are used in action and add to the visual impact of a scene but do not in themselves dictate the realisation of the performance.

19. The phrase 'performant function' is that of Jean Alter (Alter 1990: 60–90). He uses it to distinguish the physical actuality of a performance which can be fulfilled by any of the stage elements (light, sound, scenery, props etc.) as well as acts of physical virtuosity (for example, tight rope walking in a circus); he opposes it to 'referent function' consisting of signs that operate semiotically.

Alter fails to recognise the ways in which 'performant function' also communicates meaning.

20. Lehmann has noted the prominence of objects in postdramatic theatre, though he does not go so far as to designate them 'performing objects' (Lehmann 2006: 72–3).

21. In her reconstructions, Debra McCall admitted she thought she had spent too long rehearsing without the costumes (Moyniham and Odom 1984:51).

22. The visible puppeteer has since World War II, Meike Wagner points out, contributed significantly to the dramaturgy of mediatised performance. Wagner goes on to construct a sophisticated argument around Merleau-Ponty's notion that the body sees and is seen, but that we only rarely note how much the latter forms an integral part of our own seeing, which she designates an 'invisibility' at the centre of vision (Wagner 2006).

23. John Bell's little known article 'Death and Performing Objects' (1996) is devoted to the phenomenon of the 'resonant' object, and is probably one of the most important articles on puppetry written in recent years, and he takes up the theme in his latest book (Bell 2008). He concentrates on materials and the stuff of which puppets are made, exposing reciprocal interplay or, rather, fusion between the physical and the psychological.

24. 'At an early age I had occupied myself intensely with the making of masks on various materials, I hardly could say why, yet sensing dimly that in this form of creation a meaning lay hidden for me. On the Bauhaus stage, these intuitions seemed to acquire a body and a life. I had beheld the "Dance of Gestures" and "The Dance of Forms" executed by dancers in metallic masks and costumed in padded sculptural suits. The stage, with jet-black backdrop and wings, contained magically spotlighted, geometrical furniture: a cube, a white sphere, steps; the actors paced, strode, slunk, trotted, dashed, stopped short, turned slowly and majestically; arms with coloured gloves were extended in a beckoning gesture; the copper and gold and silver heads . . . were laid together, flew apart; the silence was broken by a whirring sound, ending in a small thump; a crescendo of buzzing noises culminated in a crash followed by portentous and dismayed silence . . . Pace and gesture, figure and prop, color [sic] and sound, all had the quality of elementary form, demonstrating anew the problem of the theatre of Schlemmer's concept: man in space': T.Lux Feininger quoted by Walter Gropius in the 1961 edition of *The Theater of the Bauhaus* book (Gropius and Wensinger [1961] 1996: 8–9).

25. Kandinsky at least had read Bergson, and Bergson was available in German translation from 1912.

26. The phrase is derived from Kaprow's argument: 'They will discover out of ordinary things the meaning of ordinariness' (Kaprow [1958] 1993: 9).

NOTES TO CHAPTER 6

1. Cage famously pointed out to us that there is never absolute silence (Kostelanetz 1988: 65).

2. Specifically, Wittgenstein's *tractatus logico-philosophicus*. He declared that of which we cannot speak we must remain silent. Perhaps perversely, in view of Elzenheimer's claims, this document was adopted by the Prague Circle as a cornerstone of logical positivism. See Galison 1990.

3. For synergies between Japanese sensibilities and Schlemmer, see Niimi 1999.

4. The colour wheels were based on slightly differing colour theories, of which that of Otto Runge was perhaps the most important as far as the Bauhaus was concerned. See Gage 1993: 260.

5. Oswald Spengler had published his famous and widely read *The Decline of the West* as early as 1918 (volume 1) (Spengler [1918] [1922] [1921–2] 1932).
6. See also Maur 1999: 83 on the theories of Hans Kayser and Josef Matthias Hauer.
7. This work was *Ballet Mécanique*, performed at the Concert Hall of the University of Massachusetts Lowell, conducted by Jeffrey Fischer, 18 November 1999.
8. See Anker 2005 for a refreshing evaluation of Maholy Nagy. Schlemmer, however, according to Raman Schlemmer, never really got on with him.
9. See LaBelle 2006: 24–34 for 'Exposing the Sound Object: Musique Concrète's Sonic Research'.
10. The German is 'in dem schweigsamen Bühnentanz, dieser unverbindlichen Muse' (Schlemmer [1958] 1977: 88).
11. This is similar to the range of styles spanned by his diagramic grid of performance types in 'Man and Art Figure' (Schlemmer 1925: 9 and Gropius and Wensinger [1961] 1996: 19).
12. See Chapter 4, this volume.
13. The surviving scores were performed on the piano most recently at the Tinguely Museum, Basel, by Vincenzo Pasquariello, 20 August 2009: *Metalltanz, Frauentanz, Gestentanz, Stäbetanz, Reifentanz* and *Tanz in Glas*.
14. According to Clarkson and Shin (2006), the quotation is from Wolpe Diary 11 132, which I have been unable to trace.
15. See Chapter 4, note 28.
16. '[T]echnical' ('mechanische' in the original) presumably refers to the technical structures of poetry, i.e. metre and rhyme and rhythm.
17. This discussion on the apperceptive reception of sound seems to illuminate Dada 'Sound' poems by Hugo Ball whose poems mean nothing written on the page but everything when performed out loud. Ball of course meant the poems as an Expressionistic gesture, paralleling the later Bauhaus desire to create new aesthetic 'Gestalten'.
18. This description is taken from John Collins's Keynote address 'Theatrical sound design—a binary paradigm' at the *Theatre Noise: The Sound of Performance* conference, The Central School of Speech and Drama, 22–4 April 2009, given here with his kind permission.
19. The phrase derives from that of Douglas Kahn (Kahn and Whitehead 1992) who says of early Modernism and its obsession with 'vibration' and synaesthesia: 'Because of the infiltrating and transmissive ethereality of vibrational space, the terrestrial anchoring of objects and bodies was largely ignored' (1992: 15).
20. In 1929, Schlemmer wrote about materials and costume as fellow 'performers' driving the action: 'Here is an amusing example whose formal principles are similar to those of the ballet I am about to speak of: a musical clown who is a victim of musicality as long as he does not play music himself but reacts physically and intensely to his two 'fellow players', that is, everything that plays on him and with him' (Schlemmer [1929] 1965: 20). Schlemmer, inspired by his innate comic understanding, also clearly tried to find ways of translating this comic 'terrestrial anchoring' of sound (Kahn and Whitehead 1992: 15) into his more serious pieces. This seems to have been the reason behind the grunts and whistles and groans in *Gesture Dance*. In this piece, Schlemmer attempted to synthesise Bauhaus theories on shape and colour with human actions, using the comedy of human fallibility to undercut any pretentiousness, and he avoided naturalism by the use of voiced sounds not words.
21. Audio Arts is an organisation founded in 1973 by William Furlong and Barry Barker devoted to auditory arts. See Furlong 1994.

22. The ill-fated National Centre for Popular Music in Sheffield in the mid-1990s had a sixteen speaker digital sound system in the circular *Soundscapes* room which moved sound around the audience: 'Our unique three dimensional surround-sound auditorium will take you on an amazing journey', with accompanying light show, promised the brochure. However, the sound seemed to come from no particular direction, try as one might to follow its journey round the speakers placed in the huge 360° circle around the audience. The welter of music and commentary with no directionality quickly established an undifferentiated surroundability.

NOTES TO CHAPTER 7

1. See Chapter 2, this volume.
2. See Fabbri 2001: 83 for a description of Schlemmer's scenography as more filmic (time based) than architectonic.
3. For example, J.B. Priestley's *Time and the Conways*, Tom Stoppard's *Arcadia*, Harold Pinter's *Betrayal*.
4. Exploration of the phenomenology and ontology of sound is typical of the Fluxus movement. Compare Yves Klein's *One Note Silence Symphony* described in Maur 1999: 112.
5. See the review of Bock and Vincenzi's *Here As If They Had Not Been, As IF They Are Not* (Jennings 2006: 19).
6. This reminds us of the shift in approaches to sound away from 'vibration' towards its material form that Kahn identified (Kahn and Whitehead 1992: 14–19).
7. An example would be viewing the Grand Canyon: here the normal bull's eye of the centre of the visual field vanishes.
8. It should be noted that according to Bergson *awareness* or consciousness of this past and present Gestalt at once banishes any sense of time durée (Bergson [1946] 1968: 193).
9. The father is here played by Juri Roverato.
10. I use the word silence here for the sake of clarity. For a series of essays on the idea of silence, especially in postmodern performance, see *Performance Research* 1999 4.3; and for Cage's famous declaration that silence does not exist see Cage [1958]1961: 22–3.
11. I have concentrated here on the articulation of the space by sound and by silence and its effect upon us; of course the semiotic content of what is uttered (for example, the words the boy utters in 'The Music') contributes equally to the extraordinary 'worlds' which Castellucci creates (Ridout 2009: 9).
12. The composer Varèse described music as 'organised sound' and so did John Cage and John Blacking.
13. The embodied nature of sound and its consequent capacity to reveal cultural shifts and changing social spaces, and our relationships to these spaces, was addressed by John Drever in his contribution to a discussion on Sonification in the Theatre Noise Conference, CSSD (Central School of Speech and Drama), London, 2009, specifically in relation to 'musak'. The difference, for example, between the sounds on Dartmoor with historical roots and the 'musak' in a Hong Kong shopping mall, that has no ownership at all, is a telling comment on our society; but he sees 'musak' as now changing in response to our indifference: perhaps a not altogether comforting change .
14. This was discussed in Chapter 6, this volume.
15. Shirley MacWilliam quotes Michel Chion's differently defined three modes of listening behaviour: causal, semantic and reduced (MacWilliam 1998: 33).

'Causal listening' (the most common form and equivalent to Ihde's leading edge/focused mode) 'seeks to attach sound to source and thereby acquire information'; '[s]emantic listening' (which is not dealt with here) 'is that applied to language or code' (i.e. listening to decode meaning with the intellect); and finally '[r]educed listening attends to the materiality of sound independent of cause or meaning and is most frequently practiced in relation to music'. The 'reduced listening' mode seems to correspond with Ihde's third mode of listening, the 'broad and open focus' type; both are associated (by Ihde and MacWilliam) with 'music'.

16. Once again, the problems of the notion of 'transcendent' are apparent, the pull between its definition as something that can never be reached and, paradoxically, its manifestation in a physical form through art. See note 10 of Chapter 2, this volume.

17. Susanne Langer, in contrast to Zuckerkandl, does not accept that musical space and motion are the 'same' as the space and motion of the physical world. See S. Langer 1953: 104–119.

18. See note 8

19. See note 15.

20. This refers to E.D. Hirsch (1967) 'Problems and Principles of Validation' in *Validity in Interpretation*, New Haven, CT: Yale University Press.

21. Gestalt modelling of structures within the postmodern stage has certain affinities with Patrice Pavis's notion of 'vectorization': see Pavis 2003.

22. Kaprow says of the anti-formalists: 'one is still dealing with a profound involvement in form' Kaprow [1974] 1993: 157) since they are still thinking in terms of a binary opposition.

23. See note 21 above.

Bibliography

WORKS BY OSKAR SCHLEMMER

(1925) 'Mensch und Kunstfigur' in *Die Bühne im Bauhaus*, Munich: Albert Langen, 7–20.

[1926] (1969) 'Tänzerische Mathematik', *Vivos Voco* (Leipzig) Vol V, No. 8/9; trans. W. Jabs and B. Gilbert, 'The Mathematics of the Dance' in H. Wingler, *The Bauhaus, Weimar, Dessau, Berlin, Chicago*, J. Stein (ed.), adapted and enlarged edition in English, Cambridge, MA: MIT Press, 118–9.

(1927a) 'Der Neue Bühnenbau' and 'Die Bühne im Bauhaus' in *Almanach des Theaters der Stadt Münster*, Münster, 68–71.

(1927b) 'Ausblicke auf Bühne und Tanz' *Melos: Zeitschrift für Musik*, vol. 6. 2 December, 520–524.

(1927c) '"bühne" aus einem vortrag von oskar schlemmer mit demonstrationen auf der bühne vor dem kreis der freunde des bauhauses am 16 märz 1927' in W. Gropius and L. Maholy-Nagy (eds.) *bauhaus 3*, Dessau, 1–4.

(1927d) 'Mechanisches Ballett' in *Tanz und Reigen*, Berlin: Bühnenvolksbundverlag.

(1927e) [1961] 'Abstraktion in Tanz und Kostüm' in *Die Tat. Monatsschrift für die Zukunft deutscher Kultur*, 19.8, Jena, 621, reprinted in Austellungs Katalog *Oskar Schlemmer und die abstrakte Bühne* (1961) Kunstgewerbemuseum, Zurich, 27–29.

(1928) 'Neue Formen der Bühne' in *Schünemanns Monatshefte*, Issue 10, Bremen, 1062–1073.

[1929] (1965) 'Bühnenelemente', reprinted in Austellungs Katalog *Bild und Bühne, Bühnenbilder der Gegenwart und Retrospektive*, Staaatliche Kunsthalle Baden-Baden, 10–27.

[1931] (1990) 'Mißverständnisse' in *Schrifttanz*, vol. iv, no. 11, Vienna, October, 27–9; trans. as 'Misunderstandings: a reply to Kállai' in V.Preston Dunlop and S. Lahusen (eds.) *Schrifttanz: A View of German Dance in the Weimar Republic*, London: Dance Books, 17–20.

[1969] (1971) *Der Mensch Unterricht am Bauhaus Nachgelassene Aufzeichnungen*, Mainz and Berlin: Florian Kupferberg; trans. J. Seligman in H. Kuchling (ed.) (1971). *Oskar Schlemmer Man Teaching notes from the Bauhaus*, London: Lund Humphries

[1958] (1977) *Oskar Schlemmer Briefe und Tagebücher*, ed. Tut Schlemmer, München, A. Langen-G. Müller: Verlag Gerd Hatje, Stuttgart.

[1958] (1972) *Letters and Diaries of Oskar Schlemmer*, ed.Tut Schlemmer, trans. Krishna Winston, Evanston, IL: Northwestern University Press.

(1990) *Oskar Schlemmer Idealist der Form, Briefe, Tagebücher, Schriften 1912–1943*, Leipzig: Reclam-Verlag.

EXHIBITION CATALOGUES

Oskar Schlemmer, A. Lehman and B. Richardson (eds.), The Baltimore Museum of Art, Baltimore, February 9–April 6 1986.

oskar schlemmer: tanz theater bühne, Kunstsammlung Nordrhein-Westfalen, Düsseldorf, 30 July–16 Oktober 1994; Kunsthalle, Wien 11 November 1994–29 Januar 1995 und Sprengel Museum, Hannover 19 Februar–21 Mai 1995.

Oskar Schlemmer, Exposición organizada por el Museo Nacional Centro de Arte Reina Sofía, Madrid, y coproducida con la Fundación 'la Caixa', Barcelona, Museo Nacional Centro de Arte Reina Sofía, Madrid 15 de octubre de 1996–9 de enero de 1997 y Centre Cultural de la Fundación 'la Caixa', Barcelona, 5 de febrero–27 de abril de 1997.

Oskar Schlemmer, Editions Musées de Marseille/Réunion desMusées nationaux, Musée Cantini, Marseilles, 7 mai–1 août 1999.

WORKS ON OSKAR SCHLEMMER

Blistène, B. (1999) 'Du théâtre à la danse ou la quête du soi', in *Oskar Schlemmer*, catalogue d'exposition, Editions Musées de Marseille/Réunion desMusées nationaux 262–8.

Bogner, D. (1997) 'Erinnerungen an Oskar Schlemmer und das Bauhaus' in E. Louis (ed.) *Oskar Schlemmer Tanz Theater Bühne*, Vienna: Ritter Verlag.

Bossmann, A. (1994) 'Theaterreform—Lebensreform, Ganzheitlichkeit im Kunstlersichen Schaffen von Oskar Schlemmer' in *oskar schlemmer: tanz theater bühne*, Ausstellungkatalog, Kunstsammlung Nordrhein-Westfalen, Düsseldorf, Kunsthalle Wien and Sprengel Museum Hannover, 22–30.

Fabbri, V. (2001) 'La Construction de la scène comme image-temps' in C. Rousier (ed.) *Oskar Schlemmer l'homme et la figure d'art*, recherches, Centre national de la danse, 67–84.

Flocon, A. Mentzel (1994) im Gespräch mit C.Raman Schlemmer in *oskar schlemmer tanz theater bühne*, Ausstellungkatalog, Kunstsammlung Nordrhein-Westfalen, Düsseldorf, Kunsthalle Wien and Sprengel Museum Hannover, 63–68.

Goldberg, Roselee (1977) 'Oskar Schlemmer's Performance Art', *Artforum*, 16.1, 32–37.

Günther, H. (1978) 'Die triadische Legende Oskar Schlemmers Ballet war keine Bauhaus-Schöpfung' *Stuttgarter Zeitung* Stuttgart.

Hastings, M. (1968) *Man and Mask, Oskar Schlemmer and the 'Bauhaus' Stage*, video, Munich: Herstellung Bavaria Filmkunst.

Herzogenrath W. (1973) *Die Wandgestaltung der neuen Architektur*, München: Prestel.

Kállai, E. (1990) 'Between Ritual and Cabaret' in V. Preston-Dunlop and S. Lahusen (eds.) *Schrifttanz: A View of German Dance in the Weimar Republic*, London: Dance Books, 16–17.

Kirchmann, K. (1997) 'Bühnenkonzepte der Moderne. Aspekte der Theater-und Tanzreformen zur Zeit Oskar Schlemmer' in Louis E. (ed.) *Oskar Schlemmer Tanz Theater Bühne*, Vienna: Ritter Verlag.

Koss, J. (2003) 'Bauhaus Theatre of Human Dolls', *Art* LXXXV 4 724–745.

Krystof, D. (1994) '"Die Schlemmerkostüme nehmen die Verpackung der Kosmonauten vorweg", zur Rezeption von Schlemmer's Bühnenwerk' in *oskar schlemmer tanz theater bühne*, Ausstellungkatalog, Kunstsammlung Nordrhein-Westfalen, Düsseldorf, Kunsthalle Wien and Sprengel Museum Hannover, 50–62.

Kuchling H. (ed.) (1971) *Man, Teaching notes from the Bauhaus,* trans. J. Seligman, London: Lund Humphries.

Kunz, L.E. (1991) 'Oskar Schlemmer: Bauhaus Artist Re-Examined' unpublished doctoral thesis, University of Pittsburgh.

Louis, E. (ed.) (1997) *Oskar Schlemmer Tanz Theater Bühne,* Vortragsreihe zur Austellung, Schriftenreihe der Kunsthalle Wien, Vienna: Ritter Verlag.

Louppe L. (1999) 'Les danses du Bauhaus: une généalogie de la modernité' in *Oskar Schlemmer,* catalogue d'exposition, Editions Musées de Marseille/Réunion des-Musées nationaux, 177–193.

Maur, Karin von (1972) *Oskar Schlemmer,* trans. by Anne Engel, London: Thames and Hudson.

———. (1979a) *Oskar Schlemmer Bd 1 Monographie,* Munich: Prestel-Verlag Munich.

———. (1979b) *Oskar Schlemmer Bd 2 Oeuvrekatalog der Gemälde, Aquarelle, Pastelle und Plastiken,* Munich: Prestel-Verlag Munich.

———. (1986) 'The Art of Oskar Schlemmer' in Arnold Lehman and Brenda Richardson (eds.) *Oskar Schlemmer,* exhibition catalogue, Baltimore, Baltimore Museum, 39–122.

———. (1996) 'Oskar Schlemmer and his Struggle to Achieve "Precision of the Idea"' in *Oskar Schlemmer,* exhibition catalogue, Museo Nacional Centro de Arte Reina Sofiá, Madrid, and la Fundación 'la Caixa', Barcelona, 181–184.

Michaud, E. (1978a) *Théâtre au Bauhaus (1919–1929),* Lausanne, L'Age d'Homme.

———. (1978b) *Théâtre et Abstraction (L'Espace du Bauhaus),* Lausanne, L'Age d'Homme.

———. (1996) 'New Men: One Law, The Theatre of Oskar Schlemmer' in *Oskar Schlemmer,* catálogo de la exposición, Barcelona: Museo Nacional Centro de Arte Reina Sofiá, Madrid, and la Fundación 'la Caixa',̖ 184–187.

Moyniham, D.S. with L. G. Odom, (1984) 'Oskar Schlemmer's Bauhaus Dances: Debra McCall's Reconstructions', *Tulane Drama Review (TDR),* 28.3, 46–58.

McCall, D. (1985) documentation of Schlemmer dance reconstructions, 2 vols and video, NYPL Dance Collection, MG21C 9–1567.

Niimi R. (1999) 'Oskar Schlemmer, designer anti-moderne' in *Oskar Schlemmer* catalogue d'exposition, Editions Musées de Marseille/Réunion desMusées nationaux, 296–304.

Norman, S.J. (2001) 'Corps/espaces interactifs' in C. Rousier (ed.) (2001) *Oskar Schlemmer l'homme et la figure d'art,* recherches, Centre national de la danse, 153–164

Paz, M. (1996) 'Oskar Schlemmer, Six Aspects of his Work' in *Oskar Schlemmer,* catálogo de la exposición, Barcelona: Museo Nacional Centro de Arte Reina Sofiá, Madrid, and la Fundación 'la Caixa', 187–191.

Plassard, D. (2001) 'Eine schöne Kunstfigur: masques et marionnettes chez Oskar Schlemmer' in C. Roussier (ed.) *Oskar Schlemmer l'homme et figure d'art,* n.p.: Centre national de la danse, 55–66.

Rasche, A. (1994) ' "Freiheit ist Nur in dem Reich der Traume" Oskar Schlemmer als Festgestalter' in *oskar schlemmer tanz theater bühne,* Aussellungkatalog, Kunstsammlung Nordrhein-Westfalen Dusseldorf, Kunsthalle Wein and Sprengel Museum Hannover, 31–39.

Rousier, C. (ed.) (2001) *Oskar Schlemmer l'homme et figure d'art,* n.p.:Centre national de la danse.

Schawinsky, X. (1971) 'From the Bauhaus to Black Mountain', *Tulane Drama Review (TDR),* 5.3a, 31–47.

Scheper, D. (1988), *Oskar Schlemmer, Das Triadische Ballett und die Bauhausbühne,* vol. 20, Berlin: Akademie de Kunste.

Schlemmer, R. (2001) 'Oskar Schlemmer et sa vision utopique du spectacle de danse' in C. Rousier (ed.) *Oskar Schlemmer l'homme et la figure d'art*, recherches, n.p: Centre National de la danse, 23–32.

Schlemmer, T. [1949] [1970] (1993) ' . . . from the living Bauhaus and its stage' in *The Bauhaus Masters and Students by Themselves*, ed. E.Neumann, New York: Van Nostrand Reinhold Company.

Schober, T. (1997) ' "Man setzt Hoffnungen auf mich" Oskar Schlemmer und das postmoderne Bildtheater' in E. Louis (ed.) *Oskar Schlemmer Tanz Theater Bühne*, Vienna: Ritter Verlag, 116–4.

Trimingham, M. (2002) 'A Methodology for Practice as Research', *Studies in Theatre and Performance*, 22.1, 54–60.

———. (2004a) 'Oskar Schlemmer's Research Practice at the Dessau Bauhaus' *Theatre Research International*, 29.2, 128–42.

———. (2004b) 'Sehr geehrter Herr Schlemmer . . . A Letter to Oskar Schlemmer Occasioned by a Performance of the Bauhaustänze at the Dessau Bauhaus 1928' *Performance Research*, 9.1, 81–97.

Troy, N. (1986) 'The Art of Reconciliation, Oskar Schlemmer's Work for the Theatre', in exhibition catalogue, ed. by Arnold Lehman and Brenda Richardson, Baltimore, MD: Baltimore Museum.

WORKS ON THE BAUHAUS

Ackermann, U. (1999) 'Bauhaus Parties—Histrionics between Eccentric dancing and Animal Drama', in J. Fiedler and P. Feierabend (eds.) (1999) *Bauhaus*, Cologne: Könemann, 126–139.

Akbar, O. (2008) 'Raum und Projekt der Bauhausbühne heute/Space and Project—Theatre of the Bauhaus Today' in Torsten Blume and Burghard Duhm (eds.) *Bauhaus. Bühne. Dessau. Szenenwechsel' Bauhaus. Theatre. Dessau. Change of Scene*, Edition Bauhaus: Jovis, 12–19.

Anker, P. (2005) 'The Bauhaus of Nature' *Modernism/Modernity*, Baltimore 12.2, 229–251.

Banes, S. (1982) a review of Alwin Nikolais at City Center, New York, and Oskar Schlemmer's dances at the Ethnic Folk Arts Center, directed by Debra McCall, 1982, *Dance Magazine*, February 1982, 80–2.

Barche, G. (1990) 'The Photographic Staging of the Image—On Stage Photography at the Bauhaus' in Jeannine Fiedler (ed.) (1990) *Photography at the Bauhaus* London: Nishen, 238–53.

Beardon, C. (2002) 'The Digital Bauhaus, aethetics, politics and technology', *Digital Creativity*, 13.4, 169–179.

Berghaus, G. (1986) *Gesture Dance, The Dance Theatre of Oskar Schlemmer*, University of Bristol, Author Günter Berghaus, Producer George Brandt, Director Rupert Wainwright, Bristol University Drama Department.

Blume T., and Duhm, B. (eds.) (2008) *Bauhaus. Bühne. Dessau. Szenenwechsel Bauhaus. Theatre. Dessau. Change of Scene*, Edition Bauhaus: Jovis.

Duhm, B. (2008) 'Tänzermensch—performancekörper/DancerWoMan—Performance. Body' in T. Blume and B. Duhm (eds.) (2008) *Bauhaus. Bühne. Dessau. Szenenwechsel Bauhaus. Theatre. Dessau. Change of Scene*, Edition Bauhaus: Jovis, 178–200.

Eisenhardt, G. (2006) 'Vulkanisches Gelände imMeer des Spießbürgertums: Musik und Bühne am Bauhaus' in *Musikstadt Dessau*, Altenburg: Verlag Klaus-Jürgen Kamprad Ellis.

Ehn, P. (1998) 'Manifesto for a Digital Bauhaus: vision or reality', *Digital Creativity* 9.4, 207–216.

Fiedler, J. (ed.) (1990) *Photography at the Bauhaus*, London: Nishen.

Fiedler, J. and P. Feierabend (eds.) (2000) *Bauhaus*, Cologne: Könemann.

Findeli, A. (1989/1990) 'The Bauhaus: Avant-garde or Tradition?', *The Structurist* 29/30, 56–63.

———. (1991/1992) 'Bauhaus Education and After: Some Critical Reflections', *The Structuralist*, 31/2, 32–43.

———. (1999/2000) 'The Bauhaus Project: An Archetype for Design Education in the New Millenium' *The Structuralist* 39/40, 36–43.

Galison, P. (1990) 'Aufbau/Bauhaus Logical Positivism and Architectural Modernism' *Critical Inquiry* 16.4, 709–752.

Gropius W. [1919] (1969) 'Program of the Staatliche Bauhaus in Weimar', Weimar: Staatliche Bauhaus in H. Wingler, *The Bauhaus, Weimar, Dessau, Berlin, Chicago*, translated as an adapted and enlarged edition in English, ed. by Joseph Stein, trans. by Wolfgang Jabs and Basil Gilbert, Cambridge, MA: MIT Press, 31–33.

Gropius W. and A.Wensinger [1961] (1996) *The Theater of the Bauhaus*, ed. by Walter Gropius and A. Wensinger, Baltimore, MD: The John Hopkins University Press, orginally published as W. Gropius and L.Maholy-Nagy (1925) *Die Bühne im Bauhaus*, Bauhausbücher 4, München: Albert Langen Verlag.

Haus, A. (1978) *Maholy Nagy, Photographs and Photograms*, London: Thames and Hudson.

———. (1990) 'Laszlo Maholy-Nagy' in Jeannine Fiedler (ed.) (1990) *Photography at the Bauhaus* London: Nishen, 14–24.

Jewitt, C. (2000) 'Music at the Bauhaus 1919–1933' *Tempo* A quarterly review of Modern Music, 5–11.

Kandinsky W. [1947] (1979) *Point and Line to Plane*, trans. Howard Derstyne and Hilla Rebay, ed. Hilla Rebay, New York: Dover.

Klee, P. [1925] (1953) (1968) *Pedagogical Sketchbook*, trans. and ed. Sibyl Maholy-Nagy, London: Faber.

———. [1956] (1961) *The Thinking Eye, The Notebooks of Paul Klee*, trans. Ralph Manheim, ed. Jürg Spiller, London: Lund Humphries; New York: George Wittenborn.

Krukowski, L. (1992) 'Aufbau and Bauhaus: A Cross Realm Comparison' in *The Journal of Aesthetics and Art Criticism*, 50.3 (1992), 197–209.

Lupton, E., and J. Abbott Miller (1993) *The abcs of [reproduction of symbols of triangle, square and circle] the Bauhaus and design theory*, London: Thames and Hudson.

Maholy-Nagy, L. (1925) 'Theater, Zirkus, Varieté' in *Die Bühne im Bauhaus*, Munich: Albert Langen, 45–56.

Malmborg, L. (2004) 'The Digital Bauhaus: Vision or Reality', *Digital Creativity*, 15.3, 175–181.

Meier P. (2006) 'Die Geschichte des Raumes Bauhausbühne und seine letze Sanierung vor dem Hintergrund Denkmalflegeris her Grundsätze', Berlin: n.p. 1–42.

Metzger C. (2000) 'Non-stop Music—a Brief Musical History of the Bauhaus' in J. Fiedler (ed.) (1990) *Photography at the Bauhaus* London: Nishen 140–59.

Neumann, E. [1970] (1993) rev.ed. *Bauhaus and Bauhaus people: personal opinions and recollections of former bauhaus members and their contemporaries*, trans. Eva Richter and Alba Lorman, New York: Van Nostrand Reinhold Comany, London: Chapman and Hall.

Pawelke, S. (2005) *Einflüsse der Bauhausbühne in den USA*, Regensburg: Roderer Verlag.

Prager P. (2006) 'Back to the Future: interactivity and associated narrativity at the Bauhaus', *Digital Creativity*, 17.4, 195–204.

Preston-Dunlop V. and Lahusen S. (eds.) (1990) *Schrifttanz: A View of German Dance in the WeimarRepublic*, London: Dance Books.

Schleiermacher, S. (1999) *Music at the Bauhaus*, MD & G Records.

Schmidt, J. (1984) *Lehre und Arbeit am Bauhaus 1919–32*, Düsseldorf: Edition Marzona.

Schoon, A. (2006) *Die Ordnung der Klänge Das Wechelspiel der Kunste von Bauhaus zum Black Mountain College*, transcript Verlag: Bielefeld.

Stuckenschmidt H. (1976) 'Musik am Bauhaus', Vortrag gehalten im Bauhaus Archiv, Berlin, Berlin: Bauhaus-Archiv.

Teuber, M. (1976) 'Blue Night by Paul Klee' in M. Henle (ed.) (1976) *Vision and Artefact*, New York: Springer.

———. (1979) 'Zwei fruhe Quellen zu Paul Klees Theorie der Form' in A.Zweite (ed.) *Paul Klee das Fruhwerk*, Ausstellungkatalog, Munich, Stadtische Galetie im Lenbachhaus, 261–296.

Whitford, F. (1984) *Bauhaus*, London: Thames and Hudson.

———. (ed.) (1992) *The Bauhaus Masters and Students by Themselves*, London: Conran Octopus.

Wingler, H. (1969) *The Bauhaus, Weimar, Dessau, Berlin, Chicago*, translated as an adapted and enlarged edition in English, ed. by Joseph Stein, trans. by Wolfgang Jabs and Basil Gilbert, Cambridge, MA: MIT Press.

OTHER WORKS

Alpers S. (1983) *The Art of Describing, Dutch Art in the Seventeenth Century*, Chicago, IL: University of Chicago Press.

Alter, J. (1990) *A Sociosemiotic Theory of Theater*, Philadelphia, PA: University of Pennsylvania Press.

Anderson L. (1994) *Stories from the Nerve Bible*, New York: Harper Perennial.

Armstrong, E., and J. Rothfus (1993) *In the Spirit of Fluxus*, ed. by J. Jenkins, exhibition catalogue, Walker Art Center, Minneapolis, Minnesota: Walker Art Center.

Arnheim R. (1972) *Art and Visual Perception*, London: Faber.

———. (1997) *The Bauhaus in Dessau* trans. by R. Behrens, *Print*, 51.6, 60.

Artaud, A. (1974) *The Theatre and its Double*, trans. by Victor Corti, New York: Calder.

Ash, Mitchell G. (1995) *Gestalt Psychology in German Culture 1890–1967*, Cambridge, UK: Cambridge University Press.

Auslander, P. (1997) *From Acting to Performance*, London: Routledge.

Barenboim D. (2006) Reith Lectures http://www.bbc.co.uk/radio4/reith2006/lecture1.shtml (accessed 16 August 2006).

Barrow, J. (1995) 'Musical Cheers and the Beautiful Noise', *THES*, 23 June 1995,19–20

Baugh, C. (2005) *Theatre, Peformance and Technology the development of scenography in the twentieth century*, Basingstoke and New York: Palgrave Macmillan.

Beckerman, B. (1970) *Dynamics of Drama,* New York: Knopf.

———. (1979) 'Theatrical Perception', *TRI*, n.s..4, 157–71.

Beckett S. (1973) *Not I*, video available HTTP: http://www.ubu.com/film/beckett_not.html (accessed 22 June 2009).

Bell, J. (1996) 'Death and Performing Objects', *P-Form* 41, 16–19, 24–7.

————. (2008) *American Puppet Modernism essays on the Material World of Performance*, London: Palgrave.

Di Benedetto, S. (2003) 'Sensing Bodies: A Phenomenological Approach to the Performance Sensorium' in *Performance Research* 8.2, 104–6.

Bennett, S. (1997) *Theatre Audiences, A Theory of Production and Reception*, 2nd edn, London: Routledge.

Bergson, H. [1946] (1968) *The Creative Mind*, [orig. *La Pensée et le mouvant* 1903–23] trans. by Mabelle L. Andison, Westport, CT: Greenwood Press.

Blacking, J. (1973) *How Musical is Man?*, Seattle, WA: University of Washington Press.

————. (1977) 'Towards An Anthropology of the Body' in *The Anthropology of the Body* ed. John Blacking, London: Academic Press, 1–28.

Bloomer K. C. and C. W. Moore (1977) *Body, Memory, and Architecture*, New Haven, CT: Yale University Press.

Bory, A. (2009) *Les Sept Planches de la Ruse* (The Seven Boards of Skill) programme notes, Barbican Centre, London BITE09.

Bottoms, S. (1998) 'Subsoil on the Sidewalk: Julie Laffin and the Chicago Underground', *Performance Research* 3 (1), 73–81.

Bragg, M (2008) 'Vitalism the spark of life', BBC Radio 4 *In Our Time* 16 October.

Brecht S. (1988) *The Bread and Puppet Theatre*, Vol.1, London/ New York: Methuen/ Routledge.

Bretano, Clemens [1838] (1965) *Wetke*, Band 3, ed. by W. Frühwald and F. Kemp, Carl Hanservlerlag, Munich.

Brinkmeier, M. (1997) *Die Bühnenwelt des Achim Freyer*, Frankfurt am Main: Lang.

Brookner, H. (1985) *Arena: The Theatre of Robert Wilson*, video, London: BBC Television.

Brown, R. (2005) 'The Theatre Soundscape and the End of Noise', *Performance Research*, 10.4, 105–119.

Burwick, F., and P. Douglas (eds.) (1992) *The Crisis in Modernism, Bergson and the Vitalist Controversy*, Cambridge, UK: Cambridge University Press.

Cage, J. [1958] (1961) 'Composition as Process' in *Silence, Lectures and Writings*, Middletown, CT: Wesleyan University Press, 18–56.

Campbell P. and H. Spackman (1998) 'The Terrible Beauty of Franko B' *Tulane Drama Review* (*TDR*) 42.4 (T160), 56–74.

Campen, Cretien von (1997) 'Early Abstract Art and experimental Gestalt psychology', *Leonardo*, 0024094X, 30.2, http:web.ebscohost.com (accessed 27 September 2007).

Cardeña, E., and J. Beard (1996) 'Truthful Trickery: Shamanism, Acting and Reality', *Performance Research*, 1.3, 31–9.

Carlson, M. (1996) *Performance: A Critical Introduction*, London: Routledge.

Clarkson, A. (2002) 'Stefan Wolpe and Abstract Expressionism' in S. Johnson (ed.) *The New York Schools of Music and Visual Arts*, London: Routledge, 75–112.

Clarkson, A., and H. Shin (2006) 'Zeus and Elida: Wolpe's Kunstjazz Opera', *Contemporary Music Review*, 27.2, 251–269.

Classen C. (1997) 'Foundations for an Anthropology of the Senses' in *International Social Science Journal (Anthropology Issues and Perspectives, Transgressing Old Boundaries)* 153, 401–412.

Coleridge, S.T. (1983) *Biographia—Biographia Literaria*, ed. by Engell and W. Jackson Bate, Princeton, NJ: Princeton University Press.

Conrad, P. (1998) 'Monsters of Grace', *The Observer Review*, April 19, 7.

Copeland, R. (1998) 'Fatal Abstraction', *Dancing Times Journal*, 14.1, 38–42.

Coppetiers, F. (1981) 'Performance and Perception' *Poetics Today* 2.3, 35–48.

Cumming, L. (2004a) 'Then I saw this white beautiful light', The Observer, 23 May.
——. (2004b) 'From a Whisper to a Scream', *The Observer*, 17 December.
Douglas, P. (1992) 'Deleuze's Bergson: Bergson redux' in F. Burwick and P. Douglas (eds.) (1992) *The Crisis in Modernism, Bergson and the Vitalist Controversy*, Cambridge, UK: Cambridge University Press, 368–388.
Drain, R. (1995) *Twentieth Century Theatre, A Sourcebook*, London: Routledge
Ellis, W. D. (ed.) (1938) *A Source Book of Gestalt Psychology*, London: Routledge and Kegan Paul Ltd.
Elzenheimer, Regine (1999) 'Silence, the Development of a New Musical-Theatrical Category', *Performance Research* 4.3, 25–33.
Farnell, B. (1994) 'Ethnographics and the Moving Body' in *Man, the Journal of the Royal Anthropological Institute* 29.4, 929–74.
Finneran, R. (ed.) (1984) *W. B.Yeats The Poems*, ed. R. Finneran, London: Macmillan.
Fischer-Lichte, E (1995) 'Passage to the realm of the Shadows' in J. Martin and William Sauter, *Understanding Theatre, Performance Analysis in Theory and Practice*, Stockholm: Almquist and Wiksell Int., 191–211.
Fisher, M. (1999) 'Buildings and Food' in programme notes for Lepage/Ex-Machina *Geometry of Miracles* (1999), National Theatre, London South Bank Centre.
Frank, H. (1994) 'Arabesque, Cypher, Hieroglyph: Between Unending Interpretation and Loss of meaning' in Keith Hartley et alia (eds.) *The Romantic Spirit in German Art 1790–1990*, London: Thames and Hudson, 147–54.
Franko. M. (1989) 'Repeatability, Reconstruction and Beyond', *Theatre Journal* 41.1, 56–74.
Fried M. (1967) 'Art and Objecthood' *Artforum* 10 (June) 12–23.
Furlong, W.(1994) *Audio Arts, Discourse and Practice in Contemporary Art* London: Academy Arts.
Gage, J. (1993) *Colour and Culture, Practice and Meaning from Antiquity to Abstraction*, London: Thames and Hudson.
Gardner Jnr., S. B. (1994) *Bodied Spaces*, Ithaca, NY: Cornell University Press.
George, D. (1996) 'Performance Epistemology', Performance Research 1.1, 16–31.
Gibson, J. (1966) *The Senses Considered as Perceptual Systems*, Boston: Houghton and Mifflin and Co.
Giedion, S. [1941] (1982) *Space, Time and Architecture: The Growth of a New Tradition*, Oxford, UK: Oxford University Press.
Gittings, R. (ed.) (1970) *Letters of John Keats*, London: Oxford University Press.
Goat Island (2009) website http://www.goatislandperformance.org (accessed 6 May 2009).
Goethe, J.W. (1981) *Faust der Tragödie*, zweiter Teil, Stuttgart: Ernst Klett
——. [1840] (1970) *Theory of Colours*, trans. C. L. Eastlake, London: John Murray, republished Cambridge, MA: MIT Press.
Goldberg, Roselee [1979] 1988 *Performance, Live Art 1909 to the Present*, republished as *Performance Art from Futurism to the Present*, rev. edn. London: Thames and Hudson.
——. (1998) *Performance Live Art Since the 60s*, London: Thames and Hudson
——. (2003) talk given at opening *Art, Lies and Videotape: Exposing Performance*, Tate Liverpool, 14 November 2003–25 January 2004.
Gormley, A. (2007) *Blind Light*, London: South Bank Centre Hayward Publishing.
Halkes P. (1998) 'Phantom Strings and Airless Breaths, The Puppet in Modern and Postmodern Art', *Parachute* 92, 14–23.
Hartley, K. et al. (eds.) (1994) *The Romantic Spirit in German Art*, London: Thames and Hudson.
Heathfield A. (ed.) (2004) *Live: Art and Performance*, London: Tate.

Helyer, N. (1999) 'Nigel Helyer in conversation with Melissa McMahon' http://www.arts.monash.edu.au/visarts/globe/issue7/nhtxt.html (accessed 3 March 1999).

Henderson, L. (1971) 'A New Facet of Cubism "The Fourth Dimension" and "Non-Euclidian Geometry" reinterpreted', *Art Quarterly* 4, 411–33.

Henle, M. (ed.) (1961) *Documents of Gestalt Psychology*, Berkeley, CA: University of California Press.

Hildebrand, A. von (1907) *The Problem of Form in Painting and Sculpture*, trans. Max Meyer and Robert Morris Ogden, New York: G.E. Stechert and Co.

Hofmann, W. (1994) 'Play and Earnest: Goethe and the Art of His Day' in K. Hartley and others (eds.) *The Romantic Spirit in German Art*, London: Thames and Hudson, 19–27.

Holmberg, A. (1996) *The Theatre of Robert Wilson*, Cambridge, UK: Cambridge University Press.

Howes, D. (ed.) (1991) 'To summon all the Senses' in *The Variety of Sensory Experience—A Sourcebook on the Anthropology of the Senses*, Toronto: University of Toronto.

Huch, R. (1922) *Vom Wesen des Menschen*, Heidelberg, n.p.

Hughes, R. (1991) *The Shock of the New: Art and the Century of Change*, London: Thames and Hudson.

Ihde, D. (1976) *Listening and Voice, A Phenomenology of Sound*, Athens, OH: Ohio University Press.

Innes C. (1993) *Avant Garde Theatre 1892–1992*, London: Routledge.

Jay, M. (1988) 'Scopic Regimes of Modernity' in H. Foster (ed.) *Vision and Visuality*, Seattle, Bay Press, 3–28.

Jennings L. (2006) *Here As If They Had Not Been, As IF They Are Not*, The Observer, 4 June, 19.

Johnson, S. (2002) *The New York Schools of Music and Visual Arts*, London: Routledge.

Kahn, D. (1993) 'The Latest: Fluxus and Music' in J. Jenkins (ed.), *In the Spirit of Fluxus*, exhibition catalogue, Minneapolis, MN: Walker Art Center, 101–120.

——. (2001) *Noise Water Meat: A History of Sound in the Arts*, Cambridge, MA: MIT Press.

Kahn, D., and G. Whitehead (eds.) (1992) *Wireless Imagination, Sound Radio and the Avant-Garde*, Cambridge, MA: MIT Press.

Kandinsky W. [1912] (1982) 'On the Spiritual in Art' in K. C. Lindsay and P. Vergo (eds.) *Kandinsky, Complete Writings in Art*, vol. 1, trans. K. C. Lindsay and P. Vergo, London: Faber and Faber, 114–219.

Kaprow A. [1958] (1993) 'The Legacy of Jackson Pollock' in J. Kelley (ed.) *Allan Kaprow Essays on The Blurring of Art and Life*, Berkeley, CA: University of California Press.

——. [1974] (1993) 'Formalism: Flogging a Dead Horse' in J.Kelley (ed.) *Allan Kaprow Essays on The Blurring of Art and Life*, Berkeley, Los Angeles, London: University of California Press, 154–62.

——. [1965] (1995) *Calling* in M. Sandford (ed.) *Happenings and Other Acts*, London: Routledge, 195–201.

——. (1966) *Assemblages, Environments and Happenings*, New York: Harry N. Abrams.

Katz D. (1950) *Gestalt Psychology, Its Nature and Significance*, trans. Robert Tysonm, New York: Ronald Press.

Kaye, N. (1994) *Postmodernism and Performance*. Basingstoke, Macmillan.

Kelley J. (ed.) (1993) *Allan Kaprow Essays on The Blurring of Art and Life*, Berkeley, CA: University of California Press.

Kern, S. [1983] (2003) *The Culture of Time and Space 1880–1918*, Cambridge, MA: Harvard University Press.

Kleist, Heinrich von [1810] (1994) 'On the Marionette Theatre' in *Essays on Dolls, Heinrich von Kleist, Charles Baudelaire, Rainer Maria Rilke*, trans. Idris Parry and Paul Kegan, London: Syrens, Penguin Books, 1–12.

Kobialka, M. (ed.) (1993) *A Journey through other Spaces Essays and Manifestos, 1944–1990 Tadeusz Kantor*, trans. M. Kobialka, Berkeley, CA: University of California Press.

Koestenbaum, P. (ed.) (1985) *Edmund Husserl, the Paris lectures*, trans. P. Koestenbaum, Dordrecht: Martinus Nijhoff.

Kostelanetz, R. (1970) *The Theatre of Mixed Means*, London: Pitman Publishing.

———. (1988) *Conversing with Cage*, New York: Limelight Editions.

LaBelle, B. (2006) *Background Noise Perspectives on Sound Art*, London: Continuum.

Laermans R. (1999) 'Performative Silences', *Performance Research* 4.3, 1–6.

Langer, M. (1989) *Merleau-Ponty's Phenomenology of Perception: A Commentary and Guide*, London: MacMillan.

Langer, S. (1953) *Feeling and Form*, London: Routledge and Kegan Paul.

Lehmann, Hans-Thies (2006) *Postdramatic Theatre*, trans.by Karen Jürs-Munby, London: Routledge.

Lindsay K. and P. Vergo (eds.) (1982) *Kandinsky, Complete Writings in Art*, 2 vols, trans. K. Lindsay and P. Vergo, London: Faber and Faber.

Lodder C. (1983) *Russian Constructivism*, reprinted 1987, New Haven, CT: Yale University Press.

Lynch, D., and M. Foster (1990/1991) *Twin Peaks*, ABC Capital Cities, ABC/INC Television Network Group.

MACBA (2007) *Un Teatro Sin Teatro*, Museu d'Art Contemporani de Barcelona, programme, 25 May–11 September 2007.

Mach, E. [1906] (1960) *Space and Geometry in the Light of Physiological, Psychological and Physical Inquiry*, trans. Thomas J McCormack, La Salle, IL: The Open Court Publishing Company.

Maciuika, J. (2006) *Before the Bauhaus: Architecture, Politics and the German State 1890–1920*, Cambridge, UK: Cambridge University Press.

MacRitchie, Lynn (1996) 'Rose English, A Perilous Profession', *Performance Research*, 58–70.

MacWilliam, S. (1998) 'Sound, Sense and Sensibilities', *Circa* 83, 30–4.

Mann, T. [1924] (1960) *Der Zauberberg* in Gesammelte Werke Bd1 & 2, trans. H.T. Lowe-Porter, *The Magic Mountain*, Middlesex, England: Penguin Books Ltd.

Manning, P. (2003) 'The Influence of Recording Technologies on the Early Development of Electroacoustic Music', *Leonardo Music Journal*,13.1, 5–10.

Marranca, B. (1977) *The Theater of Images*, New York: Drama Book Specialists.

———. (1996) *Ecologies of Theater*, Baltimore, MD: The John Hopkins University Press.

Martin, J., and W. Sauter (1995) *Understanding Theatre, Performance Analysis in Theory and* Practice, Stockholm: Almquist and Wiksell Int.

Maur, Karin von (1999) *The Sound of Painting, Music in Modern Art*, Munich: Prestel Verlag.

Melzer, A. [1976] (1980) *Latest Rage the Big Drum Dada and Surrealsit Performance*, Ann Arbor, MI: UMI Research Press.

Merleau-Ponty, M. (1964) *Sense and Nonsense*, trans. Hubert L. Dreyfus and Patricia Allen Dreyfus, Evanston, IL: Northwestern University Press.

———. (1974a) 'Eye and Mind', in J. O'Neill (ed.) *Phenomenology, Language and Sociology*, London: Heinemann, 280–311.

———. (1974b) 'The Primacy of Perception and Its Philosophical Consequences' in O'Neill (1974), 196–226.

———. (2002) *The Phenomenology of Perception* trans. Colin Smith, London: Routledge.

Macann, C. (2007) 'Being and Becoming', *Philosophy Now* 61 May June 2007, 20–3.

Naess, A. (1989) *Ecology, community and Lifestyle, Outline of an Ecosophy* trans. and revised David Rotheberg, Cambridge, UK: Cambridge University Press.

Nikolais, A. (1971) 'nik', *Dance Perspectives* 48 (winter) 1971, 2–59.

O'Neill, J. (ed.) (1974) *Phenomenology, Language, and Sociology*. London: Heinemann.

O'States, B. (1985) *Great Reckonings in Little Rooms: On the Phenomenology of Theater*, Berkeley, CA: University of California.

———. (1992) 'The Phenomenological Attitude' in J. Reinelt and J. Roach, *Critical Theory and Performance*, Ann Arbor, MI: University of Michigan Press.

Otto-Bernstein, K. [2006] (2007) *Absolute Wilson*, New Yorker Films.

Overy P. (2004) 'Visions of the Future and the Immediate Past: The Werkbund Exhibition, Paris 1930' *Journal of Design History* 17.4, 337–57.

Pavis, P. (2003) *Analysing Performance: Theater, Dance and Film*, trans. by David Williams, Ann Arbor, MI: The University of Michigan Press.

Quadri, F. (1984) 'Robert Wilson, It's About Time', *Artforum International* V.23, 76–82.

Quick, A. (1996) 'Approaching the Real, Reality Effects and the Play of Fiction', *Performance Research*, 1.3 (1996), 12–22.

Rainer, Y (1995) Some Retrospective Notes on a Dance for Ten People and Twelve Matresses Called *Parts of Some Sextets*' in M. Sandford (1995) *Happenings and Other Acts*, London: Routledge.

Rée, J. (1999) *I See a Voice*, London: Harper Collins.

Reinelt, J. G., and J. R. Roach (1992) *Critical Theory and Performance*, Ann Arbor, MI: University of Michigan Press.

Ridout, N. (2009) 'Creating Worlds' in programme notes, *Inferno, Purgatorio, Paradiso* Barbican Centre, London BITE09, 9–12.

Rouseau, G. (1992) 'The perpetual crises of modernism and the traditions of Enlightenment vitalism: with a note on Mikhail Bakhtin' in F. Burwick and P. Douglas (eds.) (1992) *The Crisis in Modernism, Bergson and the Vitalist Controversy* Cambridge: Cambridge University Press, 15–75.

Sandford, M. (ed.) (1995) *Happenings and Other Acts*, London: Routledge.

Sayre, H. (2004) 'In the Space of Duration' in A.Heathfield (ed.) *Live Art and Performance*, London: Tate Publishing, 38–45.

Schilder, P. (1950) *The Image and Appearance of the Human Body*, New York: International Universities Press Inc. originally published as P. Schilder *Das Körperschema* (1923) Berlin, n.p.

Schiller, Friedrich von (1954) *Letters on the Aesthetic Education of Man*, trans. Reginald Snell, London: Routledge Kegan Paul Ltd.

Schober T. (1994) *Das Theater der Maler*, Stuttgart: M & P.

Schumann, P. [1990] 1991 'The Radicality of the Puppet Theater', *The Drama Review* 35.4 (T132), 75–83 originally published Schumann P (1990), *The Radicality of the Puppet Theater* Glover, Vermont: Bread and Puppet Theater.

Schwabsky, B. (1998) '"Subject X" Notes on Performative Art Part 1' Art/Text 60, 40–43.

Schwartz, L. (1999) 'Understanding Silence: Meaning and Interpretation' *Performance Research*, 4.3 8–11.

Segel, H. (1995) *Pinoccio's Progeny: puppets, marionettes, automatons and robots in modernist and avant-garde drama*, Baltimore, MD: John Hopkins University Press.

Spengler, O. [1918] [1922] [1921–2] (1932) *Untergang des Abenlandes Gestalt and Wirklichkeit, Untergang des Abenlandes Welthistorische Perspektiven*, 2 Bänden, München: C.H.Beck; Neu–veröffentlichung (1921–2) *Der Untergang des Abenlandes*, 2 Bänden, München: R.Piper; trans. Charles Atkinson *The Decline of the West*, 2 vols, London: George Allen and Unwin Ltd.

Spiegelberg, H. (1982) *The Phenomenological Movement A Historical Introduction*, 3rd and revised edition, The Hague: Martinus Nijhoff Publishers.

Steiner, G. (1978) *Heidegger*, 2nd edition revised and expanded, London: Fontana.

Stewert, D., and A.Mickunas (1974) *Exploring Phenomenology: A Guide to the Field and Its Literature*, Chicago, IL: American Library Association.

Stoller, P. (1984) 'Sound in Songhay Cultural Experience' *American Ethnologist* 11.3, 559–70.

———. (1989) *The Taste of Ethnographic Thought*, Philadelphia, PA: University of Philadelphia.

Storch, W. [1968] (1970) *Art and the Stage in the Twentieth Century—Painters and Sculptors work for the Theatre*, ed. by Henning Rischbieter, trans. by Michael Bullock, Greenwich, CT: New York Graphic Society.

Streb, E. (1999) 'Exceptional Forces' in programme notes, *STREB*, Barbican Centre, London BITE99.

Synnott A. (1991) 'Puzzling over the Senses: from Plato to Marx' in D. Howes (ed.) *Varieties of Sensory Experience-a Sourcebook on the Anthropology of the Senses*, Toronto: University of Toronto, 61–76.

Tairov, A. (1969) *Notes of a Director*, Miami, FL: University of Miami Press.

Tisdall, C. (1979) *Joseph Beuys* London: Thames and Hudson.

Toop, D. (1995) *Ocean of Sound, Aether Talk, Ambient Sound and Imaginary Worlds*, New York: Serpent's Tail.

Treitel, C. (2004) *A Science for the Soul: Occultism and the Genesis of the German Modern*, Baltimore, MD: John Hopkins University Press.

Tuan, Yi-fu (1974) *Topophilia*, Englewood Cliffs, NJ: Prentice Hall.

Vergo P. (1994)'Music and the Visual Arts' in Keith Hartley and others (eds.) *The Romantic Spirit in German Art 1790–1990*, London: Thames and Hudson.

Wagner, M. (2006) 'Other Bodies: The Intermedial Gaze in Theatre' in C. Kattenbelt and F. Chapple (eds.) *Intermediality in Theatre and Performance*, Amsterdam: Rodopi, 124–36.

Whitrow, G.J. (1961) *The Natural Philosophy of Time*, London: Thomas Nelson and Sons.

Wilshire, B. (1982) *Role Playing and Identity: The Limits of Theatre as Metaphor*, Bloomington, IN: Indiana University Press.

Wilson, C. (2006) 'Phenomenology as a Mystical Discipline' *Philosophy Now* 56 July/August 2006, 15–9.

Wilson, R. (2000) Interview in programme notes, *A Dream Play* by August Strindberg, Barbican Centre, London BITE01.

———. (2004) lecture on the occasion of *The Black Rider*, Barbican Centre, London BITE04.

Worringer, W. [1908] [1948] (1953) *Abstraktion und Einfuhlun: ein Beitrag zur Stilpsychologie*, München: R.Piper; trans. Michael Bullock, (1953) *Abstraction and Empathy: A Contribution to the Psychology of Style*, New York: Int. Univ. Press.

Yeats, W. (1984*) The Poems, a New Edition*, R. Finnerman (ed.), London: Macmillan.

Zuckerkandl, V. (1956) *Sound and Symbol, Music and the External World*, trans. Willard R. Trask, Princeton, NJ: Princeton University Press.

Index

Note: page numbers in *italics* indicate illustrations